D1488584

CHOCOLATE THUNDER

CHOCOLATE THUNDER

THE UNCENSORED LIFE AND TIMES OF THE NBA'S ORIGINAL SHOWMAN

Darryl Dawkins
and Charley Rosen

Copyright © 2003 Darryl Dawkins and Charley Rosen

All rights reserved.

No part of this book may be reproduced or transmitted in any form or by any means, electronic or mechanical, including photocopying, recording, or by any information storage and retrieval system, without permission in writing from the publisher.

For information about permission to reproduce selections from this book, please write to:

Permissions
Sport Media Publishing, Inc.,
21 Carlaw Ave.,
Toronto, Ontario, Canada, M4M 2R6
www.sportclassicbooks.com

Cover design: Paul Hodgson / pHd
Cover Photograph: Tim Shaffer
Back Cover Photograph: © Bettman/CORBIS/MAGMA
Interior design: Greg Oliver

ISBN: 0-9731443-2-7

Library of Congress Control Number: 2002116808

Printed in United States of America

First, my thanks to God for blessing me with
the opportunity to do this book.
The book is dedicated to:
Nicholas Paul Dawkins, my first and only son;
to my daughters Dara, Tabitha and Alexis Celestine;
to my mother Harriette James;
to all my brothers and sisters;
but most of all to Nicholas Antoneli and
his family, Sue, Alexis and Nessa,
my second family for whom I would lay down my life.
Thanks so much.
To everyone in these difficult times, relax,
God is still in control,
and I owe Him special thanks for
finding Janice, my true love
after three times trying (ha, ha, ha).

Love,

Chocolate Thunder

To Daia, for the breadth and generosity of her spirit.

Charley Rosen

CONTENTS

Introduction: Chocolate Thunder and me

As a rabid hoop-o-phile, I was certainly familiar with Darryl Dawkins' on-court antics. His power and mass, his unexpectedly soft jump shots and his exuberant dunks. But more intriguing to me was his off-court persona. His extra-terrestrial fantasies and ribald sense of humor, his beguiling intelligence and his honest smile.

Q: When were you born, Darryl?

A: January 11th, 12th and 13th.

Q: What's your sign?

A: Slippery when wet.

I was also familiar with the testimony of the basketball experts. According to Pat Williams, who was originally responsible for drafting Dawkins in Philadelphia, "Darryl was an astounding combination of strength, size, and speed." Larry Brown, who coached Dawkins in New Jersey, avowed that "Darryl's basketball possibilities are unlimited." Stan Albeck, longtime NBA assistant and head coach, even compared young Dawk to Kareem Abdul-Jabbar, and claimed that Darryl had the potential to be "one of the NBA's all-time elite centers."

And I was captivated by the hows and wherefores of this prodigious man-child.

Darryl first made national headlines in June 1975 when he became the fifth overall pick in the NBA draft. The surprise was that he was only 18 years old and the first player ever to move directly from high school into the NBA. But Darryl was also a pioneer in many other ways.

Back then the NBA was in turmoil. Many of its players were abusing drugs, arena attendance and TV ratings were down, and the NBA seemed on the verge of becoming an "outlaw" league. This was four years before Larry Bird and Magic Johnson were drafted and the NBA embarked on a public relations campaign that would focus on the star-quality of these two clean-cut young men. In 1975, however, the unofficial NBA policy was that the game was supposed to be bigger than the players, and the players were supposed to be stable, grateful and unassuming citizens of Sports America.

And then came Darryl Dawkins. As much of an outlaw as any of his new peers, he was also full of fun and talking trash, unloosing rhymed couplets and backboard-breaking dunks. He was a serious player and an irresistible showman. Kind of like the basketball equivalent of Muhammad Ali.

Almost 30 years later, NBA performers routinely play to the fans and to the media. Beating their chests after a dramatic, rim-rattling slam. Waving their hands to rouse the crowd into uproarious celebrations. Encouraging even louder cheers by cupping a hand to an ear. Mugging and scowling and flexing tattooed biceps. But Darryl Dawkins did it first and did it best.

The difference was the authenticity and spontaneity of his humor. Dusting himself off after drawing a charge to show that he hadn't been injured by the collision. Running along the sideline after hitting a spectacular fall-back jumper and giving the courtside fans high-fives. Darryl had a ball playing ball and he invited the fans to join the fun. Even so, the NBA bigwigs disapproved of Darryl's cavortings. The Harlem Globetrotters played for laughs, but NBA basketball was a serious business. Laughter trivialized NBA action and was therefore deemed to be dangerous. Decorum was what counted. Behave and be thankful. Throughout his 14-year career, the NBA's referees tried to curtail Darryl's exuberance by banishing him to the bench with chronic foul trouble. They might as well have tried to still a whirlwind with technical fouls.

Eventually, the very fact of Darryl's longevity broke the straight-laced mold that the NBA foolishly, and fruitlessly, tried to impose on its players. That's why all of the subsequent high-steppers, flamboyant personalities and boisterous dunksters, from Charles Barkley to Dennis

Rodman to Vince Carter, owe a tremendous debt of gratitude to Darryl Dawkins.

Was Chocolate Thunder ahead of his time? Yes. And did he suffer for his innocence? Yes. Yet in his own way, Darryl Dawkins had a more lasting effect on professional basketball than did his all-star contemporaries—Julius Erving, Kareem Abdul-Jabbar, Magic Johnson and Larry Bird—because it was Double-D who proved that adding a healthy dose of entertainment to NBA competition made the game much more fan-friendly. So give credit to Darryl for helping to resurrect the NBA from its darkest days and ways.

When Darryl played with the Nets in the early 1980's, I was a freelance sports journalist based in New York. Through a fortuitous set of circumstances I prevailed upon the editors at the since-defunct *Inside Sports* magazine to commission me to write a profile of Chocolate Thunder.

My initial behind-the-scenes encounter with Darryl was at a New York Nets practice session. The players were lying on their backs as the trainer led them through various warm-up exercises. The arena was silent except for the trainer's occasional directions. Dave Wohl was the Nets' coach of the moment and he strode through the ranks of the sprawled players wearing a neatly pressed team sweatsuit and an air of propriety.

Suddenly the earnest silence was ruptured by a shrill falsetto voice: "Oh, Old Black Joe! Could y'all sing for me one of them Nee-gro spirituals y'all sing so well?"

The faux question was answered with a lazy, sonorous baritone: "Yas'm, Missy Viola. I'se sure be delighted to sing for y'all."

It was Dawkins, of course, who then broke into song: "Ole man river, dat ole man river ..."

Wohl was instantly apoplectic. "Let's get serious here! Darryl, practice is no time to be fooling around."

But it was too late. Whatever decorum had been evident was now destroyed as the players convulsed with laughter. Their helpless hysteria was boosted when Dawkins responded to his coach's request in the same drowsy, Ante Bellum tone: "Yah suh, Mistah Boss Man."

Q: *And what's your race?*
A: *The hundred-yard dash.*

During the subsequent interview sessions, Dawkins proved to be the forerunner of the multi-talented, irresponsible and irrepressible, too good too soon, millionaire hooplings who fill today's NBA rosters. The most profound difference being that Darryl Dawkins was also the funniest man in the history of sports.

"I take a new girl to every game," he told me. "One night a tall, well-built one, the next night a little redbone. That's because I think all ladies are beautiful, even fat ones. It's up to the man to find a woman's good qualities and build on them. The Bible says there's a proper time for all things, and there's a time for women, too..." Dawkins leaned forward and lowered his voice to deliver the punch line: "... the *night time.*"

Q: *What about esthetics, Darryl? What about beauty?*

A: *Beauty is skin deep, but ugly is to the motherfucking bone.*

The next time I encountered Darryl, he was playing with the Detroit Pistons, I was coaching in the Continental Basketball Association, and our paths crossed in the Milwaukee airport. He had been tossed for cursing a referee the night before and was already plotting his revenge: "All I did was call him a motherfucker and he slapped me with two techs. Hey, a guy his age has to be fucking somebody's mother or else he isn't getting any pussy at all. But I've got a plan. Me and Ham Dick are going to spend the off-season traveling all over the country fucking referees' daughters."

Q: *You've played both center and power forward. What do you think is your best position?*

A: *Crouched over a little, like this.*

Nearly 20 years later, an announcement was made that Dawkins had bested two other finalists, Albert Einstein and William Shakespeare, and was chosen "Man of the Millennium" by NBC's *Saturday Night Live.* Even more amazing, the anti-coach was coaching the Pennsylvania ValleyDawgs in the summertime United States Basketball League. It was time for Darryl Dawkins Redux. This time, my commission was from *Pro* magazine.

As sharp-witted and big-hearted as ever, Darryl still retained a hint of the naiveté and of the need to be universally well regarded that motivated much of his outrageous behavior in the NBA. So, too, had his natural cheerfulness and his refusal to dissemble survived his juvenile blunders. Best of all, his sense of humor was also intact.

Here's Darryl's at-large scouting report of a player he was considering bringing to the ValleyDawgs: "The guy's agent says he's a seven-footer, which means he's about six-foot-nine. He's also got a big ol' head and he's as ugly as shit on a stick, so we won't be losing no girls to him. Yeah! Let's sign him up!"

Here's Darryl talking to a player about his favorite beer: "Labatts Ice is so good it'll knock your dick in the dirt."

Occasionally, Sir Slam even took a turn on the court, mostly as a means of educating his young centers. Still running with his familiar stiff-kneed, hip-locked, slightly pigeon-toed gait, Darryl nevertheless managed to keep up with the traffic. He concentrated on throwing passes (one-handed fast balls that usually hit the mark), helping on defense, and demonstrating post-up offense and defense to the big men. Every mistake his charges made was quietly corrected, every successful sequence was loudly praised.

The Dawkman's rapport with his players was unique. He'd joke, jive and have them howling with laughter, but he was also quick to firmly discourage his young players from reprising his own much-regretted laissez-faire mistakes: When the shirts team snatched three consecutive offensive rebounds on the same possession, Darryl shouted, "Fuckin' dumb-ass skins! Everybody on the black-ass line and run me a sprint!"

Come game time and the opposing coach (Tom Hughes of the Kansas Cagerz) was wearing a red-knit shirt emblazoned with the team's logo. But Dr. Dunkenstein was resplendent in a light-gold double-breasted suit replete with a neatly folded purple handkerchief tucked into the breast pocket, a purple T-shirt, purple alligator shoes, a diamond-encrusted gold ring, gold earrings and a gold crucifix.

As the teams warmed up, several fans accosted Darryl. "Young girls comin' at me fast," he said. "It's hard work to stay straight." And he moaned when he saw one of the refs for tonight's game: "That ref is as sloppy as an elephant trying to shit in a Dixie cup."

With his hoarse voice straining to be heard over the modest crowd noise, Darryl was passionately involved in the game. "Push it," he continually chided his players. "Gimme a look at the three seconds," he begged the elephant-shit ref.

After the Dawgs raced to a 120-100 victory, the coach sat in the locker room he shared with his players. The only concession to his civilian status was that instead of a folding chair, Darryl could ease himself onto a faded gold velvet couch. First, he reminisced about his past: "If I had it to do all over again, there's only one thing I'd change. I wouldn't have fallen in love with as many women as I did."

Then he mused about the present: "Right now, I'm as happy as I've ever been in my life. My legs are okay, my knees are okay and I've even got half a brain left. There's no way that somebody who's done all the crazy shit that I've done could have survived as well as I have without divine intervention. Whoever your God is—Jesus, Yahweh, Allah, Buddha—there's got to be something in your life that's bigger than you."

Q: What is your alma mater?

A: Always do the best you can.

Spending such brief interludes in his company only heightened my curiosity. This guy was larger than life, certainly larger than the contents of two (or a dozen) magazine profiles. To do justice to Darryl Dawkins' gargantuan life experiences would require a full-length book. Through another series of fortuitous circumstances, *Chocolate Thunder* eventually came into being.

During the numerous hours of interviews for this book, Darryl was always respectful, responsible, thoughtful, enthusiastic, painfully honest and routinely hilarious. He obviously enjoyed waxing nostalgic about his past, but he was also mindful of structure and meaning. If I waited long enough, his discourses would come to a point that would either accentuate or perpetuate something special in his narrative. Although Darryl is reputed by nationally known sportswriters to "know everything and everybody," in our tapings he also made sure to separate rumors and second-hand information from his own eyewitness accounts.

So I was not at all surprised when the story of Darryl's "crazy shit" turned out to be more than the collected *bon mots* and rollicking adventures of a refugee alien from the planet Lovetron. Yet I must also confess that many of the hitherto untold specifics of his life's journey were indeed unexpected: The secrets of African-American culture; the ruthless politics of professional athletics; the dark side of some of the

NBA's most prominent personalities; the NBA's undercover police force; and the X-rated truth about sex, drugs and racism in the NBA.

Above all, I remain grateful to Darryl for so warmly welcoming me into his universe. For proving that his humor is genuine and not born of any concealed anger or malignant world view. And for not sanitizing either his misdeeds or his language. Honesty is Darryl Dawkins' only policy.

Q: If you could be reincarnated, what would you come back as?

A: As soon as possible.

Charley Rosen
Accord, NY

1

Coming Up

As deep as I can dig into my roots, I've always found religion. Both of my father's parents were missionaries and his grandmother was a minister. There were also plenty of good Christians on my mother's side, and her mother was the most religious lady I ever knew. That's why, whatever goofy, knuckle-headed situations I've gotten myself into, the Good News was always working on me somewhere in the back of my mind.

My father's name was Frank Marie Dawkins (he passed in 1993, God rest the dead). He was born in Nassau, Bahamas and right after World War II his family came to West Palm Beach, Florida, and that's where he grew up. For a while, my father was a preacher, too. When he was asked why he stopped preaching, he'd say that he found himself looking the wrong way at all the sisters in the church so he knew that God would punish him more than He would punish the average sinner. Even though his mother was only five feet tall and his father was five-foot-six, my father grew to be six-foot-seven and 270 pounds. (The family joke was that there must've been a tall milkman or mailman in the area). After he stopped preaching, my father kicked ass for a living. His job was to collect overdue debts, so on Friday he'd stand outside the bank where the welcher was cashing his paycheck, and my father was so big that everybody just had to give up the money. My father's cut was 30%. When the collection business was slow, he'd trim trees, but he never did make a whole lot of money.

Growing up, my brothers and sisters called him "Frankie" because that's what my mother always called him. When we got older, we called him "Big Daddy."

My mother, Harriette Yvonne Dawkins, was born in Orlando, and her maiden name was Massengale, which is an Indian name. Her parents had moved to Orlando from Kat Island, Jamaica. She grew to be six-feet tall and 160 pounds, and in high school she was a majorette, a track star and a real good basketball player. For a while she sold maintenance agreements in Sears, then she was a seamstress.

I called her "Mama" when I wanted something, otherwise it was "Harriette." She was so pretty I swore I was going to marry a girl who looked just like her.

Somehow my father got himself up to Orlando and met my mother at a party in 1955. One of Harriette's brothers was Candy McDaniels, a boxer who had once fought Joe Louis. When Candy saw Harriette and Frankie together, he went up to my father and said, "If you ever hurt my sister, I'll kill you." That made Frankie hesitant about going out with her, but they fell in love, got married, and Candy never laid a glove on him.

I came along a little before 9 a.m. on January 11, 1957, the second of eight children. I weighed only six pounds but I was long. That makes me a Capricorn, a loving person who cannot carry a grudge. Capricorn is also an earth sign and that's me, too; always down to earth. The Capricorn colors are tan, brown and blue, and that's what most of my clothes are. And the biggest reason why I love being a Capricorn? Because Capricorns get better with age.

Even so, my mother always says that something must be wrong with me because even though I was born in Florida I never liked hot weather. "Look at you," she says. "You're always living in places like Philadelphia, New Jersey, Utah, Detroit, North Dakota and even Canada. You must have thin blood."

Mitchell is the oldest of my brothers by a year and a half. I'm 11 months older than Chico. Then there's my half-brother Troy and three younger half-sisters, Amanda (who's now got seven kids of her own), Shawn and Puddin, who all came after my father and mother separated in 1964.

My mother carried all her babies very low so her stomach never got big. I remember one day when I was 10, Mom just got up and left me and the other kids alone in the house without even giving us a reason. We just hung around all worried and confused until my grandmother came home from work and we told her that Harriette had gone we didn't know where. We didn't have a phone, so Grandma went over to a neighbor's house, then came back after a while to say that she was also going to leave us alone, without an explanation. A few hours later, Grandma came back and said we had a brand new baby sister. It was the same thing with Troy—nobody knew my mother was pregnant so the baby seemed to come from nowhere.

We all lived in my grandmother's house on the outskirts of Orlando in what was known as a TPP neighborhood. That's a Trailer Park People neighborhood. The whole area had once been farmland but had since been broken up into small lots. Most of the houses, including my grandmother's, were set up on stones so that we could crawl underneath them and root around with the dogs and chickens that were always running all over the place. For about two square blocks all around us there was nothing but black folks. The black section was also called Little Egypt, and when we went to school the other kids would say, "Pharaoh opened the gates so you guys could come out of Egypt." The white people who lived three blocks away were also poor and struggling but weren't quite so bad off as the blacks were. And everybody, black and white, had a little garden (mostly for peas, corn and tomatoes) and also raised chickens, ducks, turkeys and some times even hogs to help feed their families.

Grandma's address was 487 West Carter Street, and it was a long walk from town—a mile and a half down a dirt road, then a mile down the Willard Gardener Highway—and she's the one who raised me the majority of the time. Her house was furnished with whatever the white people she worked for gave to her. That meant the furniture was high-quality but old. We also thought that a mark of our poverty was the fact that we had bare wooden floors. Later on I was astonished to discover that rich people pay a lot of money for hardwood floors. There was also a wood-burning stove in the middle of the living room and chopping wood was my main chore in the winter. Dead trees were scarce, so any time somebody tore down an old house, Grandma would let them dump the wood on her property. Then I'd pull out the nails and chop up the burnable wood.

When I was in the NBA, people used to ask me why my muscles were so well-developed. At what gym did I work out? What program did I follow? I'd just laugh, because all of the kids growing up in Little Egypt were all buffed and not because of Charles Atlas or any gym. If you did chores around the house, you automatically got muscles.

My grandmother's name was Amanda Celestine Jones, and she was only about 5' 4", with a big chest, a thin waistline and big hips. She had black-and-gray hair and always wore a little white cap because she was a member of a ladies' club called the Lily Whites that did charitable work. Grandma was also a member of the Antioch Primitive Baptist Church, and was so religious that she never drank and she only wore makeup once in her life, some eye shadow when she went to a dance as a teenager. After a while, the eye shadow began to drip into her eyes and she couldn't see a thing. Someone had to carry her home, and she believed the Lord had struck her blind for wearing makeup. She never went to another dance and never even put on lipstick or nail polish until she passed (God rest the dead).

I remember running outside my Grandma's house after it rained to make mud pies in the dirt road. For me, that's mostly how I picture myself growing up: a little black boy, poor as dirt, making mud pies in the road.

When it rained we'd also have to take two pair of shoes with us to school—one to walk through the mud up to the highway and the other to wear in school. And when my grandmother went off to work she'd have to do the same thing.

Once we were big enough, all the kids in the neighborhood loved to play football in the mud. Just banging and slopping around. It's funny, recently I went back home for one of my sisters' weddings and I set out to measure just how big grandma's yard really was. Six strides from the front of the house to the street, five strides from the house to the back of the property, and 15 strides across. But when we were kids playing football, the yard seemed as big as the Rose Bowl.

At various times as many as 11 people lived in Grandma's house and family matters sometimes got complicated. I was seven when my father left and I was afraid that the family was breaking up. With so many children around, and with space in the house and money so scarce, we all couldn't live in the same place. When Puddin was born,

Troy was sent into town to live with his Aunt Sally. Amanda was living with her father, Henry Clay. Shawn was living in town with her father, Welt Williams, and a woman named Miss May, and they had raised Shawn. In fact, when Welt died, Shawn took care of Miss May, thinking she was her mother. Everybody knew what the real deal was except Shawn.

Now, we had a cousin, Mama Liz Morgan, who liked to take a drink, and she came up to Shawn one day and said, "You need to go over there with your family because Darryl Dawkins is your brother." Shawn was sassy 17 at the time, so she said, "Darryl Dawkins is too ugly to be my brother." Anyway, that's how Shawn came to live with us. When she did find out the truth, Shawn was furious and we feared she might beat Miss May's ass for having her stay on after her father was gone. Even though we were scattered all over the landscape, we always had a sense of who our brothers and sisters were. When we did forget, Mama had her ways of reminding us: My brother Mitchell (a.k.a. Gator) got into a fight one day. It was a fair fight, so we just let them go at it, but Gator got poked in the eye. It wasn't serious but on the way home the eye swelled up.

Mama noticed as soon as Gator came through the door. So he told mama about the fight and made sure she understood that it was a fair fight and no one was seriously hurt.

"But none of the rest of you got black eyes?" she asked.

Then she gave all of us a beating, and screamed: "If one of you comes home with a black eye, all of you better have one, too. I don't care if it's a fair fight, when somebody touches one of your brothers, you all better help him."

It was a mistake we never made again.

We all knew about Jim Crow, because the Florida police was always accusing black men of looking at white women with malicious intent. A lot of black men were jailed or lynched because of that. And my grandmother always used to say, "Be careful, now. You just look at them white women and they'll get you for reckless eyeballing." Granddad even told us a story about a black man he knew who was beaten to death for just that reason. Growing up, we were all very much aware of segregation. We were "niggers" and they were "crackers." We sat in the backs of the buses and there were certain stores like the Publix Market where blacks believed they weren't welcomed. It was what it was. The point was not to get riled about the Jim Crow ways, just to learn how to live and survive. But Grandma also taught us that one day things would change for the better.

We were also taught that President Kennedy was working to help raise the black people, so he was a hero to us. I can remember my mother being pregnant with my sister Amanda and we went for a walk on the dirt road on a cold November afternoon. That's when a neighbor told us about President Kennedy getting shot. My mother was so upset that she went into labor, and Amanda was born almost three weeks early. Everybody said that President Kennedy's efforts to overturn Jim Crow were the reason he was killed. And later on, that was the same reason why his brother Robert was also assassinated.

In school and at home we also learned that Khrushchev was an evil man and that someday the Russians were going to come get us. The Russians weren't going to shoot any nuclear missiles, however, because that would destroy the land and the land was what they were after. So I grew up expecting a Russian invasion of Florida to happen at any time. But Grandma said if we put our faith in the Lord we would be saved.

My grandfather was John C. Scott and he wasn't quite the Christian that Grandma was. In fact, Granddad liked his taste of the bottle. We were working out in the yard one summer's day when we heard a loud noise from inside the house. BOOM! And my grandfather dropped his rake and took off running into the house. Then we heard another one. BOOM! A minute later, he came walking out carrying three big old jugs of homemade whiskey, each one wrapped in macramé. "Shit!" he said. "The heat almost got all of 'em." That's when we found out that Granddad and his buddies had a still somewhere out in the woods. He would wrap up the jugs and stash them under his bed so the whiskey could ferment properly. But it was so hot that day that the jugs started exploding. It's a good thing my grandmother wasn't around, because if she had known there was bootleg whiskey under her bed she would've raised both hell and high water.

Granddad was always drinking and cutting up. On Sunday mornings the whole family would come over, cousins and all. Grandma would cook breakfast and we'd get ready to go to church. One particular morning, my grandfather was still feeling good from the night before and he came to the breakfast table wearing a beat-up white shirt, boxer shorts, his fancy Stacy Adams shoes, his black pinstripe socks and his felt hat. He also had a transistor radio, and Rufus Thomas was singing, "Do the funky chicken, ah, ah, ah!" So my grandfather started singing along, "Ah, ah, ah! Ah, ah, ah!"

She said, "Scott, why don't you cut that out, you old fool?" All the grandkids thought it was hilarious. But when he came back for another "Ah, ah, ah!" she picked up the radio and threw it out the back door. Now he started screaming, "Woman! You're out of hand!" Then he ran out, picked up the radio, dusted it off and came back into the kitchen. The timing was perfect. Just as he switched the radio back on, Granddad chimed in with Rufus Thomas to loudly sing one more "AH, AH, AH!" right in my grandma's face.

The outcome was that she wouldn't let Granddad come to church with us, but he was happy to stay on the back porch drinking all day long.

Granddad had a gardening job at a white man's house. He'd work three days, drink four days, work four days, drink three days. And he kept telling us that Chubby Checker was his first cousin. Now, this guy had a big hit record, *The Twist*, and he was incredibly rich and famous, so we really didn't believe Granddad. But during my last season with the Sixers I met Chubby Checker in an airport and he remembered my grandfather and everything.

One of Granddad's favorite stunts was to stand in front of me and say, "C'mon, boy. Hit me in the stomach as hard as you can." And when I'd do it, he'd say, "Yeah, yeah. You can't hurt me none." It became our little routine that whenever he was away for a while I'd welcome him home with a punch in the stomach. "You're growing fast," he'd say, "but you still can't even make me flinch." So one day when I was about nine, Granddad had just gotten off the bus after a long ride from South Carolina where he'd been visiting some relatives. It was the day after Christmas and he was still bloated with food and drink. He was glad to see us, but he was also hurrying to get to the toilet. As usual, I ran up to him and punched him in the stomach. This time he doubled over and had to let it all loose. Then my grandmother started laughing. "Oh, yeah," she said. "Darryl, you just knocked the living shit outta your grandfather." That one punch became a legend in the family.

From time to time, my father would come back to town and bring money when he could. He was also very resourceful when it came to raising cash. He was driving around in South Florida one day when he noticed the gas gauge swinging dangerously close to empty, but when he dug into his pockets all he found was some lint. So he pulled his car over in front of a Baptist church. Suddenly inspired, Daddy grabbed a Bible from the trunk, entered the church and started preaching. After the congregation had passed the collection plate, Daddy was able to fill his tank and buy some lunch.

Sure, he knew the Bible back and forth, but he was also devoted to drinking. Even when Big Daddy was sober he could out-talk everybody and entertain the whole neighborhood. He was the funniest man I've ever met and was also quite a prankster.

Frankie and his drinking buddies didn't like fat women, so they swore never to have anything to do with them. But then one of the crew was seen sweet-talking a fat woman, and Frankie arranged a trial. It all seemed very serious. Frankie got a rope and a little red wagon, and the tree was right there that they were going to hang the accused from if he was found guilty. The poor guy was scared to death until his buddies finally let him know the joke was on him. Sure, it was cruel, but laughs are hard to come by in hard times. And whenever a black man violates a social code of honor, his ass is grass.

There were always people coming and going and the family kept getting bigger. My little half-brother Troy lived in town with his father, and Troy was just bad for no goddamn reason at all. He could find trouble wherever it was, under a rock or high up in a tree. Once, a lady came and told my mother, "You better go get your son from town because he's liable to get killed over there." There was a prostitute's house down the street from where Troy was living and he was always looking in the window and getting everybody all riled up. So we went and got him and he moved in with us. Grandma aimed for us to be good Christians and eventually she got Troy to calm down some.

Meanwhile, our family just kept on growing: When my Uncle

Candy was a boxer he had a girlfriend named Rosemary and they had two kids together, Twyla and Eric. But then Rosemary got tied up in the streets, drinking and carrying on so bad that welfare took her kids until my grandmother went and got them. Twyla was two and Eric was three, so they were raised as part of the family. But with his own children now at his mother's house, Candy became a frequent visitor and often showed up after he'd been drinking. The trouble was that whenever Candy got drunk he wanted to fight everybody in sight, so there was a lot of hollering going on between him and Grandma. But Candy was also a lot of fun. He'd put the kids in the backyard, box all of us at the same time, and not one of us could even touch him.

My grandmother had two basketball backboards set up in her backyard. There was no cement under foot, just dirt and grass, but we did have nets. We'd just steal the nets off the baskets in the schoolyard then go put them back up when we were done playing. And it was my mother who first taught me how to play basketball. She had a running hook shot and one of those old-time one-handers where she brought up her knee as she released the ball. All you had to do was get hit in the balls one time and you'd stop trying to block that shot of hers. Harriette was a very physical player and quite an athlete.

My grandmother had another son, Ernest Lee Jones, who treated all of us like he was our big brother, and he also taught me the game. His nickname was Bearcat and he had a motto: "Strong as a bear, quick as a cat, the women say they like it like that." Uncle Bearcat was a karate master and when he played basketball with me, he'd rough me up good. I mean beat me all to hell and back. But that's what helped make me such a powerful player later on.

Bearcat signed up to go into the military and the night before he was leaving for Vietnam he was scared that he'd never come back alive. Finally, he drifted off to sleep and had a dream. He saw his grandmother, who had passed away long ago, and she came up to him and touched the top of his head. "Don't worry, Ernest," she said. "You're gonna be all right." Well, when Bearcat woke up, his hair had turned gray right in the spot that his grandmother had touched. And it's still gray to this day.

So Bearcat went off to Vietnam where he got shot up and every-thing else, but the worst that happened to him there was getting dosed with Agent Orange. His arms were all fried up. When he got back home, Grandma got on her hands and knees and started praying. "Lord," she said, "I know you can hear me. I'm asking You to take that off my boy because he's a young man and he's got a lot of living left for him to do. Yes, Lord. Take it off him and put it on me." As God is my witness, about six months later Bearcat's skin was clear and my grandmother's arms were burned up. She stayed like that for three or four years and it always scared the hell out of me.

When I was 11, it was time for me to do whatever was necessary to make some money. Out in the country, poor people have dirt yards instead of lawns and sometimes it would rain so bad that all the dirt was washed away. Then a dump truck would have to come into the yard and unload some more dirt, which would then have to be spread. It was backbreaking work, but if I made a dollar for spreading dirt all day I was very happy.

When I was about 14, I started picking fruit. I could make fifty cents a box in the orange grove, so I'd climb a tree, throw the oranges to the ground, get back down and put them in boxes. If I picked 16 boxes I'd make $8 minus a dollar they'd keep for the government. By the time I was 16, I was the tallest guy in the orange grove, so I was also given another job. Nobody else could load and stack the heavy boxes of oranges as high on the truck as they had to be. So I would pick like 22 boxes by myself and and make $10. Then I'd load anywhere from 600 to 800 boxes on to the truck and, at three cents a box, I'd make another $18 to $24. On a real good day, I might load as many as 2,000 boxes and make $60. The extra bonus was that my arms, my chest and my shoulders got big from lifting those heavy boxes.

Whatever money we earned, we were supposed to give Mama half to help pay the bills. But here I was making over $20, telling her I was making ten, and giving her only five. This went on for about three weeks until one of my brothers turned me in. Now, when it came to money my mother didn't play games. She's a Sagittarius, and she's so good she can tell to a penny the amount of money in somebody else's pocket. That's why, when my brother told her I was holding out, I got one of the worst ass whippings of my life.

Extra money was always hard to find. We never had the latest style in any kind of clothes, but whatever we had was clean. And growing up, I knew that we were really poor.

Mama Liz Morgan had 11 kids and sometimes we had to pool our resources to make a meal. Maybe my mother had four bags of chicken neck bones, Grandma had some carrots or onions, and Mama Liz had two bags of beans, so they'd throw everything into a big pot and that was the only way we'd all have enough to eat.

Even though we were mighty poor, we didn't always live from hand to mouth. There was a black man in town named Mister Ike who wanted to raise some chickens, turkeys and ducks, so he brought them out to us and had my grandparents tend them. Every once in a while Mister Ike would let us have one of the chickens and he always gave us a turkey come Thanksgiving. We also had a garden out back where we'd grow watermelons, corn, peas and okra. In fact, looking back, those were some of the best times in my life.

Maybe once every two months, all the bills would be paid and there'd be $20 left over, so one of my uncles would drive us over to Steak 'n' Shake for french fries, a soda and a burger. The waitress would come over on roller skates and she'd hang the food tray on the side of the car. That was a major league treat for us.

All the kids had chores to do. My main ones were to keep the yard clean and to wash the dishes. There was a wood stove in the living room and another job of mine was to chop wood and bring it into the house. In colder weather, we'd open the doors to the other rooms and the wood stove would keep us warm enough. There was also a kerosene heater for the back bedroom that we were very careful with. If it ever got knocked over, the house was so dry that everything would've burned down in a jiffy.

We had a kerosene stove and a gas stove. A tank of gas that would last about two months cost $15, which was a lot more expensive than kerosene, so we used the gas stove very sparingly. Neck bones or beans would cook all day on the kerosene stove, and the gas was used special for pork chops or chicken.

Grandma's house didn't get indoor plumbing until I was in junior high school so we used an outhouse in the backyard. We had to walk through the weeds to get there, and in the south there are always frogs and snakes lurking around. At night you'd need a flashlight or a candle and every stick looked like a snake. So we'd hate it when one of us got sick because when that happened everybody would have to take a dose of castor oil. And once you take castor oil you'd better have a ten-pack of Charmin around. When we ran out of toilet paper we'd use newspaper or comic books. That's why whenever somebody did get sick the rest of us would be holding on even though he'd be so sick he was passing out. "He's okay, Grandma. He says he's feeling much better."

When we finally did get indoor plumbing we also had to have a septic tank. It cost $15 to have a truck come and drain the tank when it started to back up, which was a lot of money for us. So we just pulled up the metal sealer-slab, then me, Granddad and my brothers would dip our buckets into the tank, haul up all the stuff and go dump everything deep into the weeds.

We had three bedrooms. I slept with my grandfather and two of my brothers in the front bedroom. My grandmother had the middle room with the youngest of my sisters. The back bedroom was for everybody else. All we had were old, beat-up mattresses, and whenever they got too lumpy we'd fill in the low spots with crumpled newspapers. I had to share a bed with my grandfather and one night when I was eight he came into the bed crazy drunk and started beating me up in his sleep. Bam, bam, bam. Punching me all over. I tried to cover up but I couldn't get away from him, so I finally hit him back as hard as I could. BAM! That woke him up and he started screaming, "Manda! This boy done hit me in the face!" So I jumped out of bed and ran to my grandmother to tell her what had really happened. "Granddad was drunk and he was fighting me and ...!" So I spent the rest of the night in her bed. All the next day Granddad was walking around like he was trying to get me alone and get back at me. But, as usual, it was Grandma who kept everything together.

That was a difficult job because, besides Granddad's drinking and all the kids running around, we lived in a hell-raising neighborhood. About two blocks away was a bar (we called them "gyp joints") called Baby's. Two blocks the other way was another one called Norman's. Then there were barbecue pits all over. That meant that lots of drunken men came running and shouting through our yard at all hours of the night. Sometimes we'd even hear the crazy motherfuckers shooting at each other. BANG! BANG!

For a while, Granddad ran one of the barbecue pits in partnership with Mister Dawson and Mister Perkins. (We were taught to say "Yes, ma'am," or "No, sir" to everybody who was older than we were, whether they were black or white, and our parents' or grandparents' friends were always Mister or Missus. It's something I still do to this day.) People would come down to the barbecue pit and ask could they cook up a goat they'd just killed. Beef bones, oxtails, anything. Sure, put it right on there. And Mister Dawson (God rest him) was chopping up some barbecue one night and he chopped his finger off. He was a little drunk at the time and feeling no pain. Blood or barbecue sauce, he couldn't tell the difference. So the finger was put into a sandwich that was wrapped up and sent off to a customer. It wasn't until after the sandwich was gone that Mister Dawson realized what he'd done. When the lady got her sandwich, she just threw it away, finger and all.

Of course there were other, more tragic accidents that happened. Like the time me, my brother Chico and two friends of ours, Mark Daniels and Alan Thompson, went swimming in a nearby lake. There were houses along the shoreline that had rowboats pulled up on the beach. Since everybody was out working, we'd borrow the rowboats and return them before they came back home. So we'd row to the middle of the lake, then jump in and start swimming. But this one time, Mark and Alan got themselves caught in suck holes. There they were spinning around and around and slowly going under. We knew that Alan was a hell of a swimmer, so me and Chico climbed back in the boat and set off to rescue Mark. Which we did. "Hold on, Alan. We'll be there in a minute." But by the time we got over to Alan, he was gone.

We raced home and came back 20 minutes later with my Uncle Candy, who kept diving and diving, trying to get to Alan. Then the rescue squad came and finally pulled the body out.

Back home, Grandma told me and Chico: "You all know that boy's mother?"

"Yes, ma'am."

"You all got to go there and tell that lady what happened before she has to see it on the TV news."

So we walked the three miles to where Mrs. Thompson lived, and she came to the door when we knocked. "Missus Thompson," I said. "We saw Alan drown." And I told her the whole story.

Then she slammed the door shut and started screaming. "Oh, Lord! Not Alan!"

I was 13 years old at the time, and when I got back home, I slept with the light on for about a week. To this very day, if you come into my house or my hotel room at any time of day or night, you'll at least see the bathroom light on. I do not like the dark.

Somebody was always dying somewhere in the neighborhood, but we didn't always attend funerals. If somebody died, they died. No use getting spooked by going to a funeral. Of course if a family member passed, that was a different story.

My mother's father had split up with Grandma long, long ago and we rarely saw him, but he was still living nearby. Granddaddy Doyle Massengale was his name. One night, Troy got up out of bed at one o'clock in the morning, walked out back and grabbed a shovel. Then he started digging a hole and crying, "I'm coming, Granddaddy! I'm coming!"

Chico ran out after him. "What's wrong with you, Troy? Stop that!" But Chico couldn't bring Troy around, so he went and got Grandma.

Grandma looked at Troy and said, "Everybody stand back." Then she slapped his face. WHAP! Nothing. Troy was still crying. So she slapped him harder. BAM! Troy was still bawling. Grandma about slapped the natural hell out of him until he finally came around.

The next morning, somebody came and told us that Granddaddy Doyle had died from an asthma attack during the night. They said Granddaddy was trying to call for help but nobody could hear until it was too late.

I was 14, I'd never been to a funeral before, and I didn't want to go to that one. "Well, you're going," my mother said, "because you're also gonna go to my daddy's funeral."

So my mother made long-sleeved white shirts for all the kids (it was the first white shirt I ever had), along with black neckties and black pants for the boys, and black dresses for the girls. When we got to the funeral, I had to go up to the casket and pay my respects. And it just about scared the life out of me because Granddad Doyle looked exactly like my mother.

The services were held at the Antioch Primitive Baptist Church in Orlando. There was a woman who had lived on and off with Granddad Doyle, Aunt Sally, and we swore she had a college degree in cussing. Aunt Sally could say "shit" and the whole house would start to stink. So in the middle of the service she starts screaming, "Oh, Doyle! You should have let somebody know you were sick! Oh, Doyle!" Everybody was looking at her and wishing she'd quiet down, but she never stopped. "Oh, Doyle! I miss you so!"

Finally, the funeral director, Mr. Bruton, came over and said, "Sally, why don't you hold down some of that noise?"

"Why don't you hold down your own self?" Aunt Sally told him. "I'm at a funeral, bitch, and I'm supposed to be sad." Then she went back to wailing.

For the next week, I was looking back over my shoulder real quick to see if any ghosts were sneaking up on me.

2

School Days on Lovetron

The only things white in Eccelston Elementary School were the chalk and the toilet paper. Black teachers, black principal, black cafeteria workers. I was a pretty good student and, even though sitting still and behaving myself wasn't easy, I liked going to school. Nothing unusual happened at Eccelston until the fifth grade. That's when I discovered my Granddad's still and I snuck out and got drunk every day. So I really don't remember anything about the fifth grade.

I do remember constantly getting into trouble at home. I wasn't considered as bad as Troy, but I was bad enough. Most of my mischief was normal country-boy stuff. Like tying two cats together by their tails and hanging them over a clothesline just to see them fight. Or sticking firecrackers in a frog's mouth and lighting them. Boom! There'd be frog guts everywhere. I'd also fight with my brothers and sisters, and sometimes I'd steal money from either my grandfather's pants when he was sleeping, or from my grandmother's pocketbook. Then I'd go buy ice cream and cookies, and sometimes I'd buy lunch for a girl I liked at school. Whenever Mama caught me, she'd beat me with a belt. But I kept on stealing the money.

My grandfather had a gun that he kept under his mattress. He'd fire it every New Year's Eve, and once in a while he'd have target practice out in the backyard. One day when nobody else was around I saw all the chickens running around and I thought it would be fun to shoot at them. I got the gun and started firing away, but I couldn't come close to hitting any of the chickens. Man, I was pissed. Then I spotted a poor little hen sitting peacefully on her nest, so I snuck up on her and BOOM! I shot her all to pieces. Frightened by what I had done, I cleaned up the mess and put the gun back.

When my grandfather came back home, he smelled something funny in the yard so he went to check out his gun. "Damn," he said. "There's sand and dirt in my gun and there's seven bullets missing. That boy must've been fooling with it." Neither my grandfather nor my grandmother ever beat us kids. Grandma came up to me as serious as I ever saw her and just told me never to touch that gun again. "Yes, ma'am," I said, and I never did. I was just glad that she didn't tell Mama.

After six years in Eccelston Elementary School I moved on to Carver Junior High School, which was also for blacks only. I was 12 in the seventh grade, and that's when I got one of the most embarrassing beatings of my life. There was a tool shed out back that had an old mattress on top of it. So one day me and a young girl from the neighborhood climbed up on the mattress and took off our clothes. We didn't know what fucking was, but we were both buck-naked so we swore we were doing *something*. And my mother happened to lean out of the back window, which was the only way she could have seen us, and see us she did. She called me into the house and, naked as I was, she whipped me with a doubled-up extension cord. After that, she made me stand on one foot in the corner for an hour.

If laws against child abuse were in effect when I was growing up, my mother would be serving a double life sentence and wearing a big ball and chain on her leg.

Now getting a beating with an extension cord wasn't too uncommon for boys my age and it left thin red welts all over my body. But there were a couple of kids in school the next day who didn't know what was what, so I told them that I had fallen into a sticker bush. One guy said, "I don't know what that is, man, but no sticker bush is gonna mark you up like that." Two days later he came into school with the same kind of welts all over him, saying, "Yeah, man. Them sticker bushes is a bitch."

It was at Carver Junior High where I started playing basketball for real. I was six-foot-three in the eighth grade and the basketball coach was Jimmy Jordan. And he was eyeballing me every time we passed in the hallways.

At the time, I was playing basketball in the backyard with my brothers, my uncles and my mother, and sometimes in the schoolyard with the other guys in the neighborhood. Just shooting and messing around.

One day, Mister Jordan stopped me in the hall and said, "Mister Dawkins, you got to play basketball on the school team."

I was anxious to play because I had just beaten my mother one-on-one for the first time, but I knew that I had other responsibilities. "Coach," I said, "I can't play basketball because my brother Mitchell's playing football at Evans High School, so I've got to be home doing the chores."

"Well, after school today, I'm gonna pay a visit to your mama."

So he drove up to the house, got out of his car, took one look at my mother sitting on the porch and said "Massengale!" Then they both started laughing, because they used to play basketball against each other.

Then he told her, "This boy should be playing basketball."

"He can't. He's got chores to do."

"Mark my words," Coach Jordan said, "if he doesn't play basketball, he'll really be missing out on something good."

They went back and forth for a while, until she finally gave in just as my grandmother came home from work and stepped onto the porch.

"What Darryl needs to start off," said Coach Jordan, "is a new pair of Converse sneakers."

"What's that cost?" my mother asked.

"Ten dollars and ninety-five cents."

"We ain't got that kind of money," Mama said, but Grandma interrupted. "Don't worry. We'll go get him the Converses."

With that settled, my mother told Coach Jordan, "You can whip him if he needs it. You can kick his ass. Whatever you got to do to make him play right, you just go ahead and do."

And I looked at my mother and said to myself, *"Damn, she just gave me away!"*

Grandma only had two pair of shoes, a white pair and a brown pair, and the browns were falling apart. But she put a piece of cardboard in her brown shoes and the next day she took me to the Cut-Rate Shoe Store and bought me a pair of sneakers. That was the beginning of my basketball career.

I could make a layup, which was a big deal for an eighth grader, I had about a seven-foot range on my jump shot, and I could block shots. But I couldn't make a free throw because I shot the ball off my palm, and I was a little goofy on the court so I didn't get to play much.

We had a sprint drill where the player who finished first didn't have to run anymore. Then the player who won the second sprint was also excused, and so on. There were three guys on the team who also ran track: C.C. Coleman, Jimmy "Moose" Lewis and Donald Mobley. So while any one of them was still in the running I would be in cruise control, and I'd only exert myself when I had a chance to win. One day as we were about to start the first sprint Coach Jordan came up behind me with a big board in his hand. "I'm gonna be running right in back of you," he told me. "If I catch you I'm gonna bust your ass with this board." And I finished second.

During the following summer, my mother moved into the projects in town but my grandmother didn't want to move in with her. My mother had two boyfriends coming around and Grandma didn't want to be in the way.

By the end of the season I had grown to six-foot-five and about 225 pounds, so I was feeling all grown up. There was a fair in town, the J and V Trade Show, and I thought I was old enough to go there on my own without asking my grandmother's permission. Besides, she was only going to tell me "no" anyway. When I came back home at about six o'clock, there was Grandma rocking on the front porch and worried to death. She asked me where I had been and I couldn't lie to her. "You went there without asking me?" she said.

"Yes, ma'am. I just went to the fair on my own."

She didn't say anything else, so I ate the supper she had left for me and I went to bed at about ten o'clock. I didn't know it, but my grandmother saw my uncle Bearcat on his way to one of the local gyp joints and told him what I had done. "If you meet up with anybody who's going on into town," she said to Bearcat, "tell him to stop by Harriette's place and say what Darryl did."

So there I was peacefully sleeping, not knowing that when my mother got the news she walked the two and a half miles out to Grandma's house in the middle of the night. Now, there was a piece of broomstick always laying near the oven that we used to fasten the oven door shut whenever Grandma was baking a cake. When Mama came into the house, she snatched the broomstick, came into the bedroom and beat the shit out of me. "You don't never make my mother worry like that ever again," she said. I had heard of other kids getting beat with a stick, but that was the first and last time it happened to me.

Anyway, Grandma and Mama got together after that and decided that I was too big for my grandmother to deal with, so three weeks later I moved into the projects with my mother.

The Ivy Lane projects in Orlando were three square blocks of one-story brick buildings. Each apartment had three or four bedrooms (ours had three), which meant that for the first time I had my own room. This was major league stuff. The population was black, white, Puerto Rican and Mexican, and the one thing we all had in common was poverty. We were poor at Grandma's house in the country, but the projects added a few things. Like ass-kickings and thievery.

Everybody in the projects got food stamps on the first of the month and the young kids would walk around peeping in all the kitchen windows trying to see who'd been going grocery shopping and what they'd bought. If somebody was careless enough to leave the kitchen light on and their groceries in sight, then within a day or two their Froot Loops, Cap'n Crunch, Pop Tarts, milk, sodas and cheese would all be stolen.

Breaking in was the easy part. Most of the kids who lived in the project were experienced thieves, and shimmying a lock was no trick at all. Because nobody had air conditioners, you had to leave your windows open just a little bit. With the windows closed, it'd be hotter in there than a pot of pig feet. Plus you'd find stuff growing on the walls that you never even planted.

The bus stop was a central location where somebody could just hang out and keep track of who was leaving and who was staying. Also, if there were two newspapers outside somebody's front door then you knew they weren't in town. But the stealing was so brazen and widespread that you could be napping in a back room and somebody would come in and clean out your refrigerator.

(When I visited the projects recently I was happy to see that the city had installed air conditioners in every house. That meant the windows could be locked shut, which went a long way to reducing the stealing.)

Mama had a big yellow and blue '62 Chevrolet station wagon. Like all the other cars in the projects, Mama's was painted with house paint and it was so rusty that everybody inside got wet when it was raining outside. The only way to get Mama's car up to 50 miles per hour would've been to drive it off a cliff. But a slow ride was always better than a fast walk.

Everybody who owned a car, however, was especially vulnerable to the local thieves. These guys would steal the battery out of your car and then come back and sell it to you. "Oh, Mrs. Jones, somebody stole your battery? My daddy got two old batteries out back and he'll surely sell you one cheap."

One of my fondest memories was when Church's Chicken opened up a branch near the projects and 15 or 16 of us would pile into Mama's car to go over there for the 99-cent special: two biscuits, two pieces of fried chicken and some fries. For another 30 cents you could even get a soda. Man, that was a fast-eating, bone-sucking, greasy-fingered party.

The first of the month meant food stamps and also welfare payments, and that was another occasion for an impromptu party. Somebody would set their stereo up on a window and everybody pitched in to buy some beer. Then we'd dance and have a good time until somebody called the cops.

Living at my grandma's house, we knew we were poor but it didn't seem like such a big deal. Living in the projects was a different story. We were in government housing so we were officially poor. Still, as long as we could eat, sleep and go to school in clean clothes we figured we were doing okay.

There was also a basketball court in the projects and a lot of good players. Richard and Robert Paine were six-foot-seven twins and had been great high school ballplayers. A guy named Snake had played at Jones High. And there was a black guy with green eyes named Pistol

Pete, who was fast as all shit and was always laughing.

These guys would foul me hard on every play, and whenever I complained they'd call me "bitch." There were lots of times when I wanted to quit, but my brother Mitchell was always around and he made me stick with it. So they kept whipping me and whipping me until I finally started to get tough.

When I went back to Carver for the ninth grade, I was a different player. I had grown to six-foot-seven. I was never skinny, never, but now I was big and strong and I could rebound with anybody. We played zone so I really didn't know how to play defense, but my offensive skills were blossoming and I wound up averaging nearly 20 points per game.

There were two high schools in the area, Jones High for blacks, and Maynard Evans High, which used to be all white but had just been integrated. If I used my mother's address in the projects, I could go to Evans High. If I used my grandmother's address, I could go to Jones. My older brother Mitchell was already at Evans and on the football team. He said there was a little bit of prejudice at the school, but nothing he couldn't handle.

The basketball coach at Jones was Tampa Red, and he lived right near Carver. I had to pass by his house every time I went to school, and he'd be sitting on his porch, saying, "I see you, boy. I see you. I want you to use your grandma's address and come to the black school where you belong. Your mama went to Jones, your Uncle Candy went to Jones, your Uncle Bearcat went to Jones. So you're going to the black school, boy."

In fact, one of the reasons I was inclined to pick Jones was because, growing up, I didn't have much contact with white people.

My grandmother worked over 15 years for the Stricklands and the Davises, two of the most well-to-do white families in Orlando, and both families were very good to us. Once when Grandma got sick, Mrs. Strickland came to our house and brought three bags of groceries and some money for us. I was amazed that there was a white lady in our house. Mrs. Strickland said for all the children to gather around her, then she patted her lap and told me, "Come up here." I had never touched a white person before and I was scared at the thought of it, but I did what she said. And there I was, sitting on a white lady's lap.

I looked around at my brothers and sisters and I couldn't help smiling from ear-to-ear because I knew I had it made. The words that jumped out of my mouth were these: "Now, now." From then on until the day she died, Mrs. Strickland always called me "Now."

Even so, I must admit to being a little afraid of white people when I was younger. I remember me and Troy were standing on a corner in town just hanging out and bullshitting when a white lady drove up and had to stop for a red light. She was alone in her car and as soon as she saw us—boom—she locked all the doors. And I realized that white people were also afraid of us. But I also felt bad because whites thought that blacks were like a lower life form.

Now, I'm aware that all kinds of racial prejudice is still happening. And I can't forget about the slavery days, either. I've read about it in books and newspapers. It's sad and horrible and everything, but I don't want to relive any part of it. Lots of bad racial shit happens, and my philosophy is to learn what we can and then move on.

There was one instance, however, when I suffered my own attack of racism. It happened the first time I watched *Roots*.

When I played with the Sixers I had a buddy named George Dickinson, a white guy with a big Afro. I had a house in Somerdale, New Jersey, and George and his wife, Tomiko, lived in nearby Cherry Hill. So me and my brother Mitchell were watching *Roots* on TV and there was a scene where a slave named Chicken George had run off so many times that the white boss said, "You ain't running no more. We're either gonna cut your foot off or your dick off. It's up to you." So the slave said, "My foot," and they chopped it off. Me and Mitchell were both hopping mad. Just then George called. He was also watching the program and he said to me, "How could they be so cruel as to do something like that?"

I was so upset that I said, "What the fuck you calling me for, you white motherfucker?" And I hung up on him. So he and his wife drove right over to my house and we all wound up hugging each other, drinking vodka and crying all night long.

If I was thinking about going to Jones High, the black school, there was one major drawback: Jones had a terrible reputation for fighting. There'd been such a bad fight during a basketball game between Jones and Evans that the schools were only allowed to play each other at a neutral site, Warner Park High School. Everybody on the black side of the tracks knew that the fight had been started by the kids at Jones and was racially motivated. I really didn't want to get involved with that kind of stuff. But what really convinced me to stay away from Jones High was a visit I had from the coach of the Evans basketball team.

His name was Fred Pennington, an old white guy from West Virginia, and he called me by one of my nicknames in the neighborhood. "Diesel," he said. "I watched you play at Carver and I thought you didn't get the ball enough. Some of the other guys on the team were freezing you out. I also noticed that you shoot the ball off the palm of your hand. If you come play for me at Evans, I know I can improve your game and make sure you get the ball."

A couple of days later, Coach Pennington called and asked if I had a summer job yet. "No, sir." He said for me to catch the bus and come right down to Evans. Which I did. And I got a job filling up the holes on the football field and sweeping the classrooms. While I was down there, I also started playing pickup games with some of the holdover Evans players. They told me that I had made the right choice. That at Jones High, one or two players would be taking all the shots and everybody else had to stand around and watch. That at Evans, Coach Pennington preached team basketball. So I used my mother's address and signed up for Evans.

Well, Tampa Red didn't like that. Every time he saw me he would chase me down the street and cuss after me. "You going to the white school, motherfucker! If I catch you, I'm gonna beat your black ass till it's red!" He was real fast, but he never did catch me.

One afternoon during the summer, a bunch of us were playing against some older kids in the Carver schoolyard. I had grown to six-foot-eight but the older guys were still beating me up every time I got close to the basket. And whenever I called a foul, they'd say, "Shut up, bitch. I barely touched you." I got so mad that the next time I got the ball I just jumped as high as I could and stuffed the ball through the hoop. Everybody just stopped and stared at me. Then somebody said, "Do you know what you just did?"

"What? What? What?"

"You just dunked the ball, man!"

Watching the NBA games on TV, I thought dunk shots were really cool, but I had never been able to get my steps together to slam one myself. Mostly I tried to copy Wilt Chamberlain's finger roll. So when I did dunk that first time, I felt like a million dollars. Even so, it took me another three or four weeks before I could figure out exactly what I had done so that I could dunk again.

Before practice began at Evans we used to have scrimmages in the gym, players who'd already graduated against the players who were still there. The seniors also had a ringer, a 55-year-old guy named Mr. Hunt. This old guy was six-foot-eight by six-foot-eight and tough as nails. He used to beat me up, down, sideways and every which way. One time I was going up for a shot and he gave me a backhand that split my lip. I ran into the locker room to look at myself in the mirror and I was so mad I was crying. Then Coach Pennington came by and said, "Suck it up." And I was thinking, *"He don't give a fuck about me."*

I came back a few days later and played pretty good, so Coach came up to me again. "You wanted me to baby you," he said, "but I'm never gonna do that. Stuff like that's gonna happen in ball games, I promise you, and you're gonna have to learn how to deal with it." He was right, but at the time I too busy pouting to fully understand.

I really liked going to high school. That's where I first encountered hippies. They wore the "Mod Squad" glasses, the headbands and the tie-dyed shirts. "What's happening, brother?" Everybody knew they were smoking weed, and they were generous about sharing their stash. "Fuckin' A, dude." But the best thing about the hippies was that they knew where to buy the baddest dashikis. "Peace and love, bro."

In the classroom I was about a B-minus student, and if I was frequently criticized for being restless and talkative the teachers also took a liking to me because I meant no harm. My favorite subject was English because my compositions were always imaginative. I also did well in Social Studies and Math, and I got straight A's in spelling. History was one subject that I didn't like. For me, education had one purpose: To prepare me to get a good job. And I couldn't see how studying history would get me there. Black history was something else, and I did a lot of reading on my own. I also read westerns and I was thrilled when I found out there'd been some black cowboys. I hated typing because my hands were too big for the keyboards. Music was another favorite subject because I loved to sing. We also had a class called Mass Media where we'd watch TV and have to remember the commercials and the slogans. The only one I could ever recall was, "Everybody doesn't like something, but nobody doesn't like Sara Lee." And that's only because my all-time favorite food is chocolate cake.

I was motivated to study because Mama would shellac my butt if I came home with a bad report card. Also, the pitch was that if you didn't get a high school diploma you couldn't get a halfway decent job. Not at the 7-11, not driving a truck. So graduating was always a high priority.

I always felt comfortable in a classroom because it was easy for me to speak in front of large groups. And even if I was reading a composition on some serious subject, I'd find a way to make everybody laugh. It was on the basketball court that I felt goofy and stupid because when I first started playing organized ball I could hardly walk and chew gum at the same time.

When my first basketball season got underway at Evans H.S., I was a couple of months short of my 16th birthday, the only tenth-grader on the varsity and starting at center. Me and Harvey Thompson were the only blacks on the team, but the white guys treated us just like everybody else. The only misunderstanding was with Coach Pennington.

Playing on the grass and dirt court in Grandma's backyard, I became a really good ball handler. I could crossover, go between my legs and behind my back. When Coach wasn't around I could dribble the ball from end-to-end and the guards couldn't take it from me. But coach didn't let me dribble the ball because he said he didn't want me "showboating." So whenever I got a rebound I had to pass it to a guard. And I told myself, *"Man, he's fucking with me. I'm going to transfer to Jones."*

The best team around was Martin County High and their starting five were all seniors. All summer long their coach had them playing with ankle weights so when the season started they were flying. But we beat them, and I had 18 points and 12 rebounds. And I started thinking, *"Hey, maybe I can do this. Maybe I can be a really good player."*

Come Christmas time, we went on a road trip to play in a big-time tournament. The players were tripled-up in the hotel and my roommates were two white boys, Kevin Lingabock and Scotty Baker. The thing that most amazed me was that before Scotty went into the bathroom, he said, "I'm going to break the seal." *Say what?* I found out later that when the maids cleaned up the rooms, they put a paper band across the toilet seat, and that was the seal that Scotty got to break. I thought it was hilarious. Growing up with so many people in the same house, the toilet seat never got cold.

Near the end of the season we played Jones High, which was the first-place team in our conference, and even though they probably had better overall talent we beat them pretty easily. As I was walking off the court, some of the Jones High students were razzing the players on their own team. "You guys ain't shit. Evans ain't got but two niggers, man. You all let some white boys beat you."

At that point, I had something important figured out. There was a big difference between white and black basketball. White guys made foul shots and passed the hell out of the ball. White guys played team ball. If a guy was hot, he'd get the ball until he cooled off.

The black philosophy was something else. If you're not scoring beaucoup points, if your picture isn't in the newspaper, if you don't have a trophy, then you ain't the man and you ain't shit. Second place was just as lame as last place. And if a teammate hit nine shots in a row, the black attitude was, "Fuck him. Now it's my turn to get it on."

I used to grumble about transferring to Jones High every time Coach Pennington ragged my ass for loafing through a drill or for dribbling too much. But once I realized how whites and blacks played the game, I knew I was better off where I'd get the ball whenever I was open.

Before I started playing basketball, most of my classmates thought of me as a big, goofy piece of shit. Being the tallest guy in school, there was nowhere I could hide, and every single mistake I made was on public display. So some of the other students would make fun of me every time I walked down the hall. "Hey, you big stupid motherfuck-er. Hey, you big dummy." But now I'd finally found something I could do and do well. I was a legitimate hooper and I was feeling real good about myself.

I felt even better after a milestone event happened the following summer. I was still only 16 and I was washing windows to make some extra money. There was an older lady down the street, maybe she was 30, and I was up on a ladder hard at work and minding my own business. But then I looked in the window and there she was, buck-naked and motioning for me to come get her. *Damn!* I almost fell off the ladder. I chucked down my cleaning rag, ran into the house, took off my clothes and jumped into bed with her. Man, I didn't know what was happening or what was supposed to happen. I just pumped away until I came. Damn, it sure was good. Then the lady cleaned me up and sent me back to finish the windows. I'll tell you something, over the next couple of weeks that lady had the cleanest windows in the neighborhood.

Then my mother got suspicious. "All right," she said, "there's something more than window washing going on over there." When she finally figured out what was what, she went down there and told what she called "that ol' 'ho" to leave me be. But it was too late, because I'd already developed a hearty appetite for pussy.

Going into my junior year, however, basketball was still my first love. I'd grown to six-foot-nine, about 250 pounds, and I was naturally strong. In those days, nobody ever lifted weights, but loading those boxes of oranges had really built up my muscles. I was strictly a post-up player. I never had a hook shot or a jump hook, but because my Uncle Bearcat would knock me down whenever I was close to the basket, I'd developed a good fadeaway jumper. I had quick feet and a really strong up-and-under move to the middle. Whenever I was double-teamed, I was a good enough dribbler to bust my way through the gap.

My brother Chico was a tenth grader at the time and he started playing basketball, too. Chico was so fat that when somebody told him to haul ass he'd have to make two trips. And Chico had a girlfriend we called "Big Messa." She was even fatter than he was and the two of them were living together. But when she broke up with him, Chico was suffering so much that he lost 50 pounds. And there he was all of six-foot-seven, lean and mean, and playing on the junior varsity. Well, we were scrimmaging the JV one day and Chico was lighting everybody up until Coach Pennington had me guard him. So I started banging Chico around and he stopped scoring. After the scrimmage, Chico came up to me and said, "I'm gonna tell Mama you beat me up just 'cause that white man told you to do it."

Later on, Chico turned into a really good player and he wound up getting a basketball scholarship to Bethune-Cookman.

We had an excellent team my junior year. There was Donnie Kuhl, who was six-foot-ten and couldn't shoot a ball out of a cannon, but could rebound and play defense. His brother Eddie Kuhl was six-foot-four and a great shooter—he could stand in the corner and wear your ass out all day long. Slack Taylor was six-foot-seven, Vernon Hale was six-foot-two and Dave Krazit was six-foot-five, and we were still one of the shortest teams around. Our point guard was C. C. Coleman, who couldn't piss in the ocean if he was standing on the shore, but he could run. No matter how far downcourt I threw the ball, C. C. would run it down and make the layup.

For my junior year I averaged around 18 points per game and we only lost two games. One of them was against Littlebrook High when I missed a layup that hit off the back of the rim and bounced out. The only other game we lost was because C. C. screwed up: The score was tied and we were playing for the last shot. C. C. had the ball and was calling out the play, "Two! Two!" The trouble was that he had three fingers sticking up. The rest of us were confused and we started yelling at him, so C. C. took his eyes off the ball to look at his fingers, and the guy guarding him stole the ball, raced downcourt and scored a layup that beat us at the buzzer.

After the season, I got together with C. C. and I said, "The only games we lost was because each of us fucked up. We gotta play basketball all summer." And that's what we did.

That was the summer of 1974, and my mother had a new boyfriend, who I knew as Mr. Henry. Now, Mr. Henry was my man. He was into smoking weed and when his pipe was empty, he'd give me $30 and I'd ride my bike and pump my ass all over town looking to score for him. Naturally, I'd take a few hits now and then.

Mr. Henry worked for Cagill's Chicken Farm and he taught me how to drive a tractor-trailer. Some days when he was too hung over to drive, he'd call me. Then he'd sleep while I drove the truck over to Daytona. And we had a little angle going. Some restaurant would order 20 cases of chicken, so we'd stash two cases somewhere, then load 18 full cases on top of two empty ones. When the guy at the restaurant would sign us out for 20 cases, we had two cases to sell. There's 26 chickens in a case, so we'd go back and pick up our stash, then park behind the Melody Bar and sell the chickens for a dollar each. We'd sell out in about 30 minutes. We never got caught and we never got in any kind of trouble.

One night that summer, Mama had a fight with Mr. Henry. There was another suitor, Mr. Chief, sniffing around and trying to get in solid with her. Mama got into Mr. Chief's car and she said to me, "If Henry comes looking for me, you don't know where I am or who I'm with, okay?"

"Yes, ma'am."

Sure enough, a while later Mr. Henry comes by the projects. "Hey, boy. Where's your mom?"

"I don't know, sir."

He kept at me until I said, "She don't want me to tell you where she is."

Now his eyes light up and he hands me a $20 bill. Now my eyes light up and I say, "She's hanging out with Mr. Chief at the Melody Bar." Then he left to go get in Mama's face.

Mama was real mad when she got back home at two in the morning. "If you think you're gonna sleep in this house tonight," she said, "I'm gonna take my gun and shoot you. You heard me right, boy. I'm gonna shoot you."

I knew she had a gun and I was really convinced she was going to use it on me. So when she went into her room and closed the door, I climbed out of the window and ran like my ass was on fire. I knew I couldn't go to Grandma's house because that would be the first place Mama would look. So I went over to my cousin Hook Smith's house. Around noon that same day, we were hanging out and eating french fried potatoes when Mr. Henry came up to the door. He just looked at me then got back in his car and drove away. Uh oh. That was the end of me. I thought maybe if I surrendered Mama would only shoot me in the leg or something, so I went back home.

She looked at me with disgust and said, "I can't believe you ran away, boy. This is the maddest I've ever been at you. I'm so damn mad at you that I can't even beat you." And she let me be. Talk about dodging a bullet!

By the time my senior year came around, I was up to six-foot-ten and 265 pounds (I'd grow another inch and a half by the end of the season) and we were kicking everybody's ass. The quarters in high school games were only eight minutes long and one time I scored 42 points in 24 minutes. I averaged about 27 points per game and it would have been much more if I didn't get shut out in one of the two games we lost. It was against Oakridge High and I had read my horoscope in the newspaper that morning. The message was that I was going to get exactly what was coming to me that day, so I was expecting to score 50. But the first time I touched the ball I made a quick spin to the basket, somebody stuck his finger right in my eye and I had to sit out the rest of the game. But for the most part, I was killing other teams.

I was having a wonderful time and my imagination ran wild. I loved to read comic books—Superman, Daredevil, Batman, the Green Lantern, Spider-Man, Thunderbolt. All these guys had a secret identity, and when they'd put on a special uniform they'd become superheroes. When I put on my basketball uniform I'd be slamming down four or five dunks every game, so I started calling myself "Chocolate Thunder." And if Batman had the Bat Cave, and if Superman came from the planet Krypton, why couldn't I have my own planet, too? Chocolate Thunder from the planet Lovetron. That was me.

My brothers and sisters were happy for me because I had finally found my niche. My mother came to see me play a few times, but my grandmother never did because she knew nothing about basketball. Grandma called up my father in New York and said, "Frankie, you need to come down here and see your boy Darryl. They tell me he's running more touchdowns on the basketball court than anyone." And Frankie did come down to see me play about three times that season.

Even though she never came to a game, Grandma knew exactly where I was at. She came up to me one day and said, "Darryl, you got a gift. God gave you a gift." I thought she was talking about basketball. "No, it ain't that ball," she said. "Your gift is that you can work with people. Especially with the kids."

I hadn't noticed it until then, but it was true. Anytime there were kids on the playground I was always out there with them cracking jokes and entertaining them. If I had money and the ice cream truck came by, I'd buy them all ice cream. Grandma was a wise old woman.

Just a few days later, the word around school was that there was some kind of racial war about to bust loose. So I happened to walk into the bathroom just in time to see a black guy sticking a white guy's head into the toilet bowl. And the black guy was saying, "Give me your money. All of your money." I really didn't know what I was doing, I certainly wasn't trying to be a hero, but I grabbed hold of both of them and took them into Coach Pennington's office. I think all I had in mind was that one kid was running over another one. Anyway, the coach took them into the principal's office. Both of the kids got suspended and had to spend a couple of days picking up trash around the school grounds. Afterwards the coach called me in and said, "Diesel, it would have been real easy for you to go ahead and help beat up that white boy, but you did the right thing bringing them in here." And his saying that to me felt even better than making a dunk shot.

Even so, there was still a lot of weird racial stuff going on in Evans. There was a white guy in my brother Mitchell's class who was always staring at him in a crazy way. So Mitchell went up to this guy and said, "Why are you staring at me all the time?"

The guy said, "I was just trying to figure out where you keep your tail."

"What? I ain't got no tail."

"No, no. I'm not trying to be funny. My parents said that all you black guys have tails that you roll up when you come to school."

Well, he finally made the football team and when they were in the shower together, he could see Mitchell really didn't have a tail. Later on, they became good friends.

There were a lot of strange goings-on in my senior year. Streaking was popular at school, and one day I was sitting outside when a streaker came racing across the football field. So I jumped up, chased him down and threw him to the ground. Damn if it wasn't one of my basketball teammates, Vernon Hale. "Let me go," he begged me, "and don't tell anyone or Coach'll throw me off the team."

When the word got around that I had caught a streaker, the coach called me in and asked me who was it. "I don't know, Coach. I didn't recognize the guy."

"Diesel, if you don't tell me who it was, you're gonna have to run 50 laps around the track carrying a 20-pound weight."

"I don't know who it was, Coach."

I did the laps and kept my mouth shut. From then on, Vernon bought me lunch every day and did all kinds of errands for me.

We had a team banquet when the season was over and the coach saved one last trophy until the very end. "This award goes to the streaker of the year," he said. "Vernon Hale." We all fell down laughing. How did Coach know? "I saw him running around getting you sodas and bringing you cups of water during practice. It had to be him."

With me feeling better about myself, I also got up the courage to ask a girl I liked for a date. She was on the girls' basketball team and she was tall, about five-foot-ten. All the guys were saying how we'd make such a good couple and they encouraged me to approach her. So I did, with a bouquet of flowers and a box of candy. But she wanted nothing to do with me. "I don't even like you a little bit," she said. Man, that girl broke my heart. Sitting nearby was another girl who overheard what had happened. So this other girl said to me as I passed her, "That's a damn shame." And I gave the flowers and candy to her. This one was only five-foot-four and we dated for several months. That's why, to this day, I only go out with short women.

Anyway, we were running through every team we played and I was scoring points like they were going out of style. The day after I set the school record by scoring 44 points, Coach Pennington called me into his office. I knew there were college scouts and even a few pro scouts tracking me, so I figured he wanted to talk to me about that. Man, was I wrong.

The thing was that I had gotten to be good friends with a white girl named Vicky. Not screwing or nothing, just talking and holding hands. So the coach said, "Darryl, a lot of people are talking about you. You're really causing a lot of ruckus around here."

I still figured he was trying to find out which college I was favoring. "I want you to tell me the truth, Darryl."

"Yes, sir."

"Are you taking Vicky to the prom?"

Say what? Here's a guy who came to get me from Carver, who taught me not to worry about white and black, and now he confronts me with this bullshit? But all I said was "No, sir. I'm taking Dot Williams to the prom." She was a black girl.

"That's okay, then," Coach said. "All right."

Throughout the season, several big-time colleges recruited me, and most made me illegal offers of money. One coach from a big-name school took a wad of $100 bills out of his pocket and put it on the table between us. Wow! It was $3,000 "I can't give this money to you," he said, "but I can put it right here." I'd already decided that if a college gave me money, they couldn't be telling anybody if I took it, right? So, sure enough, when the coach looked away, I picked up the cash.

There were a lot of schools that ran the same routine. I was promised three thousand bucks every month, a car, a job for my mother and another car for her. Kansas was just about the only college that played it straight. Ken Owens was the coach there and he said, "I don't know what other colleges are offering you, Darryl, but what you're gonna get here is a good education, room and board, $20 a month for laundry and a summer job." Most everybody else was crooked and, making the rounds, I wound up with about $12,000 in my pocket.

I gave almost all of the money to my mother to pay the bills. She also went out and bought new clothes for all of her kids. No more third-generation hand-me-downs. For myself, I was too smart to arouse everybody's suspicions by buying a car. So whatever cash I could hide from Mama I used to buy a moderate amount of clothing and also to provide my brothers and sisters with some spending money. But it was all kind of hush-hush.

I was trying to choose between two major schools and was on the verge of committing to one of them because they made everything seem so attractive. I mean, it was hard to walk away from what they were offering.

In addition to the college coaches at our games, there were scouts from the New Orleans Jazz, the Chicago Bulls and the Philadelphia 76ers. In 1974, Moses Malone had been drafted out of high school into the American Basketball Association, but nobody had ever been drafted out of high school into the NBA. So I never gave those pro scouts a second thought.

The biggest surprise was the money offered by sports agents if I'd turn pro. One guy told me that if I signed with him, he'd give me $100,000 as soon as the ink was dry on our contract. A little while later, another agent showed up offering me $200,000. Then a third came along promising $300,000 if I signed with him. That's when I began to think that turning pro might be a good idea.

My mother came into my room one night and said, "Whether you go to college or go pro, Darryl, it's your decision. Whatever you choose I'm with you 100%." What she did not say was, "You got to go for the money to help your family." The only pressure was what I put on myself. I'd seen my mother, my grandmother and my grandfather working so hard for me and my brothers and sisters to have clean clothes and food on the table. Now it was my turn to pay everybody back. To buy my mother and my grandmother decent homes. To help my brothers and sisters through college. To buy everybody some of the luxuries we'd never had.

I also thought that the only reason why anybody went to college was to improve their earning power anyway. But now I had the chance to get the big money right away.

Another factor was the way I played the game. Running and diving into the stands after loose balls, recklessly trying to jump over people to rebound or to block shots. I couldn't change the way I played, but I really believed there was a good chance that I'd hurt myself so badly that my career would be ended prematurely.

That's why I had no hesitation about making myself eligible for the NBA draft. And it's a decision that I've never regretted.

It's a decision facing more and more high school kids these days, and in general I'd encourage them to go ahead and take the plunge. But only if they've got good people they can trust to help invest the money, and only if they're level-headed kids to begin with. Take somebody like Kwame Brown, who was the top pick in the 2001 draft. The Washington Wizards gave him $11.9 million over three years but it seems to me he does nothing but complain. At 19, he's not old enough to go drinking in clubs, all of his friends are still in school back home and he's tired of playing Nintendo in his hotel rooms. Damn! With all that money, he can hire somebody to travel with him, buy a bigger, better Nintendo, and find creative ways to entertain himself. A lot of these kids think that money will solve all of their problems and they'll live happily ever after. It ain't necessarily so. Rich or poor, it's all about what you do with what you have.

Meanwhile Evans H.S. kept winning and winning until we were playing against Miami Jackson for the state championship. And I had a great game. I stole the ball from a guard at halfcourt, then executed a reverse dribble and a hardass dunk. At the end, when the outcome was up for grabs, I hit a bunch of jumpers that won us the game and the championship. For the season, I averaged 32 points and 21 rebounds per game.

Afterwards, Coach Pennington said, "You're gonna get a lot of offers, Diesel. You're gonna need somebody to guide you, to make sure you keep your feet on the ground."

Well, Coach was right, so I went straight to a man I knew I could trust, the pastor of my church, Reverend W. B. Judge. We decided that I needed a professional agent, so Reverend Judge did some investigating and was recommended to Herb Rudoy, a big-time agent out of Chicago. Rudoy flew into Orlando, met with us, explained that he had already found out Philadelphia was going to pick me with the fifth selection in the first round, and told us what he could do for me. It sounded good so I signed a contract with Rudoy.

In those days, the draft wasn't such a media event. I was just told to be in the principal's office at Evans at two o'clock and someone from the NBA would call and let me know what had happened. Sure enough, it all went down exactly the way Rudoy had predicted: The Atlanta Hawks picked David Thompson from N.C. State. The Los Angeles Lakers got David Meyers from UCLA. The Atlanta Hawks picked Marvin Webster from Morgan State. The Phoenix Suns had the fourth pick which was Alvan Adams from Oklahoma. Then the Sixers picked me. (Bill Willoughby, another high school player, was picked by the Hawks in the second round.) Philadelphia's thinking was that I could easily grow to be seven-foot-two or -three and become another Kareem Abdul-Jabbar.

The season before (1974–75), the Sixers had won only 34 games and two years before that they'd gone 9–73, the worst record in NBA history. I was happy to be drafted by a team that had been down but was coming back up. It was an excellent opportunity for me to get a lot of playing time right away.

But before I went to training camp I had to sign my first pro contract, and that was an experience onto itself. I had always intended to share my good fortune with my family. What I hadn't anticipated was all the other people with their hands out. Reverend Judge got 2.5%, my agent got 5% and even Coach Pennington got into the act, although his reward didn't come from my pocket. Ever since he'd questioned me about bringing the white girl to the prom, Pennington had been a different person, much more distant. But he remained part of our inner circle and, in order to keep him happy, the Sixers gave him some sort of scouting contract. It seemed to me, though, that there was plenty of money to go around. I signed a seven-year contract worth more than $2 million, starting at $200,000 for my first year.

Signing that contract sure did wonders for my social life back at Evans. Instead of wearing jeans and T-shirts, I was wearing fancy suits and hats and shoes with tassels. It hadn't been so long ago that the only tassels I had on my shoes were when the shoes started falling apart. All the pretty girls that I liked but wouldn't give me the time of day were now crawling all over me. There was one really beautiful girl that I was just crazy about. Not only would she not talk to me, but she also had a steady boyfriend. Well, there were about ten days left before graduation and I'd just bought myself a blue and white Lincoln Continental convertible. After classes I was about to drive back home when this girl came up to me.

"Would you give me a ride home?" she asked.

"Hell, yeah."

So we're in the car, driving to her house and she put her hand on my leg. "Darryl," she said. "I always did like you." *Damn!* And when we got home she gave me some pussy.

Hot damn!

But Reverend Judge was a wise man. "I tell you, son," he told me, "all kinds of women are going to come over to you 'cause you got money now. All the ones that didn't like you before, now they're gonna love you. You got to be careful, son. You got to protect yourself. Understand?"

I understood. Growing up, none of the guys ever used a condom.

The worst thing you could catch was the clap, and a couple of shots from a doctor would cure that. But I was fortunate that I didn't get anybody pregnant, because, believe me, I did some fucking.

Suddenly, I thought I had all the money in the world. I bought my mother a five-bedroom house at 434 Rock Lake Drive and a yellow-white Coupe de Ville, and I bought my grandmother a house. "I don't care how much money you got," Grandma said, "you're still my sweet ugly boy." (Later on, I also put all of my brothers and sisters through college.) I was 18 and I was going to play in "The League." I had seven years of guaranteed big-time money. So I was happy. Very happy. And while I was waiting to go to training camp, it was time to party.

One night, to celebrate Mitchell's birthday, we went to a bar for some drinks. While we were there we met two girls we had known from school and we all got really friendly. My brothers and my sister Shawn were living with Mama in the new house, but Mama and Shawn had gone out of town to a church convention, so me and Mitchell decided to bring the girls home with us. Chico was hanging around the house and he agreed to keep watch on everything, sound the alarm if Mama came back early.

My bedroom was right across the hall from Mama's, so I moved my stereo into the middle of the hall and put one speaker in her room and one in mine. It was Mitchell's birthday, so I let him take my room while I went into Mama's. So me and this girl were drinking and rolling until we both fell asleep.

Then about five o'clock in the morning someone started banging on the bedroom door. I was dead drunk, but I staggered out of bed and opened the door. Guess who?

"Hello, Mama."

"What's that? Who's that? You get that stinking whore out of my bed!"

And she kept on screaming while I was desperately trying to wake the girl and get her dressed. So I was hurrying and I was scared of what Mama would do to me, and then I got sick and started throwing up on the bed. "Get that whore out of here!"

"I ain't no whore, Mrs. Dawkins," the girl said.

"You're a whore, goddamn it."

On my way out to drive the girl home, I stopped into Chico's room and there he was snoring away. I woke him and told him to go outside the house, knock on my bedroom window and tell Mitchell that Mama's home. Okay. He knocked on the window and when they didn't respond, he opened the window. "Mitchell! Mitchell! Mama's home!" But Chico couldn't wake them.

When I came back to the house I holed up in Chico's room. Mama came and got me at about 11 in the morning. "I ain't gonna beat you," she said to me. "But you're gonna buy me a new goddamn mattress."

"Yes, ma'am."

Then she got into her car and drove to the store for some groceries. While she was gone, Mitchell and his girl came sashaying out of my bedroom. "Hey, what's happening?" Mama never checked the room they were in and they got a free pass.

We called my mother "The Warden," and our bedrooms were "Cell Block One," "Cell Block Two," and so on. She would get out of bed early in the morning and wake up everybody else no matter how late we'd come in the night before. "Get on up," she'd say. "Ain't nobody gonna be sleeping till noon in this house." She didn't care that I was a hotshot professional athlete. Me and my brothers would have to cut the yard or wash the cars or do something.

It was almost a relief when Rudoy called in the middle of the summer to say the Sixers wanted me to come up to Philadelphia and play in the Baker League.

3

Smoked Pork
on the Loose

The Baker League was played at Temple University, right in the middle of a black neighborhood. A couple of NBA teams had squads in the Baker, mostly made up of draft picks like me, the eleventh and twelfth players on last season's rosters, some free agents looking to make enough of an impression to get invited to somebody's training camp, plus some established veterans who lived nearby and were just looking for a good run. The Sixers' team was coached by Jack McMahon, who was an assistant to head coach Gene Shue, and his son Jack Jr. Our most experienced players were Harvey Catchings and Coniel Norman, who'd both played the season before with the Sixers. We had only three days of practice before the games began so things were kind of loose and everybody was mostly freelancing. I didn't know anything about anybody's reputation. All I knew was that I was going to play basketball with some NBA veterans.

The first game was against a bunch of players from New York: John Shumate, Earl Williams, Jocko Jackson and a rookie the Sixers had drafted in the second round, Lloyd Free (who later changed his name to World B. Free). All right. I had my headband on, and my fucked up Afro hairdo, and I was flying high from the opening tip. Bang! I hit my first jump shot. Pow! I busted loose for a dunk. I was jumping to the moon, rebounding like I was a wolf and the ball was a lamb chop, and the Philly crowd was going crazy. Then Shumate tried to dunk on me and not only did I block the shot but I snatched the ball right out of his hand. Earl Williams tried to dunk on me and I did the same thing. Now the fans were chanting, "Dar-ryl! Dar-ryl!"

So I said to myself, *"Damn! I like this shit!"*

After the game, World came over to me and said, "I can't wait to play with y'all." That was the start of a life-long friendship.

We either had a game or a practice session every day except Saturday, so I rented a one-bedroom apartment a short distance away in Voorhees, New Jersey. As a second-round draft pick, World didn't get near the money I got, so to economize he was driving back and forth to New York every day. When it was time for him to play, he was always tired. So I said, "World, you can stay with me."

"You'd do that for me?"

"Yeah. I can only sleep in one room at a time."

So Jack McMahon took us over to A to Z Rental and we got a cot for World. We set him up right in the living room and we started hanging out together. Then World said, "You know why I'm wanting to play with y'all?"

"Why?"

"Because before we played against you that first time, all the guys on my team were talking shit about you. Shumate was saying, 'I'm gonna make that motherfucker wish he'd gone on to college.' And Earl Williams was saying, 'Yeah. I'm gonna bust his young ass.' After y'all dunked on them and caught their shit in midair, they were all sour and shit and saying nothing. It was all I could do to keep from laughing."

I was on a roll that whole time and we won the league championship. I said, *"Damn! Bring on the motherfucking NBA!"*

A couple of weeks later, it was time for the Sixers' training camp. As soon as I walked in the door, I saw Harvey Catchings. "Welcome to hell," he said. "Shue's gonna run the shit out of us."

Gene Shue was straight as an arrow and he never bullshitted the players. And Catchings was right on—Shue would have us run and run and then run some more and then keep on running. I was young and energetic, but some of the older guys were always sucking wind.

In high school my teammates were also some of my best friends and I expected the same situation with the Sixers. But I eventually discovered that true friendship is rare among NBA players.

In a real NBA friendship, the guys are always there for each other.

"Hey, man. I need a couple of thousand dollars until next payday Tuesday." "You got it." True-blue friends will compliment each other about how their games are improving and make suggestions in that direction. "You've got to square up more when you set those baseline picks." And a real friend will also take you to task if necessary. "Hey, man, you didn't play hard enough tonight 'cause you're much better than so-and-so but you let him tear your ass up."

Sometimes, however, if a couple of players get too tight they can create disharmony on a ball club. Then you'll have a situation like the Orlando Magic a couple seasons ago, where it often looked like Tracy McGrady and Darrell Armstrong only wanted to pass to each other. As close as World and I were, we'd always look for one another whenever we played together in practice sessions. But we were rookies after all, so we spent most of the ball games sitting side-by-side on the bench.

One big obstacle to NBA friendship is when two guys on the same team play the same position and are competing for playing time. What they're really competing for is money. That's because the more a guy plays, the better his personal statistics will be (points scored, rebounds, assists, etc.), and better numbers usually generate high-end, long-term contracts.

Over the course of my NBA career, I can number only three other players who I consider to be bonafide, heart-to-heart friends: Earl Cureton, Bobby Jones and World B. Free. It was my good fortune that World and I were rookies on the same team at the same time so we could grow into the league together.

Anyway, I really liked my new teammates and I managed to get along with just about everybody. Of course, some guys were easier to get along with than others, and Harvey Catchings was one of the easiest. Catchings was in his second year in the league and, even though we were both centers, he was always looking to show me the ropes. Harvey couldn't shoot himself in the foot, but he was one of the best defensive players ever. He was the only big man who'd get up in Bob McAdoo's ass. Man, Harvey used to have McAdoo running around in circles like a dog chasing its tail.

Billy Cunningham was on the ball club until he tore up his knee just before Thanksgiving. He was a hell of a player, but he kept his distance from the rest of the guys. Billy was also about as nervous as a rabbit in a dog pound. Imagine my surprise when I saw Cunningham (and Freddie Carter and George McGinnis) smoking cigarettes in the locker room at half-time of a ball game. *Damn! These guys smoke in here right in front of the coach? What the hell. If they're all smoking, then I'm drinking.* So I went over to the cooler and got a beer. Everybody started laughing. Then they told me I couldn't drink the beer until after the game.

Steve Mix was always a wise guy who also kept his teammates at arm's length, and he'd talk shit about anybody. If somebody shot an airball, he'd say, "Next time you feel like shooting, it'll be less embarrassing if you pass the fucking ball to me."

Freddy Boyd was one of the quickest guys I'd ever seen. The trouble with Freddy was that he was too fast. He'd jet to the basket and once he got there he didn't know what to do.

Fred Carter's nickname was "Mad Dog," and he's another guy who loved to talk shit. He didn't like my Afro, so he said, "Hey, man, you gotta get yourself a fucking haircut." But I wasn't taking anything from him. "Suck my dick, motherfucker," I told him. "You don't tell me what to do." Fred was too stunned to come back at me. A rookie facing up to a veteran? From then on, I started busting on Fred every day. I called his kids "little doggie dogs" and he'd just sputter and tell me to go fuck myself.

Joe Bryant (Kobe's father) was strictly on his own page, but he loved playing with me and World and Coniel because we just went out there and had fun.

Raymond Lewis had an excellent training camp, but got cut apparently for political reasons. Philly had picked both Lewis and Doug Collins in the first round of the 1973 draft. But the Sixers decided to give Collins the big money and Lewis was so pissed that he didn't want to play at all. Collins was apparently also pissed because he thought that Lewis was showing him up for being greedy. After sitting out for two seasons, Lewis finally agreed to play and he was tearing everybody up. The rumor, which was never substantiated, was that Doug didn't want to play with Lewis and would ask to be traded if Lewis made the team, so Lewis walked the plank and never did get to play in the league.

Even with all this bullshit going on, I thought Doug was a great guy and I knew he was a great player. If he would've stayed healthy, Doug would've been every bit as good as Larry Bird. We were both represented by Herb Rudoy, so Doug let me stay in his house until I got squared away with a place of my own. Doug was a fitness freak and he'd try to convince me to go out running with him. Every day he'd run his two and a half miles and I'd run with him for about a mile before I quit. It's much easier for thin guys like Doug to do that kind of stuff. I was just a shade under seven feet and weighed 265, and too much extracurricular running wore me out.

But I must say that Doug was also very jittery and I got the impression that he was always on the verge of going over the edge. I remember seeing him sitting in the locker room after a ball game and crying because he said his feet were hurting so bad. But I thought he was really afraid that his career was over and he was more scared than hurt.

Nowadays, Doug's more jittery and less friendly than he used to be, but if we live long enough all of us are bound to change. In Doug's defense, he's undergone some tough shit in his coaching career. Like when Michael Jordan reportedly got him fired from the Chicago Bulls. That's why everybody couldn't understand Michael hiring Doug to coach the Washington Wizards.

Anyway, not that I always took it, but Doug always gave me good advice. "When the team is on the road and you get to your hotel room," he'd say, "you should just lock the door and mind your own business." And he also warned me about how ruthless the business side of the game could be. Whenever a player got hurt, management's attitude was to go out and get another piece of meat to put on the slab. Preferably a white piece of meat to make the fans happy. Throughout the league, management always talked about loyalty between the players and the team, but in reality this was strictly a one-way street. The players were supposed to be loyal, but management hardly ever was. So Doug would tell me, "You've always got to take care of yourself, Darryl, because nobody else in this league gives a shit about you."

In truth, the Sixers' management started busting my chops that first season. After ball games there was always a bunch of kids hanging around near the exit of the lot where the players parked their cars, and

I'd always roll down my windows and give them a hello. One rainy night there was a raggedy-looking black kid out there just getting soaked to his skin, and when he asked me to give him a ride home I said okay. Not surprisingly, he lived in an all-black neighborhood on the poorest, roughest side of town. The same kid was waiting for me after our next game, but this time there was a party waiting for me at his house. His mother had made some delicious fried chicken, a mess of greens and some cornbread. It was the closest I'd been to down-home cooking, and I had a good old time.

Sure, the neighborhood might have been dangerous, but there were about 40 people who had gathered just to check me out. What kind of car did I drive? What was I wearing? Would I sign some autographs? Everybody was as friendly as they could be. Just because they were poor didn't mean they weren't good people.

Somehow, the Sixers' brass found out about my little adventures to the wrong side of the tracks. So someone from the front office came up to me and said, "That was a bad neighborhood, Darryl, and you've got to stay out of there and stay away from those people." Now, I never did have an antagonistic attitude toward authority, but this time I got pissed. I hadn't done anything to cause any trouble for anybody. And, besides, wasn't I a good person who was raised in a bad neighborhood? So I told the guy that the ball club had no business trying to tell me that certain places and certain people were off-limits. And, in fact, I drove that same kid home a few more times.

There were a lot of players, however, who'd act like assholes to try and ingratiate themselves with the Sixers' front office: George McGinnis was the high-scorer and star of the team, and management's favorite player. Most of the players were also McGinnis fans and went out of their way to please him. Every time he made a nice move they'd fall all over themselves. "Did you see that move? Man, George is so great." Whenever me and World heard this kind of bullshit we'd give each other disgusted looks. Being a city-wise New Yorker, World had his own explanation: "Everybody's sucking George's dick because they think if they get in good with him then the ball club won't trade them or fuck with them."

So there I was in my first NBA training camp and going up against two experienced centers, Leroy Ellis and Clyde Lee. They had a lot of little veteran tricks and they made me look bad a time or two. Tugging on my pants, stepping on my feet, hooking my arms. But I was a quick learner and soon enough they'd have to come up with some new tricks. Which they did.

I wasn't all that surprised when I discovered I could compete with the veteran big men. I could run and bang with them, and I could pull up and shoot from 18 to 20 feet. Big guys don't like going outside to guard other big guys and most of them just won't do it. So I could get off a jumper just about whenever I wanted to.

Even with World to pal around with that first year in Philly, I was as lonely as I could be. I missed my brothers and sisters. I missed my mama's cooking. I missed somebody telling me, "Come on, get up out of bed. It's time to go here, it's time to go there." I missed somebody else doing my laundry.

Back home, I'd have to go to church on Sunday mornings or else my mother (or grandmother) wouldn't let me go to the movies, or go to a friend's birthday party. I used to resist and get all grouchy, but after a while I came to enjoy church. When I got to Philly, I thought, "Man, now I don't have to go to church, so I'm not going to go." And for a while I slept late on Sundays. But then I started feeling guilty so I'd start back to going and start back to liking it. Then once the season got into gear, the Sixers had a game scheduled just about every Sunday afternoon, so I couldn't go to church even though I really wanted to. Later on, there was a hullabaloo in the media when my mother came to Philly for a visit and I was late for a Sunday afternoon game because we went to church.

It didn't help my homesickness any when Steve Mix and Fred Carter would always look at me kind of funny, like, "What's this young motherfucker doing playing up here in the NBA and making more money than us?" All of the veterans tried to bully me to see how I'd react. Dave Cowens used to be really physical when we played the Celtics. Sometimes he'd go over the line and be downright dirty. "If you don't like it," Cowens would say to me, "then get your ass back to high school." But I never backed down from Cowens or anyone else. We'd just bang the shit out of each other. WHAM! An elbow to the chops. SLAM! Body against body and bone against bone. After one game, Cowens came over and said, "You know what? You don't have to go back go high school, big fella. You belong here."

All right! I passed the ultimate initiation!

Before and after practice, me and World would play lots of one-on-one. He's only six-foot-three so we had to make up our own rules. World had to shoot inside the paint and I could only shoot from outside. Playing with World helped me with my jump shooting and my ball handling.

Too bad Shue didn't like me taking jump shots. In his day, Gene was an all-star guard and he knew the little man's game cold. But Gene only wanted his big men to rebound, play defense and give up the ball to the guards. Catchings set me straight early in training camp: "If you want to score, you're gonna have to get some stick-backs on the offensive boards, because Shue ain't gonna run no plays for us big men."

There was an early-season game where somebody was in foul trouble so Shue had to put me in with the game on the line. My only job on offense was to step up to the foul line, receive the ball from one wing then reverse it to the other wing. When I caught the ball, though, my defender just backed off so I took the shot. BAM! The very next time downcourt, the same thing happened again. My man backed away so I fired it up and BAM! I was two-for-two. So Gene called a time-out and said, "Stop fucking around, Darryl."

"Gene, I ain't fucking around. I made both of those shots."

"I don't care. Quit fucking around and just swing the ball."

After about ten or twelve games into the season, I realized that I could definitely play at this level. But looking at the record book, I only played 165 minutes in 37 games during the entire season. That's because Gene did not like to play rookies until we were either 20 points up or 20 points down. His attitude was that a rookie's job was to sit on the bench, look and learn.

We were playing in Washington one night and we were 20 points down at the end of the third quarter. During the quarter break, Gene got into it with a referee and got tossed. Jack McMahon was now in the command seat and as Gene was walking toward the locker room, Jack sent me, World, Joe Bryant, Jerry Baskerville and Wali Jones into the game. The rookies and the benchwarmers. So we're playing our asses off, running up and down like it's a fire drill, and with five minutes left we're only down by six points. That's when Gene sent a message to McMahon from the locker room. "Take those motherfuckers out and put the veterans back in." The windup was that we lost by 13.

On our way back in the locker room after the game, me and World were complaining to McMahon. "We could've beat those motherfuckers." But McMahon only shrugged and said, "Speak to the boss."

When we reached the locker room, the boss spoke for himself. "Fuck you, Jack. Can't you at least let me get outta the fucking building before you put your fucking boys in the game?"

But I did have my moments. We were in New York, the game was winding down and we were down by 20 when Gene sent in the shock troops. On the first play I jumped out to block a shot by Earl Monroe. Right after that, I blocked one of Spencer Haywood's shots. Then I hit a jumper. Then I jammed a rebound. At the end, we lost by only ten.

Fred Carter came up to me in the locker room. "You know what, man? You just played four incredible minutes against some of the greatest players in the game. Coach got to start playing you more." And toward the end of the season, he did. Hell, Gene even relented and put in a play for the center. "But we're never gonna run it for Harvey," he said. "It's only for when Darryl's in the game."

Early in the season I bought a house in Cherry Hill and got myself all set up. And I was coming out of my country thing and into a city thing. Instead of, "Hey, y'all, where y'all fixin' to go?" it was, "Wha's up, man? Whachu gonna do?" I was getting more city savvy, but I made sure to call home as much as I could. I was also smoking some pot, taking an occasional snort and fucking my brains out. Anyway, as much partying as I was doing, I was also trying to control myself because I felt that if I went too far Grandma would come get me.

I tried getting Grandma to fly up to Philadelphia to see me play. She'd never been up north in her life. "I'm not coming up there," she said. "If God wanted me to fly He would have gave me wings." And Grandma didn't know anything about what a telephone answering machine was. *This is Darryl. I'm not here right now, but if you leave a message I'll get back to you as soon as I can.* Then I'd hear her hollering, "I know that's you, Darryl. You answer me! You pick up the phone! You hear me?"

Grandma would watch the games on TV and shake that old broomstick at the referees whenever they made a call against me. As little as I played she did a whole lot of stick shaking that year. From the very start, I never liked referees and they returned the favor. I might've liked a ref when he was in his civilian clothes, but once he put on that striped shirt he turned into an asshole. The only referees I respected were Hue Hollins, Hugh Evans, Jake O'Donnell, and Earl Strom. The ones I hated most were Mike Mathis—he should take the whistle and stick it up his ass because that's the only way he's gonna blow it—and Darrell Garretson. Whenever the big men were smacking each other around in the pivot, Garretson would come running over with his little mincing steps and say, "No, no, no, gentlemen. We're not gonna do that tonight." Guys like Garretson thought the fans had come to see them. When they called a traveling violation, they'd skip over to the scorer's table and make a big fuss waving their arms and saying, "No, no, no."

I don't think the NBA referees had ever seen a player like me, a big guy, built like a football player, handling the ball like big men hadn't done before. I was so big and so strong and so young and so cocky. Plus I was talking trash all the time. Like when I was defending somebody who was trying to back me toward the basket, I'd say, "You can't back me down, motherfucker. It ain't that easy." Refs didn't like that and always told me to shut up.

Throughout my NBA career, referees were always looking to nail me. They gave everybody a license to beat on me, but every time I so much as scratched my ass, a foul was called on me. Jim Capers once called a foul on me while I was sitting on the bench. *Tweet!* "Foul, number fifty-three. Five-three." Everybody was confused and looking around for number fifty-three, so I stood up and said, "I'm over here and the only thing I'm fouling is the water bottle." Then Capers started stuttering and looking around for another number. "I-I mean thirty-one. Yeah, that's it. Three-one."

I saw Sam Lacey, who'd been in the league for ages, get in a referee's face and say, "That's a fucking shame how you fucked up that call, you son of a bitch!" And the ref just turned and walked away. I also saw another veteran, Norm Van Lier, say to a ref, "That's bullshit you're calling, man. That's fucking bullshit and you can suck my dick!" Again, the ref walked away. Then when I blocked somebody's shot and said to myself, "Get that shit outta here," I got teed up.

The best thing a referee ever did? We were playing in New Jersey and the game was on the line. Earl Strom and Dick Bavetta were the senior refs, and Strom made a call that went against the Nets and won the game for us. But Bavetta came running and jumping from half-court, saying, "No, no, no! I got a push off against McGinnis!"

Strom said to Bavetta, "Are you overruling my call?"

"I got pushing off right here," Bavetta insisted, and the Nets wound up winning the game.

We were just walking into our locker room when the door to the referees' locker room came flying open and I saw Bavetta come staggering out. His shirt was torn, he had a big knot over his eye and he was running any way he could find to run. Then Strom stepped out into the runway and shouted after him, "You'll take another one of my fucking calls again, right, motherfucker?"

I also came to believe that many of the white refs were racists. White guys always got away with more shit than black guys did. For example, after I was in the league for a couple of years, I was playing in Detroit against Bill Laimbeer, the master of the cheap shot. So I jumped to shoot the ball, and he ran up to me and punched me in the nuts. Almost knocked me out. I'm doubled over in pain and I said to the nearest referee, "Didn't you see that?" The ref said, "No, I didn't see it." Okay. A couple of plays later, I'm under the basket with Laimbeer and I punched him in the kidney. BOOM! He fell down like a little bitch and started screaming, so the referee called a foul. Then the ref came up to me and said, "If you hit a white boy like that, I got to call the foul."

No matter who had position, it seemed that if a black player tried to draw a charging foul against a white player, it was always a blocking foul. Switch them around and the black player was always called for charging into a white player. It also seemed hard for a white guy to foul out because not too many fans were willing to pay to see nothing but blacks out there. The referees must have also realized that the black guys were better athletes than the whites so the white players had to have an edge somewhere. The refs haunted me my whole career. Stan Albeck, who coached me later with the New Jersey Nets, couldn't believe some of the referees' calls that were going against me. Unlike my previous coaches, he decided to do something. After spending hours at the tape machine, Stan put together the very first Darryl Dawkins video. Eight beautiful minutes of my side of the story. A total of 76 fouls called on me that never warranted a whistle. There were hacks that never happened, invisible bumps, imaginary extra steps, clean blocks that turned into free throws for other teams. Then Stan sent the tape to officials in the NBA league office but nothing changed.

According to the league, even though I may have had perfect position to draw a charge I was inevitably called for a block only because I was so big. Whenever I fell down after drawing what really was a charge, the logic went like this: "If a guy as big as Dawkins falls after being hit by a smaller player, then Dawkins must be faking." And what about all the times I was fouled in the act of shooting? "Dawkins is too strong for anything but a karate chop to interfere with his shot." That's the same reasoning that keeps Shaquille O'Neal from shooting 30 free throws every game.

To make matters worse, the referees never took me seriously. Common referee wisdom held that a player wasn't really playing hard unless he had a hangdog look on his face. The look you get when the finance company repossesses your car, or when the landlord raises your rent, or when your wife tells you she's ten weeks pregnant and you've been on a West Coast trip for three months.

On the court and off, I've always got a smile on my face. And why not? It's great to be alive. Even when I'm mad I don't scowl too long before my grin takes over. Unfortunately for me, the refs decided early in my career that I was only out there to clown around. Yet there were other guys, like Magic Johnson and Dominique Wilkins, whose standard game-face included a shit-eating grin, and the refs gave them the benefit of every close call.

I tried everything to establish a rapport with the refs. I even swallowed my pride and tried complimenting them. When I said, "Nice call," they shot right back with, "I know." When the nice-guy approach didn't work, I yelled at them to try and make them think more about the next call. Besides a sore throat, all that got me was more quick fouls and early exits. In all, I played in the league for 14 seasons and I could never completely understand the referees' continuing and personal bias against me. In hindsight, though, I think the answer to the mystery was very simple: Somehow the referees figured out that I really thought they were all dickheads.

So fuck referees and everybody who looks like them.

My rookie year also showed me some surprises off the court as well: My father was living in New York where he had a company called Automatic Platers that could put gold-plating on any kind of raw metal. He called me up in Philly one day and said, "Come over here to New York, boy. I want to show you something." We had a day off so I drove up there in a Mark IV I had bought. I'd never been to New York by myself before and I was scared to be there. I don't know, there's something about New York that I didn't like. Even when I was playing across the river with the New Jersey Nets, I rarely ventured into New York. So I met Frankie at the Flash Theater in Harlem, a classy soul food joint with a garden in front. We were sitting at a table and even though I was still scared to death, I was trying to maintain my composure. We were looking at the menu when a black guy walked over to us. He looked exactly like me except he was about six-foot-four. So he pulled out a chair and sat down with us. "Hey, man," I said. "This is me and my father's table."

"That's my daddy, too," he said.

Then my father took his gin and tonic and poured it down his throat before he said to me, "I got to tell you something, boy."

That's when I found out that I had another half-brother who was only a year younger than me. Meaning that when Frankie was living with Harriette, he was fooling around somewhere.

And that wasn't even the end of it: We were in Washington, D.C., to play the Bullets when a tall girl came up to me after the game. She must've been a six-footer. "What's up, brother?" she says. "How you doing?"

"Yeah, yeah," I said, thinking she's just another girl trying to hit on a rich NBA player.

"No, no," she said. "I really mean it when I said 'brother'."

What the fuck? "Get away from here, girl. Go put that routine on somebody else."

Then she said her name was Gerry Lynne Dawkins and that Frankie was her father. Frankie lived here and he worked there and this was his phone number. Then she called him up and put me on the phone. "Pop, this girl is here and she's says you're her father."

"That's your sister," he said. "Take her to dinner. I'll see you later." Then he hung up.

During my rookie year, the surprises never stopped: The team was checking into a hotel in New Orleans and while we were waiting in the lobby for our room assignments I was drinking a soda and entertaining all the guys like I always did. Talking trash, talking in rhymes, talking about all the pussy on Lovetron, talking about what I'm gonna do to this girl and that girl. All of a sudden this beautiful girl walked up to us and said, "You hot. You're cute." The guys were looking around to see who she was talking to because she was a real knockout. I had a really good mirror in my house so I knew I wasn't anything close to cute, and I was looking around, too.

"You right there," she said. "You. You're cute." And she was looking at me. "Yeah, you." So even though I dropped my soda, I immediately became cute.

"What you doing tonight after the game?" she asked.

"I ain't doing nothing."

"You want some company?"

"Yeah, yeah."

When I went back to the front desk all the guys were cheering me on. "You just got chosen, man. You better be knowing what to do with that fine looking pussy."

"Yeah, man. I'm gonna bust that pussy tonight. Yes, I am."

After the game, the girl came by my room, we jumped into bed, rolled around and had a hell of a night. When we woke up the next morning she said, "That'll be a $100."

What?

"That's right. I'm a prostitute, and if you don't pay up my pimp is gonna come up here and put a bullet in your ass."

Damn!

After that, I decided to be more careful. I knew that I was raised better than what I was doing, so I tried to back up and not sleep with just anybody. This was a hard thing to do because being in the NBA, and traveling from town to town, there were girls coming at me from everywhere. A few times I've even been scared by a girl. "What's with it, big name? Can I get that dick?" Get the hell away from me. Most guys are like that. If you're pursued too hard, then you don't want it. But if you're the pursuer, then you want it bad.

I've played with some world famous players who talked to the media about how dedicated they were to their wives and how happily married they were. And whenever we went on a road trip they'd take off their wedding rings. When I was a rookie, Gene Shue told me the rule of the road: "What you see on the road stays on the road."

Gene also had another rule: If any player came into the hotel bar and Gene was entertaining someone the player had to turn around and walk back out. Well, we were in Houston the night before a ball game and me and World came into the hotel bar. Gene was there, but we were pissed at him because he wasn't playing us, so we sat right down at the bar and ordered some beers. Gene looked at us and said, "You guys know the rule."

"Fuck the rule," World said.

"Yeah," I chimed in. "You ain't playing us, so why do we give a shit?"

Gene said, "Be careful what you ask for." Then Gene and his guest left.

Came the ball game the next night, Gene put me and World in the game and left us in for nine straight minutes. Now, when a player's only been playing in practice he thinks he's in shape, but being in game shape is altogether different. So me and World got tired in a hurry and we motioned for Gene to take us out, but he just looked the other way. During the next time-out I was pissed. "Coach, you seen I was trying to get out of the damn game."

"You guys wanna play?" Gene said. "You wanna be a man. Okay, so be a man."

When Gene finally did yank us, me and World sat at the far end of the bench and hoped he wouldn't call us again. And that was the last time either of us ever broke that particular rule.

The team won 46 regular season games, which was 12 games better than the year before. Philadelphia also made the playoffs for the first time in five years. All the veterans kept telling me about how intense playoff games were and I was anxious to see for myself. Turned out that's when I played longer and better. Gene gave me 10 minutes per game and I averaged 5.3 points and 3.2 rebounds.

We didn't get past the first round, losing a mini-series to Buffalo, two games to one. Gene gave me more playing time against the Braves than he had in the regular season and I was balling. I even took it coast-to-coast and threw it down a couple of times. After we'd lost, the media asked Gene where I had been all year. Gene told them blah then he said to me, "If you had played the right way from the beginning, Darryl, you would have played more."

"Then I should've been playing," I said, "because I was kicking ass all year."

Then Gene said, "Aw, c'mon, Darryl. Fuck it," and we both laughed.

If I wasn't happy about all the pine-time I'd had, I expected that I'd be in the regular rotation next year. Yeah. That's when I was really going to kick ass.

Over the summer, I went back down to Florida for a short visit. I had gone to Boyd's clothing store in Philadelphia, so I was dressed like a rich pimp. A tan suit with brown stripes that cost $450, two-tone shoes, a stylish shirt and tie, and a brown hat. I also had a new car, a black Fleetwood Broughman with white-wall tires and all the extras money could buy. First off, I went to see my mother and my brothers, sisters, uncles, aunts and cousins, and we had a great time. Just to have something to do, my mother was still working off and on, but she took the time to make my favorite meal (fried chicken with hot sauce) and we all ate like we'd just been rescued from a desert island. Afterwards, I was anxious to go out partying, but I drove into the country to see Grandma.

She was rocking on the front porch as usual. "Hey, Grandma. How you doing?" Then I peeled off three or four $100 bills, gave them to her and said, "Well, I'd like to visit, Grandma, but I can't stay right now."

"Wait, wait. Where you going? Sit down, boy. You ain't got nothing to do and nowheres to go."

"But, Grandma, I gotta ..."

"Sit down."

"Yes, ma'am."

"All right, then," she said. "Don't you come around here with a big head, 'cause easy as you got it, that's how easy the Lord can take it away. You gotta keep your feet on the ground, boy, and stay humble. You gotta get back to going to church. Now come inside and let me feed you right."

Even though I had just eaten a big meal at my mother's place, I had to eat at Grandma's. It was always like that. She had retired completely, and she'd spent all day cooking up some ham hocks and greens and cornbread, so I had to sit there and stuff myself again.

But Grandma always kept me under wraps. Because of her I never did go as buck wild as I could have. She was the wisest person I ever met. God rest the dead.

After visiting with my family, I had to take care of my buddies, so I went to the bus station where they were all hanging out and I told them stories about the NBA. First they wanted to know about the girls. Yeah, I had this one and that one and the other one. All the winos and the druggies I had played with were also there, just sitting in the shade and scratching. "Hey, man, you made it," one of them said. "But you owe it all to us, motherfucker. Am I right? If we didn't beat your ass out on that basketball court you still wouldn't've been shit." Then the other winos started to chime in. "Yeah, motherfucker. You owe us something."

So I bought them about six bottles of wine and they were as happy as a pig taking a shit-bath. About two hours later, they were all still sitting there, but fast asleep.

While I was back in Florida I stayed at my mother's house. The only good thing about that was she didn't make me do any chores. It was good to be home and get reconnected to my own roots. And I was really sensitive to the difference between how white people lived and died and how blacks did the same.

Most white men have some kind of life insurance, so when the head of the family dies he can leave some money behind. At least enough to bury him. When a black man dies he leaves bills and outstanding loans, so everybody's got to scramble and hustle up funeral money. I saw a hat passed around a bar or a barbecue pit dozens of times. "My so-and-so died and we're trying to buy him a casket."

When a white guy starts making big money, all he usually has to do is help out some at home. Most of the time his parents will even keep their jobs. But when a black man strikes it rich, he's got to support his whole family. That's why it's so hard for a black ballplayer to save any money. His agent's stealing money out of one pocket and, out of the other pocket, he's taking care of his family. Comes the day when his playing career is over and his income is drastically reduced, I've seen retired players trying to help their families to the point where they were hurting themselves.

As much as I liked being back home, I did have a hard time making certain adjustments. After ball games, NBA players don't get to bed until three or four in the morning anyway, so I was in the habit of sleeping late. The only way I'd be getting up at eight or nine is when there was a plane to catch. But there was Warden Harriette knocking on my bedroom door and saying, "Come on. Time to get up. Come on, you lazy boy."

"Aw, Mama. What do I got to get up for?"

"'Cause this is my house and nobody lays around till noon here."

Another problem was that I couldn't walk around wearing just my drawers like I did in my own house. Mama didn't like that either. "Put some clothes on, boy. This ain't no peep show here."

I love my mother, so I hate to say that she could get on my nerves. With her being a Sagittarius and me being a Capricorn, we could get along for a while. But we were both happy when it was time for me to get back to Philadelphia.

4

Scoring Off the Court

The 1976-77 team had some important new players (including a guy named Julius Erving), and one of the more interesting ones was Henry Bibby, who had been in the league for four years with the Knicks and the New Orleans Jazz. He was a scrappy scoring guard and, like Doug Collins, he was always doing something to stay in shape. Stationary bikes, treadmills, he wore them all out. And Henry worked just as hard to get laid. Every girl he saw he gave the same line: "Hey, my name's Henry. You want to fuck?" Baggage girls at the airport, limousine drivers, desk clerks, maids, waitresses. One day I wanted to know why he kept on asking the same question. "Because I have it figured out," he said. "One out of nine girls says 'yes'."

Henry had a phone book that was second to none. I mean, you could wake up at four in the morning, look out the hotel window and see Henry walking across the street with a girl. We called him "Henry the Hound."

There was a lady reporter for one of the Philly newspapers who used to come into the locker room after the game. The guys would walk around with their dicks flopping just to see her blink. The trouble was that this lady was getting inside information about the team— who had a fight in practice, which married man was caught on the road with another woman, who was pissed at the coach and why—and she was printing it in the paper. When we asked her who her source was, she said "Deep Basket." Now all the players are looking at each other. Deep Basket? Who could that be? At first, everybody thought it was me, but then a better explanation appeared. The reporter was seen going in and out of Bibby's hotel room. Yep, we figured he must have been screwing her and giving her the dirt on the rest of us. Because of that, I always thought Henry Bibby was only out for himself, and that he was a slimy kind of guy.

I think that NBA players get hooked on sex for the same reasons they get involved with drugs—too much free time and too much money. Yet what really makes guys into pussy hounds is loneliness. People usually don't think of NBA players as being lonely, but they are. The loneliness comes when you don't trust women. All the guys are constantly warning each other to be wary of bad women who're just looking to grab some of their money. So you start looking for one-night stands with beautiful women. Then you cast about for days for redheads with titties, or big-assed blondes, or skinny brunettes, or whatever. So it's loneliness that leads to lust.

Love is something entirely different. Love is something you find when you're not looking for it. You might be in a club and see a woman and you like her looks. Then you go over and talk and you seem to get along. Then you go out a couple of times, simple things like a movie or dinner, and sometimes she pays and sometimes you pay. You'll go to a house party and then to church together, and the next thing you know, you're in love.

For pure, lustful sex, though, the late '70s to the early '80s were the best of times. Nobody ever heard of AIDS back then. The worst you could catch was the clap, and the team's trainer had pills for that. That's why it was so hard for married guys to be faithful. No matter how pretty or sweet-smelling your wife (or your girlfriend back home) was, there was always a girl on the road who was prettier, smelled sweeter, had that certain walk that made her ass pop, and knew how to come at you. It sometimes got so crazy that girls would compete with each other. "That bitch ain't got shit. I got all the pussy you need right here."

Then, now, and forever, the NBA's pussy haven was Salt Lake City. Ummm-umm. That's the main reason why black guys want to play for the Utah Jazz. The second-best pussy capital was Atlanta, with New Orleans a close third. By far the worst place to get laid was New York City, only because the girls there couldn't be trusted. I couldn't number how many times a teammate would come up to me while we were partying somewhere in New York to say this: "Hey, Dawk. Do me a solid, man. I got this hot chick for tonight and I don't know her that good. So keep my wallet and my jewelry for me, man." And the next morning on the bus, he'd say, "Hey, Dawk. Give me back my shit. Thanks, man." Only in New York.

There have also been lots of times when a ball club was destroyed by lust. One famous example happened in the mid-'90s when Jason Kidd and Jim Jackson were both playing for the Dallas Mavericks. The papers reported that Toni Braxton was going out with both of them at the same time. When the news got out, Kidd and Jackson were apparently pissed, not at the girl, but at each other. It looked to me like they stopped passing to each other and that they didn't care whether Dallas won or lost because they only wanted to win the girl.

It's all about competition, and when sex is involved, friendships go out the window. Everybody had their special hangout buddies at home, and also on the road in cities where (or close to where) they either lived or went to college. When the cliques of two or more teammates happen to be in the same nightclub, they're both competing for attention and for women. Hey, who's the fucking star here? It's the same old thing about black guys getting caught up in trying to be the man everywhere they go.

Not having gone to college myself, my friends were mostly in Philly, Orlando, and Detroit, where I had played some summer ball. (Nowadays guys have "posses" that can fill a small room.) One of those friends was Earl Cureton, who I first met after the Sixers drafted him in 1979. Even after he was cut, we remained close, and we never worried about competing for the ladies' attention, not in Philly and not even in Earl's hometown of Detroit. Our philosophy was like this: There's enough for everybody. Your boys will get some pussy. My boys will get some pussy. Now let's me and you sit back and get drunk.

Who could argue with that?

It's fair to say I sampled just about everything sex-wise during my career, but certain moments can't help but stand out.

During a disappointing 1978-79 season, the best thing that happened to me all year long took place in a hotel room in Washington,

D.C. Since Philly was only a short bus ride away we normally didn't stay overnight in D.C. except during the playoffs, but this one night we did. The players were at the hotel bar laughing and yakking and trying to get something going with the girls. There was one beautiful girl who caught my eye, and she seemed to be bored by the whole scene. And I liked that. She was different, not just some giggly bitch trying to hook on to a rich athlete. Now, I wasn't near as good looking as the other guys, and I didn't have long curly hair that most girls like. But I was clean, I knew how to dress, and I could be funny. So I stepped up and just entertained the drawers off of her. Her name was Glenda and she was in her early thirties. I made her laugh until she had cramps in her stomach.

When it was time to leave, a couple of the guys were on her, but she said, "No, I'm going with him." And she pointed to me. All right! We went up to my room and we got to rolling, rolling, rolling, and I'm jumping up and down and doing all I can do. Yeah! So then we laid back in the bed and I was ready to go to sleep.

"I'm warning you," Glenda said, "if you fall asleep, I'm gonna put my pussy in your face."

Now, a black country boy from Florida ain't eating no pussy. Not me. I ain't bringing my dinner plate to the dump. Most black guys just won't eat pussy. Never. And those that did had to be very careful because if you ever ate a redhead's pussy then you were sure to get sick. (That's exactly what happened once to my brother Chico.) And if a black man was foolish enough to go down on a woman who was having her period, then he'd be under her spell and he'd be in love with her forever. So I said to Glenda, "Girl, if you do that, I'm gonna have to get up and knock your ass out."

"Well, I'm gonna do it. I promise you."

I thought she was just bullshitting, so I closed my eyes and I was gone. Next thing I knew, I woke up to find nothing but ass in my face. What? Huh? What the fuck? Hmmm. Long as it's right here. Lickety-split. Damn! This ain't half bad! And that was the start of my pussy-eating career.

Coincidentally a couple of days later I got a call from *Playboy* magazine asking if I would do an interview. Sure, bring it on. So the writer was asking me about black guys and white guys and black women and white women, and then he said, "What do you think about eating pussy?"

I said, "Yum-yum, gimme some."

When the interview was published, my mother saw it and she was very embarrassed. "Darryl, you just told all of your innermost secrets. I can't believe you did it."

But when the team got to L.A. there were a bunch of messages waiting for me. Stuff like, "I got the biggest, prettiest pussy you've ever seen. Do yourself a favor and let me come on over and I'll let you take a look and a lick."

From then on, lots of incredibly beautiful women would come up to me saying, "I hear you eat pussy." Hell, yeah! "Okay, then let's go."

So I was starting to go around with gorgeous women, starlets and models, and players on other teams who didn't know what was going on would say, "Man, what's an ugly motherfucker like you doing with that beautiful girl?" I'd just wiggle my tongue and do like 'Aaah, aaah,' and all they could do was to laugh.

Of course, there were other sexual possibilities available. I know of about five or six NBA players who were gay, and there probably were even more. And since the rest of us were in prime physical condition, there were always homosexuals hanging around the clubs that we frequented.

In Philly, some of the players hung out in Kim Graves' nightclub, and a flaming homosexual we all got to know was sure to be there, too. He loved to dress up like Mae West with a white wig and a red dress, and he was always cracking gay jokes. "There's that big mother-fucker, Darryl Dawkins. I'll bet he dribbles before he shoots." Well, he would sometimes come over to my house to do some decorating with curtains and drapes. He also cooked a delicious spaghetti sauce and he smoked weed without trying to force his asshole on me or anything like that. The point is that he was a nice person and fun to be with.

My sister Amanda has a lot of gay friends and the ones I've met were wonderful people. Hey, they're different from straights the same way blacks are different from whites, or Chinese are different from Japanese.

The way I always saw it was that God created Adam and Eve, not

Adam and Steve. However, if a man chooses to be with a man, that's his prerogative. But it sure ain't mine. I mean, sometimes after I eat bad food it hurts when I fart or take a shit. Now why would anybody want to force something in their ass that's not supposed to be there? I don't even want a woman's asshole. I don't understand gays, but at the same time it's their private business what they do with their private parts. The only problem I have is when a homosexual forces himself (or herself) on somebody else.

I was in Atlantic City one night and a homosexual scared me worse than a man with a gun. I was playing the slot machines when this guy came over looking like an albino Sam Elliott, wearing a white jacket, white pants, white shirt, and white shoes, and with his white hair pulled all the way back.

He said, "Oh, you're winning! You're winning! You know what? I'm gonna touch you for more luck." Then he reached out and grabbed my dick!

I yelled out, "Security! Security!" Then I said to the guy, "You better get away from here before I put my foot in your ass."

"Oooh," he said. "The whole foot? The whole foot?"

I got up and hid out at the blackjack table.

Another incident showed just how un-smart basketball players can be. After a game, the players all went out to a nightclub. Right away, two of the guys connected with two good-looking girls. Before I started sniffing out the available pussy, I was surprised to see a guy I knew from Detroit, Greg Guy. "Hey, Popeye. What's going on, man?" But he couldn't even talk for laughing. When he saw my teammates leave to go back to the hotel with the girls, Popeye was laughing so hard he was crying.

"Let's go, man," I said to him. "I got to smoke some of that shit that's making you laugh so much."

When we got to my room, Popeye rolled up a joint, but he still couldn't stop laughing. I took a couple of tokes, and it was good shit, but my funny bone wasn't tickled even a little bit. " Popeye, what the fuck's going on?"

"I gotta tell you, Dawk. Go tell your teammates that those two girls they're with are really boys."

"What?"

"No lie."

So I went to their room and knocked on the door. "Hey, it's me, Darryl."

From inside, one of the guys yelled, "We're busy. Get the fuck away."

"I gotta talk to you, man. It's very important. Believe me, you want to hear what I have to say."

So he opened the door and I stepped into the room. The he-shes were sitting on the couch drinking Hennessy. Their dresses were hiked up to their panties and the guys were getting all excited.

"Guys," I said, "those two ain't got one pussy between them 'cause they're both faggots."

"What?"

Then one of the he-shes said, "It's that motherfucker Popeye saying bullshit about us. If I see that bitch, I'm gonna cut him."

"They can't be faggots," said one of the players. "They already drank up all of our liquor and ate a whole bucket of chicken wings."

"Check out their drawers."

When one of the guys went over to have a close look, the he-shes clamped their legs tight. "Open your legs, motherfuckers," he said. Of course they refused. Then he started muttering about booze and chicken wings and how horny he was. So he said to the drag queens, "Listen, I know you ain't girls, but we already spent so much goddamn money ..." Then he grabbed his crotch and said, "Couldn't y'all do something for us up in here anyway?"

He had to be joking, but I laughed so hard I almost peed my pants.

Thinking about the game and about the NBA culture was something that increasingly occupied my attention. And with all the sticking and licking I was doing, I finally began to see what all the agreeable women had on their mind: Like Don King always says, it was nothing but M-O-N-E-*MOTHERFUCKING*-Y!

Sometimes a guy will meet what he thinks is a really together woman on the road somewhere. She'll be wearing a fur coat, an expensive dress and shoes, a couple of gold rings on her fingers, and she'll be driving a Jaguar or a BMW. She'll come up to a player and say, "I don't need anything. I just want to suck your dick and give you some pussy." And the guy thinks, "Finally here's a girl who's got her own shit and won't be looking to mooch anything off of me." What the guy doesn't know is that the dress and shoes belong to her sister, the rings belong to her mother, the car belongs to a cousin, and she's going to bring the fur coat back to the store the next day. He doesn't know that she's got two kids, her sister's got three kids and they all live together in a two-bedroom apartment in the projects. He doesn't know that what she's looking for is to have his baby so she can sue his ass and get child support for the next 18 years. Or else she'll want a lump-sum settlement. Unfortunately, I know all about this, and similar sad scenarios, from personal experience.

The first time I got involved with something like this was on my birthday in 1979 when I saw a pretty girl sitting behind the bench during a game. She had her titties up, her red blouse, and her red lipstick, so I took a second look. Later, when I was at a club to celebrate my birthday, she came up to me and started talking. Her name was Penny, but I was mostly interested in getting drunk so I brushed her off. When I moved on to another club, she turned up there, too. "Don't be following me around," I told her. By the time I arrived at still another club I was tanked, and there she was. So we went over to my place and bounced around.

Penny came from a nice respectable family and we actually became good friends. We saw each other for a few months then she told me that she was pregnant and wanted to have the baby. Okay. I wasn't going to force Penny into having an abortion and I was willing to accept my responsibility. So I gave her money for maternity clothes, and when she had the baby, I gave her money for a crib and baby clothes. Now I had a baby daughter named Dara, and by the looks of her there was no doubt that she was mine. Just to make sure, I sent a picture of the baby to my mother. "No question," Mama said. "That's my granddaughter right there."

Instead of siccing two lawyers on each other, we went to court and settled things by ourselves. Penny had Dara dressed up in a little Sixers' uniform, so the baby looked even more like me. We decided on a one-time, lump-sum settlement of $70,000.

After I paid it, we were on much better terms. I would go over to her place to spend time with Penny and the baby and it worked out. Penny and I matured much better apart then we would have together.

A lot of unwed mothers try to turn their children against the father. "Your daddy don't want you. He left you and he left me." But Penny was very respectful to me in the way she raised Dara. She'd call me every so often to remind me that I hadn't seen Dara in a while, so I'd make the time to go visit them whenever I could.

There was another time where a girlfriend got pregnant that didn't have such a happy ending. When this girl found out she was pregnant, she said to me, "I got your baby. It's in here and it's a boy. And I'm gonna get your money, you motherfucker." I didn't see her for a couple of months so I braced myself for a lawsuit. Then I ran into her sister, who told me there had been a car accident and the baby hadn't survived. I was sad for the baby, but happy that the girl hadn't been able to hook me.

Sometimes the whole thing gets even more low-down and dirty. A friend of mine on another team was in his hotel room just punishing some girl's pussy, while another girl was standing outside, knocking on the door and saying, "Hurry up and put that bitch out! She ain't got no pussy! I got all the pussy out here!" Twenty minutes later, the first girl left and the other girl walked in.

Or you're with a girl somewhere on the road, maybe Chicago, and she keeps telling you that you're the only one for her, and you believe her. You don't know that when the next team comes into town she's saying the same thing to another player. Now let's say your team loses to Indiana in the playoffs so your season is over and you're thinking that you want to go hang out with this girl who really loves you. So you call her and call her and she's never home. Since you're in Indianapolis you drive down to Chicago, but she still won't answer the phone. So you decide to go see the Bulls game and hang out with the guys. Then you see her after the game, waiting for one of the players. "Hey, Susan, how're you doing?" And she says, "I can't talk right now. I've got something going on here." And she leaves with somebody else.

Bitches like this may not walk the street wearing see-through blouses and pink hot pants, but they're still prostitutes.

All right. What about using a rubber to make sure a girl doesn't get pregnant? Well, there's a couple of things working against this. The first is that more black guys than white guys believe that pussy isn't the same if you're wearing a glove. And it's true. You can still get your shit off, but it doesn't feel near as good as doing without. The black guys want to go raw dawg. Remember that AIDS wasn't a problem back in those days. The second thing is that most of the younger guys didn't even know how to use a rubber. My mother made sure to show me how to put one on. That's right. She got a banana and showed me how it's done.

There are all kinds of horror stories. I've heard lots of times about a girl supplying a rubber, only she's already poked holes in it. Or a guy got a girl pregnant, and when she sued him he discovered that the name he knew her by wasn't even her real name. There are so many girls coming at a pro athlete from so many different angles just looking for a meal ticket.

I had one girl, who I'll call Gail, stay overnight at my house and in the morning she wouldn't leave. She stayed around and cooked, cleaned the house, scrubbed the floors, everything. When I brought another girl home for the night, Gail just slept downstairs on the couch. Then she made breakfast for me and the new girl, and kept on cleaning and cooking like a hired maid. This went on for about six weeks, and even though I had several other girls stay the night, Gail never complained. One day I came home with a girl but I threw her out after we had a fight. Then I went downstairs, put a bottle on the table and started drinking. That's when Gail came over. "I never asked you for nothing," she said. "All I want to do is take care of you, because I love you. I really do." Damn! Maybe Gail is for real. Maybe she's the one I've been looking for. Uh uh. Turned out she was just plotting to get me all along.

All kinds of respectable women come after NBA players: Doctors, lawyers, even judges and talk show hostesses. Because I was in the limelight, some of them got off on fucking celebrities and some wanted to use me to boost their careers.

Some women who are celebrities in their own right also like to fuck other celebrities. One ex-player had just gotten married, but then he appeared on a very popular talk show and started fucking the hostess. When his wife found out, she threatened to sue him for $6,000,000. "Man," I said to him, "how could you be so stupid?" His only defense was, "Neither of us could help it. I have a thing for famous women and she has one for famous men."

With all the goings and the comings, I was always looking to fall in love. One African woman said to me, "I'm about to lose my citizenship. If you marry me I'll give you $10,000. We'll have to live together for a year, then you can go your way and I'll go mine."

I said, "But what happens if I fall madly in love with you?"

"That's a chance you'll have to take."

"Maybe you'd better find somebody else."

Girls would even cozy up to my brothers to get close to me. One night, my brother brought a girl to my house in Philly and they were doing their thing while I was sleeping. Then in the middle of the night, his girl just jumped into my bed and went to work on me. "You're the one I want to be with, Darryl." This happened several times. Now my mother and my grandmother both used to tell me not to fool around with any girl that any of my brothers were seeing. Doing that was nasty and disgusting. So in the back of my mind, I knew that what I was doing was wrong. At the same time, once I put my dick in there what was wrong felt awfully right.

Now, one of my nicknames was Big Freak because I was always sexually adventurous. Putting whipped cream on a girl's titties, chocolate syrup on my dick, I did all that stuff. And I thought, well, if I'm a freak, then fuck it, I'm a freak. And sometimes all the guys would be out at some club, a beautiful girl would come around and they'd be shooting the come-on shit at her. Then when I walked in, the guys would say, "Here comes the Big Freak." Bet your bottom dollar the girl would come over to me and say, "How come they call you that?" She'd be interested because she might get something from me that she couldn't from the other guys. That was fine with me because the both of us were just looking to have a good time without anybody getting hurt or feeling used.

Now, I never considered myself to be a low-down pussy hound. Wilt Chamberlain used to say that he'd had 20,000 women. Maybe I've had a 1,000, so I was never more than a button on Wilt's shirt. But I never did anything to manipulate a woman so that she felt obliged to give me her pussy. I never bought a woman groceries, or jewelry, or clothes, or fixed the transmission in her car, just to try and buy her pussy. A lot of guys would do shit like that. If I didn't like a girl then

I never slept with her. There had to be a mutual attraction and a mutual willingness or else there'd be nothing doing. That's because I've always had the utmost respect for women. I've seen too many single women raising families for me to take advantage of them.

There were always different kinds of team functions where the players and their wives and girlfriends would get together. Everybody would tease each other and we'd all have a lot of fun. I'd always come there by myself, and I'd make everybody laugh, but it got to the point where I was beginning to feel like the court jester. So I began to be interested in trying to find a long-term relationship with a woman who could dig me for who, and not what, I was. The trouble was that with all the women coming at me just for a good-time one-night stand, or else to get their hands on my money, it was hard to recognize a good woman when I saw one.

I met a girl at a club in Philly, a former southern beauty queen who was ten years older than me. I mean she was gorgeous. She stayed with me for four days, both of us sleeping buck naked and kissing and hugging, but she wouldn't give me any pussy. I did a lot of begging, but I went along with her program until I couldn't take it any longer and I brought home another girl who was ready to go. "Miss Beauty Queen," I said. "You got to get out." Before she left, she said, "I was holding out because I wanted to see if you really liked me as a person. And I was gonna give you some pussy tonight."

Damn! I fucked it up.

Maybe so. But the truth was that I was only 24 and still too young to know what was good for me.

5

The Doctor
is In

No player brought more attention to the 1976-77 Sixers than Julius Erving, Doctor J. The American Basketball Association had folded and the Sixers' owner, Harold Katz, bought Doc's rights from the New Jersey Nets. Doc had been the whole show in the ABA and although he was only 26 when he got to Philly, he had an old man's knees. I mean, he had about as much lateral movement as a fire hydrant. But Doc still had great moves with the ball and the refs also cut him some slack by letting him walk whenever he drove to the hoop. (Guys like Moses Malone, Karl Malone and Alonzo Mourning were also allowed to dance the European Mambo.) Doc's specialty was flying on the fastbreak, and he was a great finisher in the open court, but he struggled in a half-court game because he didn't have a jump shot. Later on, Doc developed a little bank shot that made the defense have to get up on him.

Doc was a surprisingly good passer, but he felt a lot of pressure to try and score on every possession in every close situation. He had to be the man. I don't think that sat too well with George McGinnis. A split developed on the team. Doc's boys and George's boys. Each side would rave about their guy's latest move and then snicker when the other guy fucked up. The guys in Doc's corner were Doug Collins, Steve Mix, Fred Carter and Caldwell Jones. George's partisans were Joe Bryant, Harvey Catchings, Terry Furlow and Mike Dunleavy. Henry Bibby was still a committee of one. And me and World were just kicking back and laughing at everybody. It got so bad that George's guys would seldom pass to Doc's guys and vice versa. And what was Gene Shue doing while all this was going on? Nothing that I could see.

The other big development was Gene's realization that he couldn't keep World buried at the end of the bench. Now, my judgment is extremely biased because World is my brother, the closest friend I ever made in the NBA. That said, World had the ability to change a game by himself. He had a long rainbow jumper that looked like an accident whenever it dropped through the net, but he could hit that shot all night. Better than that, World loved to drive. Even if he was wide open, he'd taunt his defender into coming out and guarding him. "C'mon," he'd say. "C'mon out here and let me do you." One-on-one, I never saw anybody come close to stopping World.

He got a rep for being a selfish, one-dimensional player. But Chuck Daly once told me and World, "If you aren't selfish, you'll never be a superstar."

If that's what we both wanted to be, World was certainly a lot closer than I was. Remember, I was still only 19, but Gene was giving me much more daylight than I'd had in my rookie season. In 1976-77, my playing time per game was up to nearly 12 minutes (in 59 games). I shot 63% from the field, which ain't too bad, averaged 5.3 points per game and scored a season-high of 20 against Phoenix. Sure, the referees were still busting my chops (that would never stop), but I was having much more of an impact on ball games.

I also made a solid impression on the Philadelphia media. I was always very quotable so they'd be sticking microphones in my face after almost every game. And I'd show up for ball games wearing a yellow-green-and-blue dashiki, or some rainbow sweat pants, or I'd be wearing a baseball cap turned backwards (which nobody else was doing in those days). When they'd ask what I called my latest outfit, it would be my Flop-A-Do or my Lovetron Tuxedo. And they just loved it. In fact, even when I had a bad game I got less criticism from the media than any other player in the league.

As good as the Philly media treated me, the New York media absolutely catered to me. I'd get calls from New York asking me to speak to some media convention at the Waldorf Astoria. TV and radio stations wanted me to be on this show and that show. I was so popular in New York that I thought if the Sixers ever traded me it would be to the Knicks.

Meanwhile we were running through the league like a dose of castor oil. Doc and George were both getting over 21 points a game. Doug missed a few games because his feet were messed up, but he was good for 18.3 points per game. World was coming off the bench and doing 16.3. Steve Mix and Henry Bibby were also scoring in double figures. We were also pounding the shit out of the offensive boards and wound up leading the league in that department.

Me? I was still toking and snorting and fucking and having a high time.

When the smoke cleared, I felt I could compete with every other center I faced except for Bob Lanier and Kareem Abdul-Jabbar. Lanier was the hardest player for me to defend. He was as big as me, he was left-handed, and he wore a size 22 shoe so he could plant himself in the pivot like the Statue of Liberty. Lanier also had a lazy eye that drove me crazy. I'd be guarding him and trying to figure out which way he was headed, but I could never tell exactly where he was look-ing. Lanier's secret weapon was a button that he had in his side. If I got caught behind him, he'd push that button and his ass got bigger. There was just no way to get around him. Add it all up and I had more trouble with Lanier than with anybody else.

Guarding Kareem was no picnic either, but Lanier gave me the key to controlling him. Kareem scored 40 on me one Mother's Day and I was still moaning when we came into Detroit to play the Pistons. "Here's what Kareem did to you," Lanier said to me. "Tell me if I'm wrong. He walked into that box on the left side of the lane, then he squared up to the ball, caught the pass and shot his skyhook going to the middle. Right? What you've got to do is not let him get to the goddamn box. It ain't his, is it? Do you see his fucking name on that box?"

Okay. The next time we played the Lakers, I hustled downcourt ahead of Kareem and just stood on the box. When Kareem got there, he said, "Move."

"I ain't gonna move."

"Move, goddamn it."

"Not me. That box don't have your name on it."

"Shit," Kareem said. "You've been talking to Bob Lanier."

From then on, I'd pick up Kareem early and keep on bumping him so he had to fight to approach his favorite spot.

Nowadays, you rarely see a true center anymore. Shaq's a center. Patrick Ewing is another one. Hakeem Olajuwon played center but he's really a power forward. Back when Olajuwon was playing with Ralph Sampson, Hakeem got stuck in the low post because Sampson couldn't take the beating down there. If he'd stayed at his natural position, Hakeem wouldn't have gotten so worn out and he'd have had another three or four outstanding seasons left. Alonzo Mourning is another power forward masquerading as a center. David Robinson is just a jump-shooting powerless forward. Arvydas Sabonis has the size and the build to play down low, but he's effective only as an outside shooter and passer.

Big kids growing up today don't want to play with their backs to the basket and have to pass out of double teams. They want to be out there running and handling and shooting threes. That's one reason why the NBA is drafting more and more big guys from European countries. They can play that outside game better than the American kids and the big men here are uncomfortable playing defense so far away from the basket. If all of the European players are Mister Softees, they have the advantage of being as white as a fish's belly. That's really the biggest consideration for the NBA—getting more white players into the league.

The increasing number of fair-skinned European players in the league is a sore point for me. The United States government spends billions of dollars every year feeding and taking care of kids all over the world; don't get me wrong, it's a good thing to do. But what about all of the sick and hungry kids right here in America? By the same token, NBA teams will go overseas to find a diamond in the rough while there's plenty of those kind of players here. Charity, along with equal opportunity, begins at home.

Traveling around the league and checking out the NBA itinerary, I couldn't avoid noticing a lot of bad business going on between the black and white players. According to Steve Mix, when he played with the Detroit Pistons in the early '70s, the white and the black players were divided along color lines. He said they didn't get along with each other and that the blacks would sit on one side of the locker room and the whites on the other. That certainly wasn't the case with the Sixers. In fact, Mix was always cracking racial jokes. Like he'd point to a black player and say, "Hey, look at that guy with no ass. He's got midnight-colored skin and he's on the NBA's all-black team, but he's got an ass-less white ass." There was nothing mean-spirited about the racial stuff, Steve said. It was just part of the team's camaraderie, and he always made everybody laugh. But even though about 80% of the players in the league were black, there were only three black head coaches when I started playing: Lenny Wilkens in Portland, Bill Russell in Seattle and Al Attles in Golden State. A few teams had a black assistant coach to deal with the brothers, and that was a great idea. But Philadelphia had no black assistant so there was nobody we could talk to about our problems. Whenever we went to Gene, he'd always say the same thing: "You guys are all grown men so you've got to deal with it."

If the Sixers were color-blind off the court, once the lights were turned on it seemed to me things often changed. George McGinnis would always shoot first and never ask questions. World used to complain about his sticky hands: "Sometimes I'm so wide open that I'm getting lonely out there. But all he sees is the basket. Except when Mike Dunleavy comes in the game. Then he passes to Dunleavy every fucking time."

When World went to Gene he got the same "you're a grown man" bullshit with a new twist: "If you're not getting enough shots to suit you, then go get a fucking offensive rebound."

So the black players were mostly on their own. And when we did get together we'd talk about how few white players really deserved to be in the NBA. Among these were Bobby Jones, Gus Gerard, Bill Walton, Dan Issel, Rick Barry, Paul Westphal, maybe Don Buse and Pete Maravich (not that Pistol Pete was such a great player, but he was talented and he did put booties in seats). Most of the other whites in the leagues were there only because of their skin color. The white centers in particular were so basic that they were easy to guard and even easier to score against. Tom Burleson, for example, was a seven-foot four-inch stiff who I just loved to play against. I'd kick his ass from endline to endline, and from tip to buzzer. But if I got too close to Burleson when he had the ball, he'd wind up shooting free throws.

Rich Kelley was another white center who I believe the refs had to protect.

White guards could sometimes present a problem, especially someone who could handle the ball, who had a little juke in his game, and who could also talk shit. I'm thinking of guys like Johnny Neumann, Ernie DiGregorio and Gail Goodrich. Playing against them could be hazardous for a black player. "I can't let that white boy embarrass me. I got to stop this motherfucker." But the black guy would then become more concerned with the white guy's game than with his own, so he'd get himself all fucked up.

There's always talk among the brothers in the league that certain white guys play like they're black, and vice versa. White guys who could jump were always admired: Billy Cunningham was called "The Kangaroo Kid." Bobby Jones could get up. So could Tom Chambers. Danny Vranes had long-ass arms, a pet boa constrictor and a pet tarantula. He was a weird motherfucker, but that white boy could jump.

Big guys never like to get dunked on. But the worst thing that could happen to a black center is to get dunked on by a white guy. When you go back to your old neighborhood, the first thing you're going to hear is that some white guy dunked on your ass. So what you do is just sit back and let them shoot their jumpers.

In the playoffs, when the Sixers squared off against the Portland Trail Blazers for the championship, all the racial undertones seemed to come to a head. It's not politically correct to make this kind of definition these days, but we played black basketball and Portland played white basketball.

The white players at the core of Portland's success were Dave Twardzik, Bobby Gross, Larry Steele and Bill Walton. It seemed like Twardzik missed maybe three shots that whole series and that's because our guards underestimated him. Aw, he's just another little white boy with no game. Not only was Twardzik making big shots, he was also beating our guards to the basket and forcing our big men to come over and help. At the small forward spot, Gross and Steele were in constant motion and broke loose for open shots. Both of them just ate Doc's lunch. (We didn't find out until after the season was over that Doc had a strained stomach muscle and was getting cortisone shots. Doc's injury was kept secret from his teammates and from the media so that the Trail Blazers wouldn't take advantage of him. But that's the way it worked out anyway.)

The hub of Portland's team was Walton, and I always thought he was full of baloney. I still get pissed today when I hear him on TV saying negative things about everybody, because he was a big dope smoker. He had this mountain-man image and I don't think he bathed regularly. And the league let him play with a red bandanna tied around his head. To say nothing of his involvement with Patty Hearst. If a black player ever tried any of that stuff, he would've been banished from the league. But Walton was a good player who could really pass and had a nice jump hook. What made Walton so effective was that he was surrounded by talented players who wanted to win and weren't concerned with being stars. I played him physically and tried to beat him to his favorite spots. For the series, I think I played Walton as well as anybody else did.

The black guys on Portland also played white basketball. Maurice Lucas was a good, strong power forward, no doubt, but it was Lloyd Neal who killed us. I mean every time George McGinnis tried to move, Neal was there to beat him to death. Our guards never did figure out that Lionel Hollins was left-handed because his favorite move was to dribble right and shoot. Nobody on Portland was making a lot of money except for Walton, and we had one of the highest payrolls in the league (second only to the Lakers), which made the Trail Blazers hungrier than we were. And nobody was hungrier than Johnny Davis, who played like a man possessed.

All of the Trail Blazers, white and black, played a controlled style of ball. Whereas we used picks just to set up isolation situations, their picks were designed to give their shooters enough time and space to get their feet set before shooting. Too bad Bibby and World always had trouble getting over picks. Portland also liked to dump the ball into Walton in the low post, and then everybody would start cutting and slashing toward the basket and into open spaces. Our mentality on defense was to knuckle down and control our man when he had the ball in his hands. Playing off-the-ball defense wasn't natural for us, so we'd be turning our heads to peek at the ball and ZIP!, our man would be gone. Jack Ramsay was the Trail Blazers' coach, and they weren't fancy, but they worked hard and were fundamentally sound.

The Sixers, on the other hand, were much more flamboyant. We had more individual moves, more off-balance shots, more fancy passes, more dunks, more entertaining one-on-one stuff. We just wanted to run and gun. Everybody wanted to shoot and everybody wanted to be the man (including me). We had too many stars and not enough role players willing to do the dirty work—like setting picks, making the pass that leads to the assist pass, getting back on defense and boxing out.

If you look even closer at black ball (or street ball or ghetto ball), this is what you'll see when somebody is trying to sucker his defender into biting for a fake: The only parts of the player's body that're moving are his head, his arms and his shoulders. The feet aren't doing anything. Kevin Porter used to come to the basket and do a little kick that would get the defense all nervous. But that little kick wasn't shit. It didn't take Porter anywhere. So if a player is shaking and baking with the ball, just keep your balance and watch his feet. That's the way to figure out what's really on his mind.

I believe that competitive black basketball (as opposed to the Globetrotters show-biz bullshit) originated in the Rucker Tournament in Harlem. The games there are played in a bad-ass neighborhood on an outdoor court where it's always hot and steaming. The Rucker is like a little oasis in the ruckus of the city, and the people who come to see the games want to be entertained. They don't want to sit in the sun and see nice pass, nice pass, jump shot, so the players have to put it down and put it over.

The predominance of the black style in today's NBA goes back to Billy Ray Bates, who played with Portland in the early eighties. Billy Ray could run and jump with anybody, but he wouldn't execute a play to save his life. I figured all he wanted to do was create a shot for himself. Whatever play the coach would call—Two, Fifty-three, Fist Left, or the 1812 Overture—as soon as Billy Ray touched the ball he was gone. Largely because of Billy Ray, black players got the reputation of being too stupid to remember a play.

Of course, with more and more schoolboys coming into the NBA, the league's coaches also have to dumb down their offenses to accommodate these younger, less experienced players. That's why Reggie Miller, Allan Houston and Glen Rice are just about the only jump-shooters around. Everybody else is trying to take it to the hoop.

World was injured in the Eastern Conference finals against Houston, suffering a collapsed lung that kept him in the hospital for seven days. Even though he played his normal minutes against Portland, World just wasn't himself. I think if World had been healthy we might have won the championship. But there were other reasons why we lost.

Jack Ramsay outfoxed us in many ways. The home team usually has its game-day shootaround from 11 to 12, then the visitors take the court. (A shootaround is where the players break a sweat so they're not just sitting around all day and getting logy, and also where the coaching staff makes adjustments in the game plan.) In Philly, if our shootaround ran one minute past 12, Ramsay would have his players walk onto the court and start shooting. Gene should have said, "This is our home court, we're not finished, and you guys have to wait." Instead, it was, "Come on, guys. We gotta go." When the situation was reversed in Portland and Ramsay's shootarounds went overtime, Gene had us stand in the hall and wait until they were done. The message was that the Blazers thought they were better than us.

Even so, the series got off to a good start. All season long we'd been tough to beat in Philadelphia. Our home record of 32-9 was fourth best in the league. The first two games were in Philly—so we rebounded, we ran, we were extremely physical, and we beat them by six to open the series. Then we blasted their ass 107-89 in Game Two. Man, was I having a good time. If the media attention is brighter during the finals, if the on-court competition is more intense, the available pussy is also of a higher caliber. I mean me and Ham Dick were on a pussy rampage.

The only problem was that during the second game I got into a fight with Bobby Gross. There was a helter-skelter battle for a loose ball and Gross was kicking and scratching me like a little bitch. So I turned to Gross and said, "Man, what the fuck are you doing?"

"What do you want to do?" he said.

Then we squared up and I swung. I hit him a glancing blow and his head bounced back and cracked into Doug Collins' face so bad that Doug needed stitches.

While this was going on, Maurice Lucas was away at half-court and he came running at me from behind. I had two of my teammates, George and Doc, standing back there and doing nothing but watching. Neither of them said, "Darryl! Look out!" So Lucas came up and blind-sided me with a sucker punch. We started throwing punches but, by that time, everybody jumped in and we never got to each other. That didn't stop the refs from throwing us out of the game. Man, I was hot. When I got back to the locker room, I took it out on a toilet. That's right. Tore it right out of the floor. What a sight. Water gushing out of the hole in the floor and shoes floating all over the place. The guys were mad as hell when they saw the mess, but they were so freaked out they didn't say anything.

I said to George, "Why the fuck didn't you tell me the guy was coming?"

George said, "I didn't see him."

"What the fuck were you looking at then?"

And what was Doc doing when the tussle started? Sitting his ass down on the court and being an eyewitness.

In the post-game locker room, Gene Shue just said some bullshit about how we're all a team here and we gotta watch out for each other. That just disgusted me even more.

Man, was I pissed. I'd already had several straight-up face-to-face fights in the NBA. I had one with John Brown one night in Atlanta when he tried to slap me and I had to pick him up and throw him to the floor. But where I came from, your boys always watched your back. I was so mad that I didn't want to play with those guys any more. So I called up my agent and said, "Fuck it, I'm not going to Portland." Of course, he talked some sense into me, but I was still mad as hell.

When the series moved to Portland, Ramsay made several critical adjustments and I thought Gene appeared overmatched. First off, Ramsay slowed the pace of Portland's offense. That only made us antsy, more anxious to bust out and run, and less interested in playing sustained defense. Secondly, Ramsay slowed our running game by having one of his big men linger in the backcourt whenever we grabbed a defensive rebound to pressure the ball and delay an outlet pass. Also, our point guard was always in the same place looking to receive that outlet pass and start the fast break, but Ramsay also kept a guard back to block the other end of that pass. What Gene should have done was have the rebounder take a few dribbles to prevent being jammed, and then have the point guard move to a different spot. But Gene made no such adjustments and our running game was stymied.

Another adjustment Ramsay made was to put his team in a hotel. This reduced their hometown distractions and kept them focused on the job of winning. Meanwhile, we were feeling cocky. There was no way those suckers were going to beat us with their dull, candy-ass style of play. So while the Blazers were getting their shit together, we were out on the town partying with all our might.

Before Game Three in Portland, Lucas came over and apologized. "I'm sorry, man," he said. "I never blind-sided a guy like that before. I don't know what got into me. Probably just the frustration of losing." Okay, so now me and Mo were cool.

The third game started out as a battle because the Trail Blazers finally found their rhythm. Then George McGinnis picked up a bag of apples. I mean he choked big time. He was passing up two-foot shots and trying to force passes into Caldwell Jones instead. George didn't score much, or rebound, or defend. That made Gene desperate. He kept running plays for George, hoping he'd get off, but George kept shooting zeroes. Meanwhile, the Portland fans were getting into it, and the Portland players started playing with confidence. We thought all we had to do to win was show up, but the Blazers played harder than we did.

All the plays that weren't run for George were run for Doc, and Doc wasn't passing the ball to anybody. Portland had our running game stopped and we couldn't do shit in a half-court game. So guys just started going off on their own, and we were completely gone. And me? I was still in a funk. I had no heart to play with these guys, and since I wasn't getting the ball anyway, I stopped rebounding and playing defense.

After we got murdered 129-107, George said that he had a pulled groin muscle. Say what? He sure didn't play like he was hurting in the first two games. To me, it looked like George was just looking for an excuse for playing like dog shit.

The Blazers also destroyed us in the next game, 130-98, to even the series at two. The pivotal Game Five was in Philly, and since no

NBA teams had chartered flights in those days, both teams were tired. Even so, we were still confident we could beat them at home. But once again, they played with more fire than we did and squeezed out a close game, 110-104. They closed us out back in Portland, 109-107, and suddenly the ride was over.

My honest opinion then and now is that black players are more talented than white players, and we certainly were more talented than Portland. And the rock-bottom reason why the Trail Blazers beat us was because they played white basketball better than we played black basketball.

The team got together after we returned to Philly and talked about how we had let ourselves down and also let the Sixers' fans down. Then Doc made a public announcement, saying to the fans, "We owe you one." And we did play much better team ball the following season.

I wasn't planning to drive back down to Florida until the middle of the summer, but some bad news got me there in a hurry: My mother was having serious trouble with her new husband. His name was Argie Neil and he stood only five-foot-six, nearly six inches shorter than Mama. During my rookie season I'd spent about $6,000 for their wedding even though none of my brothers or sisters had anything good to say about Argie. "How come you're marrying him, Mama?"

"I can't help it," she said. "I love Argie and I can't do without him."

They'd been married for two years and he'd been pissing off everybody except my mother. He didn't want anything to do with my grandmother or anybody else Mama had been close to and sometimes he'd even slap her around. "Mama! Get rid of him!"

"I can't help it. I love Argie and I can't do without him."

One night, my mother went out on her own to a neighborhood bar to have a few sociable drinks with some friends. Argie showed up and told Mama, "Come on, Harriette. Darryl just got here from up north and he's waiting for you back at the house." My mother was a little tipsy, but when they came home she was sober enough to realize that I wasn't there at all. That's when they had a big fight. As soon as the word got around, me and the rest of my brothers made a fastbreak for home. But by the time we got there, Argie was gone, and Mama was crying that she wanted him back.

The next Sunday, Mama went up in her bedroom closet to pick out a hat to wear to church. She must've had 70 or 80 church hats, some of them with feathers going this way, others with the feathers going that way. Suddenly something dropped to the floor, a little black leather pouch. So she took it over to my grandmother's house.

Grandma was sitting and rocking on the porch when my mother showed up. "Mama, what is this that fell out of my closet?"

"I know what it is," Grandma said. "Get in your car and drive yourself out of the yard. That's right. Go out on the street right now."

When Mama did like she was told, Grandma struck a match and held it to the black pouch. WOOF! The pouch flashed up in a big flame and there was black smoke everywhere. When the smoke cleared, the pouch had disintegrated into nothing.

"Okay," my grandmother said to Mama. "You're all right now. You can go ahead on home."

Since that day, my mother ain't talked about that man, ain't ever seen him, ain't nothing. Yeah! She'd been rooted, and Grandma broke the spell.

That's right!

With so many poor Southern blacks hailing from Jamaica, Haiti and other Caribbean countries, it's no wonder that they brought along some of the islands' black magic practices. That's why "rooting" somebody was a normal part of my upbringing. There were root men and root ladies in the backwoods all over Florida, South Carolina and North Carolina. If you wanted someone to fall in love with you, and to stay that way, then you sought out a root man and he'd tell you what had to be done. And my mother wasn't even the first person in the family who got rooted for love.

When my brother Mitchell was in the navy, he fell in love with a light-skinned girl from New Orleans. Mitchell was so much in love that he couldn't keep his mind on anything else. He couldn't keep his rifle clean, his shoes shined, or his left foot from stepping on his right foot. Mitchell's buddies wanted him to break up with her, but he couldn't. "I love her too much to let her go." After a while his friends finally convinced him to go visit a root man, so that's what Mitchell did. When Mitchell came back to the barracks he sprinkled salt all around his bed, poured lighter fluid on the salt, then lit it up. When the fire went out, he swept up the ashes, went to see the girl, and said, "I can't stand your ass and I never want to see you again."

That's right!

Sometimes a married man or woman got rooted if they were out fucking around and their spouse was upset. One method was to convince the wayward partner that they were going crazy and make them afraid to leave the house. Every old house in the neighborhood had spider webs in all the nooks and corners, with big brown spiders and big white eggs somewhere on the webs. So the woman whose husband was out tomcatting would put some of the spider eggs into the spaghetti. Because most people don't thoroughly chew their food, the husband would swallow the eggs whole and they'd hatch in his stomach. Then the husband would get sick and go to the doctor, saying, "I'm throwing up spiders." And the doctor would tell him he was crazy.

Frog's eggs work the same way.

That's right!

In addition to these kinds of home remedies, more serious problems called for more serious rooting. Go to a root man with some of your spouse's hair and blood, and it'll get put into a jar along with a rusty nail, some hot peppers, and secret herbs. Bury the jar in the yard just outside the front door. Whenever the guilty party leaves the house, they'll start to sweat like blazes and feel like they're on fire. After a couple of times with the same reaction, they'd rather stay home than go anywhere.

That's right! I've seen these things and more!

6

Dunk You Very Much

M y third season was when I came of age as an NBA player, but it sure got off to a bad start. Even though we had essentially the same roster, we stumbled out of the gate, winning only two of our first six games. That's when Gene Shue pulled me aside and said, "They're gonna get rid of me, Darryl, because it's not working out the way they want it to. And one day they're gonna do the same to you. When it happens, you've got to think of it as a transfer, not as a demotion. It happened to Doc in New Jersey. It happened to Wilt Chamberlain twice. It happened to Kareem in Milwaukee. No matter how good you are, if you play this game long enough, you're gonna get traded." Two days later, Gene was replaced by Billy Cunningham.

The word from the Sixers' front office was that Gene had lost his edge, that he wasn't working hard enough. But many of us figured there was some other reason he'd fallen out of favor with management. While the front-office maneouvring was playing itself out, Cunningham had begun hanging around the team. We all assumed he was making it known that he wanted to coach. I was told that Cunningham had even spoken to the Sixers' owner, Harold Katz, and said that he could get us to win a championship. Katz also liked the idea of Cunningham coming back to the scene of his all-star playing days. Gene got into enough trouble on his own, but I always suspected Cunningham stabbed him in the back.

Cunningham didn't change much. Like Gene, he tried to make both George and Doc happy, an impossible job. But at the beginning of his coaching career, Cunningham wasn't very good. Although he'd been successful as a player and as a businessman, he didn't strike me as a people person. From my perspective, it seemed his attitude was that people approached him to get something from him. He struck me as standoffish and often suspicious.

We had our first hassle early in Billy's tenure, when he was still in the locker room while the horn sounded to start the game. All the players were itching to get it going and the other team was already on the court, but still no Billy. Manny Goukas was Billy's assistant and he was reluctant to do anything by himself. Finally I said, "Manny, have some balls, put a starting five out there, and let's go." Which he did. Billy showed up when the game was already a couple of minutes gone and he immediately called a timeout to ask Manny what was going on. Manny pointed at me and told Billy what had gone down. When play resumed, Billy came over to where I was sitting and said, "Who the fuck are you to tell Manny to get started without me?"

I just said, "Fuck you, Billy." And I sat at the end of the bench for the rest of the game.

But he couldn't keep me on the bench forever, because my game had really developed. I had the drop-step and the fall-away jumper. I could put the ball on the floor and get to the basket. I could block shots and keep the ball in bounds. Up till then I never liked to run the court, but now I was hauling ass and enjoying it. For the season, I averaged almost 25 minutes and over 11 points per game. I was also second in the league (to Bobby Jones of Denver) with a .575 field goal percentage. Billy knew I would never back down from any other player in the league, and he knew that I never got tight nuts when the pressure was on, but like Gene he very seldom called a play designed for me to shoot.

What the fuck? But I didn't have to love my coach to play hard for him. I just ignored most of what Billy had to say to me.

It was also easy to con Billy. When I didn't want to run in practice I'd just start panting like a dog in a heat wave and Billy would give me a water break. How could I respect a coach I could so easily chump?

My respect for him was also tested in the huddle because early in his coaching career he seemed easily ruffled during close games. One time we were losing by a point with only a few seconds left in the game, and Billy was frantic. "Doc," he started yelling. "Where's Doc? Doc?"

"I'm right here, Billy."

Like where the fuck else is he gonna be?

So Billy diagrammed a play. "Darryl, you go stand over here. George and Doug, you stand over here. Henry, you stand over here. Doc's over here and we're gonna give you the ball and you go one-on-one. You just take it, Doc. You j-j-j-just take it." Then he went over the same thing again. "Darryl, you go stand over here ..."

Just then a beautiful girl walked right behind the bench, and I said, "Goddamn, World. You see the ass on her?"

And Billy went off. "That's your fucking problem, Darryl. You're never serious. That's your fucking problem."

I just said, "Aw, Billy, just go ahead and diagram your bullshit play."

"I don't want anybody but Doc going to the goal. Anybody."

So we went out there and four of us were standing near the sideline with our fingers up our asses and Doc got the ball with eight seconds left. And Doc went di-di-di-di-dit and finally made his move. As he went up for the shot, I saw the ball starting to slip out of Doc's hand so I took off toward the basket. The ball hit the back of the rim, bounced off, and BOOM! I was there to throw it down and win the game at the buzzer.

In the locker room, Billy charged up into my face. "You broke the play, Darryl! You weren't supposed to go to the goal!"

"Billy," I said, like I was talking to a child, "We won the fucking game."

"Yeah," he said. "But you're never fucking serious."

Billy was partially correct, because me and my buddy World were always yapping at each other during a ball game. My name for World was Shortcake and he called me Stovetop Stuffin'. He'd come down the court dribbling the ball and calling out to me, "Hey, Stuffin'! You need a shot?" Yeah, I always needed a shot. "Well, here it is, motherfucker. But you better make it." Sometimes he'd tell me that he was going to fool the refs into sending him to the foul line, so he'd flop and squeal like Reggie Miller made a career out of doing, and the refs would always take the bait.

One night I told World that I was aiming to catch somebody's shot, and that's what I did. Billy was always after me to block a shot lightly and then go chase it down. He didn't want me sending somebody's shit into the mezzanine. I don't remember who shot the ball, but I jumped straight up, caught it one-handed like a shortstop spearing a line drive, then came down with it. I'd done the same thing several times in the Baker League, but the NBA referees had never seen anything like it before, and they were so stunned that they just kept sucking on their whistles. So I threw a long pass to World and he scored a layup. Instead of two points for them, it was two for us, but Billy was bugged out. "Darryl, don't do that."

"It wasn't goaltending, Billy. The ball was still on the way up and I just caught it."

"But the referees will think you're a hot dog and they'll start making crazy calls against you."

"Shit," I said. "They've been doing that for the last three years so what's the difference?" But I never did it again.

Doc (20.6 ppg) and George (20.3) were still our leading scorers, but we had enough firepower up and down the lineup for Billy to go to any one of a bunch of guys in the clutch. Doug Collins was healthy for the entire season and he shot over 53%, scored 19.7 ppg, and could always either find a good shot or get to the foul line. World was outrageous, still impossible to guard one-on-one, and scored 15.7 ppg. But Billy didn't run too many plays for him either because he said World could only play street ball. Bibby and Mix also averaged close to double-figures. In fact, we led the NBA in scoring. Too bad we were also one of the league's worst defensive teams.

There was no defending my dunk shots, however, and I was getting so many of them that I started giving them names:

Yo Mama
In Your Face Disgrace
Cover Yo Damn Head
Earthquake Breaker
Left-Handed Spine Chiller Supreme
Sexophonic Turbo Delight

The media started calling me Sir Slam and Dr. Dunk and I was all over the highlight tapes on the evening news from coast to coast. And

I really liked the idea of entertaining the fans. Sometimes when I took a charging foul from a guard I'd back up and slide on my ass like I'd been hit by a freight train. Or when I'd make a jump shot, I'd run downcourt with big eyes and a hallelujah smile. Or else when a referee make a bad call against me, I'd storm over to him like I was about to rip his head off, but then I'd smile and bow and tell him that he'd made the right call. I used to listen to George Clinton and Parliament-Funkadelic, so I talked to reporters about my interplanetary funksmanship.

Making people laugh was something that always pleased me and was something that I had a talent for. But I wasn't putting on a show to sell myself to the public and make money. Not me. Carrying on like I did just came naturally. I was a basketball player but I was also an entertainer. This was something unheard of in those days. Basketball players were supposed to go to work wearing a grim gameface and never let on that hooping is a fun thing to do. Looking back, I can see that I was way ahead of my time.

Even so, I was totally frustrated with my role on the Sixers. I wanted to be a go-to player on offense, not just a rebounding janitor who was supposed to clean up everybody else's mess on the offensive glass. Billy kept telling me that the organization wanted me to be a great player, a franchise player. So I'd be out there killing guys, shooting the lights out and shaking the building with monster dunks. But whenever the game was on the line, I never got the damn ball. It was like Gene Shue revisited: If I wanted a shot, I had to get an offensive rebound. Added to all of this was the hard time the referees were still giving me. It was difficult for me to develop any kind of rhythm because I was always saddled with foul trouble.

Damn! I wished somebody would just let me PLAY!

I think my overall frustration was the reason why I started doing more drugs than I'd ever done before. Which was very easy to do. At that time, I didn't know of more than a handful of players in the NBA who didn't snort cocaine or smoke weed or take the green uppers that we called Christmas trees. And plenty of guys were doing all three.

We managed to stay straight enough to win 55 games in the regular season. Only the Trail Blazers, with 58, had more. So we thought we'd just breeze into the finals once again. We started out by sweeping the Knicks, then Washington busted us in six games. The Bullets had Elvin Hayes and Wes Unseld on their frontline so we couldn't overpower them on the boards and get our running game in gear. Like Portland the year before, the Bullets also whitewashed us with a station-to-station half-court strategy. Another reason why we lost was the continuing disharmony between George's and Doc's cliques.

All in all, I was so frustrated with the way the Sixers were holding me back that I was almost happy when the season ended. Almost.

I spent most of the summer of 1978 in and around Philly doing basketball camps for kids. Sometimes I'd get just my expenses, sometimes four or five hundred bucks, but most of the time I worked just for the kick of teaching and entertaining young kids. White kids or black kids, it didn't matter. Throughout my career, I'd say I've done more kids camps than any other player in the history of the NBA. And I can't think of any other situation where I've had as much fun. Once again, Grandma had me pegged right.

I also got into some big trouble that summer, trouble that never made the news, but that I can never forget. I'm not naturally a violent person, but I do have an evil twin named Darnell. As Darryl I would rather try and talk my way out of any kind of problem. Darryl can be personally insulted, and can even discover that somebody's been stealing my money, but none of this is enough to make me want to physically hurt somebody. Of course, if my family is involved, or if I'm backed into a corner, then Darnell *will* beat somebody's ass.

And that's what happened that summer in Philly. I don't want to get into the details, but I wound up punching a guy in his face so hard that he was out cold before he hit the ground. The problem was compounded when his head hit the sidewalk and split open like a ripe melon. There was more blood than I'd ever seen and the guy almost died. Since then, Darnell's been chained in the basement and I hope he never has to see the light of day again.

My fourth season in the NBA brought about a lot of changes, on the court and off. My brother Troy was so crazy and wild that he couldn't finish high school in Florida. The only thing to do was to bring him up to New Jersey and have him live with me. And I made sure that he not only went to school every day, but that he graduated in June.

Another good change was the Sixers trading George McGinnis to Denver for Bobby Jones. Even though he had epilepsy, Bobby could run, jump and play defense big time. But if he played more than 28 minutes in a game, it would take him several days to get his strength back. And I'll say it flat out: I love Bobby Jones. He was the best guy I have ever met in the NBA. Nobody's game was more unselfish than his.

Bobby was a Christian, but if someone would tell a funny story using bad language, he would laugh as hard as anybody. I used to tease him all the time: "Come have a drink with me." He'd get a shocked look on his face just thinking about the possibility. "No, no, no." I once asked him if he ever had a drink of alcohol. "I had half a beer one time in college," he said, "and I didn't like it." Whenever a female reporter was allowed into the locker room, Bobby would run through the shower and get dressed before she got there.

Bobby was just about an 80%-free-throw shooter and I only saw him miss two-for-two once. It was in Los Angeles, and when he stepped to the foul line the fans under the basket held up big pictures of naked women. JA-BAM! JA-BAM! He was so shaken up he almost broke the rim.

For me, the addition of Bobby Jones almost made up for the subtraction of World. I don't think Billy ever did like World's personality or his game. No matter how good World played, Billy would often be chewing him and chewing him, just screaming and hollering. "Don't do that. Do this. You're taking too many jumpers. You're taking too many shots." World would just grimace like Billy had the world's worst halitosis and then walk away. That's when Billy would come to me to complain: "What's the matter with World? I'm talking to him and there's nothing there. Nothing." I didn't want to hear that bullshit either, so I'd also ignore him. Then Billy would get red-eyed mad and finally leave me be.

Even during the preceding season, every time he had a shitty game, World would say to me, "Ham, they're gonna trade me. I know it." I told him that he was averaging nearly 16 points a game so the Sixers couldn't afford to deal him. But they did. During training camp they exiled him to one of the worst teams in the league, the San Diego Clippers. Almost single-handedly, World turned that team around. He scored 28.8 his first season there, 30.2 the year after.

So now I was alone and without a running mate. I was still playing only 26 minutes a game, less than one minute more than in '77-78. Sure, my stats were up and I was now scoring 13.1 (with a high of 30 points against Phoenix), but that was only because I was naturally getting better. I felt that I was now 21 and coming into my prime, so I kept telling Billy that I needed to play more. His response was to tell me to shut up. So I decided that I wanted to be traded to some team that would appreciate me more, and I spent too much of that year pouting.

The Sixers didn't have a first round draft choice in 1978, but they lucked out by picking Maurice Cheeks out of West Texas State in the middle of the second round. Mo was a point guard and Billy spent a lot of time in practice trying to develop him, so Henry Bibby wasn't too happy. In practice sessions during the season, players are only supposed to scrimmage at about three-quarter speed to avoid injuries and to save themselves for the games, but Bibby would come full-speed at Mo. The rookie wasn't a very good shooter, so Bibby played him for the drive and used all his veteran game-time tricks to try and make Mo look bad. Whenever Mo beat Bibby with his quickness, POW! he'd be fouled much harder than practice protocol demanded. I mean Bibby was ruthless. And I never heard Billy say shit. However, Billy did compromise by playing Bibby a lot at the two guard.

As the season progressed, I had my own problems with Mo. It seemed as if all he wanted to do was pass the ball to Doc. Now, Mo might just have been following instructions from Billy. Just the same, the guy guarding me could've had a heart attack and I'd be standing under the basket by myself, but Mo would try to find Doc even if he was stranded in traffic. So I'd yell at Mo, "Doc ain't the only player on the floor besides you. Give me the damn ball when I'm open!" Nope. Didn't do any good. It was still Doc, Doc, Doc. "Goddamn fucking rookie! What am I, fucking invisible?"

So Cheeks must have gone and complained to Billy because Billy told me to lay off the rookie. That only pissed me off more. "I can't believe you went running to the coach," I told Mo. "You're a punk motherfucker."

Things got better only when, instead of throwing a nice catchable outlet pass to Mo, I started firing cannon shots at his head. He got the message then.

But the season was already fucked. We had too many guys on that team who didn't know how to win, who didn't play hard enough for long enough. We won only 47 games then we zipped New Jersey in a mini-playoff series, and faced off against San Antonio. The Spurs' center was Billy Paultz, a big round white guy who I could easily beat to the basket. But, of course, I never got the ball enough to do much damage. We were down three games to two and we had to beat them in Philly to force a seventh game in San Antonio. It was a really tight game all the way through and come nut-cutting time George Gervin was just backing Mo Cheeks into the pivot. Gervin was six-foot-seven and, if Mo was wearing his mama's high heels, the rookie was maybe six-one, so the Ice Man was chilling us right out of the playoffs. In the final minute, I came flying from the weak side to block two of Gervin's shots and we won the game. Billy was all over me, telling me what a great job I did. Then in Game Seven I couldn't even smell the ball. Doc was trying to win the game by himself and Mo was the accessory to the crime. We lost 111-108.

Another season bit the dust.

7

Wham-Bam-
I-Am Jam!

The single most dramatic event of my career happened on November 13, 1979 at the Kansas City Municipal Auditorium.

I read somewhere that Gus Johnson of the old Baltimore Bullets had dunked hard enough to break a couple of rims during preseason games. It sounded like a fun thing to do and I'd been thinking about the possibility of trying the same stunt myself. But I wanted to do more than just break a rim. I wanted to smash a Plexiglas backboard to smithereens precisely because it was considered to be the ultimate and unattainable proof of strength. I'd seen guys dunk so hard the rim vibrated like a diving board but everybody said that tearing one down was impossible. Fooling around in practice I figured out that the rim was weakest where it was connected to the heel that attached to the backboard.

When I told the media about my plan, everybody laughed at me. The Sixers' trainer, Al Domenico, said, "You're nuts, Darryl. Backboards are unbreakable. You'll just wind up pulling your arm out of its socket."

So we were playing the Kansas City Kings, I was being guarded by Bill Robinzine, and we were only 38 seconds into the third quarter when I caught a pass and made a two-step approach to the basket, and CRASH! I got it just right and the whole backboard just disintegrated. I was the do-er so I just kept moving, but Robinzine was the do-ee so he had to haul ass to get away from the broken glass. *Damn! That felt good!*

After about ten minutes, the arena staff showed up, swept up the broken glass, and wheeled what was left of the backboard off the court. I sort of wandered by and asked what they were going to do with the broken glass, and one worker said it was headed for the garbage. Somebody else joked about selling the pieces as souvenirs, so I tried to scoop up some of the biggest chunks. Later, I arranged for the pieces I had collected to be sold at a charity auction.

"I didn't mean to destroy it," I told the sportswriters after the game. "It was the power, the Chocolate Thunder. I could feel it surging through my body, fighting to get out. I had no control."

I wound up calling my most famous dunk "If You Ain't Groovin' Best Get Movin'- Chocolate Thunder Flyin'- Robinzine Cryin'- Teeth Shakin'- Glass Breakin'- Rump Roastin'- Bun Toastin'- Glass Still Flyin'- Wham-Bam-I-Am Jam!"

Naturally, every TV station in the country showed the tape and I became a national celebrity. More importantly, the guys around the league were impressed. Even Doc said to me, "You're the strongest motherfucker I ever played with."

Yeah! Let me see if I can do this again!

The general manager of the Kings, Joe Axelson, was furious. The Kings were winning when the game had to be interrupted to find and position a new backboard, and he said I'd deliberately done the deed to break the home team's rhythm. We lost the game anyway, but nobody, not even Axelson, seemed to notice.

Nobody else seemed to be upset. A couple of fans at the game said to me, "I got home an hour late because of you, but it was worth it." Other guys came up to me to say they'd been laying in bed and watching the game on TV, then had to stand up because they thought they'd been dreaming. One guy thought my dunk was an hallucination due to some bad weed he'd been smoking until he saw the replay on TV. Nobody had a discouraging word. Not even the basketball purists complained that I was ruining the game. The beat writers who covered the Sixers made up a pool to pick the exact game I would break another backboard. Las Vegas started setting game-by-game odds. When we got to Detroit, a maintenance man begged me to break the backboard because his crew had been practicing and could replace a broken backboard in under 15 minutes. But I wasn't inter-

ested in breaking backboards on request just to get myself some chea_
publicity.

Three weeks later we played San Antonio in a nationally televised
game in Philadelphia. Once again, I caught it just right and BAM!
This time the rim broke right off, leaving a big square hole where the
rim used to be connected to the backboard. There was no big explo-
sion or shower of glass, but the effect was the same.

I called this one the "Chocolate Thunder Ain't Playin'- Get Out
of The Wayin'- Backboard Swayin'- Game Delayin'- Super Spike!"
And I was also inspired to give myself another nickname, "The Master
of Disaster."

Suddenly the Sixers were the biggest draw in the league. The TV
ratings went sky-high and every arena we played in was SRO. I was
the darling of the fans and I really got a chance to check them out: I
always liked the Philly fans the best because they'd be with you when
you're on top, and when you're on the bottom they will get your ass
going. Utah had great fans only because there's nothing else to do in
Salt Lake City except go see the Jazz. The most knowledgeable fans
were in New York, Chicago, Boston and Los Angeles. The Detroit fans
loved to see one player embarrass another. "Oh, man," they'd scream.
"He shitted on you."

New York had the most die-hard fans—they'd usually come out in
full force whether the team was good or bad. The only time the Knick
fans stayed away was in the '80-'81 season when the team had 12 black
players. That's when the New York fans were talking about the
"Niggerbockers."

In those days, not as many black fans attended NBA games as
today. I'd be looking for black in the stands in Seattle, for example, and
see three brothers and a white guy in a tuxedo. Boston was the same
way. In Philly, there was nothing but white fans around the court and
I'd have to look up to the third level to see where the members were
sitting. None of this affected the way I played as long as I heard some
fans somewhere rooting for me.

When I came into the league, the black players were flat-out better athletes than the white players. The white guys were buried far
down on the bench and the fans would go crazy whenever one of
them got into the game. They'd rather see a white player make a basic

wide-open jump shot than a black player dunking over two guys. That's why, except for that all-black Knick team, a ball club's twelfth man was usually white. He might not play much, but he'd come to practice every day and he'd go out into the community making speeches at the Boys' Club and the Chamber of Commerce. These days, the white players are catching up to the black players. And counting the Canadians and the Europeans, there are more white players in the league than there have been since the 1950s.

Michael Jordan is justly credited with making black athletes acceptable to white fans because his talent transcended race and he was the first brother to be spotlighted in nation-wide television commercials. Even white kids wanted to wear Nikes and "be like Mike." But in a way, my basket-breaking dunksmanship was definitely a forerunner to MJ's national celebrity.

Wherever the Sixers played there were all kinds of signs and posters, and even the white fans were screaming for me to go ahead and tear down another backboard. But then things got a little crazy. Every time I dunked, no matter how nice and polite I'd do it, the refs would nail me with a technical foul for swinging on the rim. Even when I wasn't dunking, the refs were putting me in a straightjacket. Then the NBA summoned me to New York and I was told that the next time I broke a backboard I'd be fined $5,000. Okay. That's cool. It's their fucking league after all. Right? Then a short time later I saw a commercial on TV: The NBA is exciting, blah, blah. Go out and see a game, blah, blah. Then there's a shot of me breaking a backboard! *What the fuck?* That was just pure, unadulterated, hypocritical bullshit.

On New Year's Eve, Billy Cunningham announced that we were going to practice on New Year's Day. Why, Billy? We don't have a game until the Third? "'Cause I'm gonna run that liquor outta you guys."

The trouble was that Billy couldn't find an open gym. He finally hooked up with Don Casey, who was coaching at Cherry Hill High School, and that's where we were going to practice. (As far as I could tell Don Casey knew jack shit about coaching. Eventually, he went on to become a longtime NBA assistant for several teams, and even the head coach of the New Jersey Nets.) So we showed up for practice on this small high school court after partying on New Year's Eve, and true to his promise Billy was running us to death. And all the guys, even Bobby Jones, started agitating for me to bust up a backboard so Billy would have to send us home. To try to convince me, they started putting money in a pile on the scorer's table. A hundred dollars. Nope. Two hundred. Not me. But when there got to be three hundred at stake, it was time to go to work. The backboards were puny little half-moon jobs, and BLAM! It came down like it was made of matchsticks. The easiest three hundred bucks I ever made.

Billy was pissed. "Whoa, Darryl. You did that on purpose."

Who, me?

Then Billy said, "Everybody get the hell outta here. But tomorrow I'm gonna run your asses off even though we're playing the next day. I'm willing to lose the game to make my point."

That was just more bullshit. In fact, Billy babied us through the next day's practice because he never wanted to lose a game for any reason.

And we didn't lose many. The Sixers just about ran away and hid from the rest of the league in 1979-80. The Sixers' first-round draft pick was Jim Spanarkel from Duke, a white boy who couldn't score with a pencil. Doug Collins missed a load of games with his aching feet. But even so, we had the third best record in the NBA—59-23, only a game behind the Lakers and two games behind the Celtics. We were 36-5 at home and for the first time since I'd been with Philly we had a winning record on the road.

For me personally, the '79-'80 season was my best so far. Even though I played for several weeks with a shoulder separation, I was the team's second leading scorer (behind Doc's 26.9 ppg) with 14.7, and the second leading rebounder (behind Caldwell Jones' 11.9) with 8.7. In addition, I dished out 1.9 assists per game, which turned out to be a career best. Why had I so suddenly blossomed? Only because Billy was giving me almost 32 minutes per game even though I still wasn't in the starting five.

For the first time in my career I also led the NBA in something. Unfortunately, the category was personal fouls (328). Who knows how much better my numbers would have been if the refs hadn't continued to pick at me? Usually, the more veteran a player is, the more the refs adjust to his game and give him the benefit of close calls. With me, I was in the NBA for 14 years and I was always whistled like I was still a rookie.

In the playoffs, we cruised through three series, losing a total of only two games (none to Washington and one each to Boston and Atlanta) until we reached the final round again, this time against the Los Angeles Lakers. It was Showtime in Hollywood and the Lakers were in the middle of their dynasty. They were a powerhouse team that featured Kareem, Magic, Jamaal Wilkes, Norm Nixon and Michael Cooper, but I believed we could take them if we worked for good shots, pounded the boards, and made Kareem have to work hard on defense.

I certainly tried to follow the game-plan. The first couple of games I was hitting my jumper from the foul line and, as expected, Kareem wouldn't come out after me. No matter how well I was shooting, he'd just hang around the basket. Bang! Bang! Bang! I couldn't miss. But then the same problem with Mo Cheeks came up. He only wanted to look for Doc. I even yelled at him, "Mo, you stupid motherfucker! Pass me the ball!" Nothing. And once Doc touched the ball, I just started moving to the offensive boards in case he missed his shot. What did Billy do about the situation? He thought I was just out for myself and trying to hoist up as many shots as possible. Then he told me to stop yelling at Cheeks.

It got so bad that the Lakers were saying, "Diesel, why aren't they going to you?" And every time Mo ignored me and forced a pass to Doc, the guys on L.A.'s bench would bust out laughing. In seasons past, I would've hung my head, but I just concentrated on rebounding, defending, and scrabbling after every loose ball.

In L.A., we stayed at a Hilton hotel right near the Forum, and Billy rented a big suite for a "serious" team meeting. We were going to straighten out all our difficulties and renew our focus and shit. So Billy said, "Somebody get on the phone and order up some hors d'oeuvres and some drinks."

Henry Bibby said, "I'm on it, Coach." And Henry ordered over a thousand dollars worth of cold lobster and shrimp, Perrier water and a case of beer. Billy almost had a heart attack when the order was delivered. We all started laughing, drinking and chowing down, and that was the end of our serious meeting.

As always, the referees favored the team that was supposed to win, so the Lakers got every close call. That's always the way it was and still is—the better team, not necessarily the home team, gets all the breaks.

I was really on my game for the entire series, and I practically won Game Five on my own, but I was frustrated by the refs and by my teammates. We finally lost in six games and it was the same story as it had been against the Trail Blazers two years back. I'd controlled my man—first Bill Walton and then Kareem—but the other team's guards and small forwards killed us. It was a question of season-long tactics. Our guards and small forwards were called on to do so much scoring that by the time the playoffs rolled around, they were all drag-ass tired. Had we gone to me for some points, the little guys would have had fresher legs. Against the Lakers, Doc's knees were killing him while he was trying to chase a young guy like Wilkes up and down the court and around a maze of picks. Doc just didn't have the energy. Plus we had Mo Cheeks trying to guard Magic, who was nine inches taller and 50 pounds heavier.

Of course, Kareem was hurt and missed the sixth game, and because Magic jumped center to start the game, the media got the idea that Magic played center and busted my ass. More media bullshit. People in the sports media see a lot of ball games so they think they really know what's going on. The truth was that I played center against Jim Chones and I didn't see Magic down there at all. Magic was guarded by Doc and went for 40-something points in Game Six. The centers never beat us.

After my best year ever, that's the way my fifth NBA season ended. Filled with frustration, misrepresentation and doubts about how much I could improve my game in Philadelphia.

8

The Drug Store, NBA style

J ust a couple of years ago, Charles Oakley said that 60% of the NBA players were smoking pot, and he was probably right. But in my rookie season it seemed to me that the number was more like 90%. They felt safe because at the time the NBA was testing for cocaine, crack and heroin and wasn't really concerned with weed. Also, along with the hippie movement, free love and all that, smoking marijuana was almost an accepted part of American culture. Doctors, lawyers, judges, politicians, and even some ministers were blowing weed. It was a cool thing to do—you smoked, you got high, you ate everything in sight, then you slept real well and you were okay.

In the NBA, the smokers knew who the other smokers were, so it was commonplace for an opponent to sidle up to me during a ball game and say, "Man, I just got a batch of Tijuana gold. I'll turn you on to some later." After the game he'd come into the Sixers' locker room and pass me a couple of joints. And if I'd score some sensimilla, say, then I'd reciprocate.

There was one guy I knew who'd get high right before a game. As soon as he got to the arena, he would disappear into the toilet to smoke some last-second weed. But one night he came into the locker room wearing a rabbit-skin jacket that was leaking so much smoke it looked like it was on fire. Even the coach could recognize the smell: "Have you been smoking that shit?"

"No, no, no," he said. "My car broke down and I had to ride over with some motherfuckers who were smoking it. What was I supposed to do? Miss the game?"

The coach just stared at him, and then at me and World. We just about fell out laughing. He didn't say a word, but none of us played that night.

If smoking pot was relatively harmless, snorting coke was downright sinister. You snorted, you got high, you're messed up for two days and your body's tired for a week. Even so, in those days, I figured half the players were snorting. It was so bad that if a guy was into pussy, liquor or weed he was considered to be a straight arrow.

One day during my rookie season, a bunch of the guys were heading out together after a practice session. "Yo, brother. Where y'all going?" Being a dumbass rookie, when they said they were going to get some "girl," I asked them to bring one back for me, too. I found out later that "girl" was the code name for cocaine.

I didn't party with all of my teammates, but I saw lots of them boarding a plane with their eyes looking like pinwheels and wearing that stoned-out, shit-eating grin. There were guys on the Sixers who cared more about getting high than they did about playing basketball. Thank God I never got that bad.

One of the players experimented with different kinds of pills, and sometimes they would really fuck him up. One night he came into the locker room at half-time and didn't know where he was. When I told him about the ball game, he just said, "Is the game over yet?" Afterward, he said, "I ain't taking that shit no more."

Everybody says that cocaine was brought into the NBA by the black players, but that's not how it was. As a black kid growing up in the country, all I knew was moonshine and marijuana, and it was the same for poor white kids. Back then cocaine was cool. It was a recreational drug that rock stars did and were expected to do. But coke was expensive, a $100 for a gram that would give you just one pop. Weed cost only $10 a bag and you'd have enough to get you high for a week. So when the average black player from a poverty background came into the NBA, he didn't know much about white drugs. In fact, it was the white players who could afford coke in college and then brought it with them into the league.

It was easy to tell when any player was abusing coke because of his erratic behavior. A guy would come to practice and be all bright and lively. "Hey, man. How's everything? Talk to me, man. Yeah, what's up?" The next day he'd come in and he'd be, "I don't want to talk to you, man. I ain't talking to fucking nobody." Or else a guy would come to practice and tell the coach that he was hurting. There were no MRIs in those days, so even when there was no swelling, if a player said his knee or ankle was sore he was allowed to stay on the sideline. I've also seen plenty of guys coming to games with their noses running. In fact, there were a couple of white stars who used to sit on the bench with towels over their heads and the talk among the players was that their noses would start bleeding whenever they sat down.

As long as only white guys were getting fucked up, the NBA appeared to have no beef. It seemed to me that it was only when the black guys started making enough money to join in the fun that the NBA started making anti-drug rules. I talked to one white franchise player who was busted by the league and instructed to tell everybody that he was going to Europe during the off-season. Meanwhile, he spent the summer drying out in some private clinic and the drug busts were never hung on him. The talk among the players was that if a guy was being promoted as part of the NBA's marketing program the league couldn't afford to have him disgraced. There was also talk that the same easy deal also went down for a couple of black Hall-of-Famers, but when the average black player got busted he stayed busted.

And the black guys knew which of the whites were cokeheads because the morning after they'd be just as fucked up as we were. But we made believe we didn't know shit. "Hey, man. Where were y'all last night? I didn't see you anywhere." They'd always say they were hanging out with an old college buddy.

The blacks would do most of our coke in a teammate's house before we went out clubbing. Hey, man. Stop by the crib and have a toot or two. Or five or ten. And it was easy to connect in any of the clubs we frequented. Just check out the guy whose girl comes back from the bathroom with her nose running.

Of course, we'd all be careful not to get stoked the day of a game because we knew we couldn't play right when we were fucked up. But there were plenty of off days.

There were some guys, though, who couldn't do their drugs in moderation. Terry Furlow was a great player who got done in by drugs. I played with and against Terry and as far as I could see all he was doing was smoking weed. But other players would tell me, "Oh, man. Terry gets so high that when we're checking out of a hotel in the morning he's throwing up all over the front desk." To my mind, the NBA had to know that Terry had a drug problem, but they never got him any help. The result was that one night Terry got so high he couldn't control the car he was driving and was killed in an accident.

In the mid-'80s, there was also a nasty business about a bunch of the Phoenix Suns doing drugs. Johnny High and James Edwards were the only players caught red-handed, but the talk was that the mob was involved along with lots of big-name people. Johnny was set to testify to a grand jury when he was killed in a car crash.

"Fast" Eddie Johnson was an outstanding player with the Atlanta Hawks who died of an overdose. John Drew was the Hawks' high-scorer for a couple of years until drugs cut short his career. Drew would get so fucked up that all during a ball game he'd be saying, "You see 'em? You see 'em, man? They comin', man! They comin'."

Not only was the NBA failing to provide help for players with drug problems, we started to believe the league was using undercover agents to nail drug users. Walter Davis ended up in rehab and the story that made the rounds was that he was probably set up by a female agent that he'd taken up to his hotel room to do a couple of lines. Later on, we believed the NBA was targeting Micheal Ray Richardson.

For a while, I believed that the NBA was tracking me. I was balling a girl who was constantly around the 76ers and she warned me to be careful. So I just chilled out for a few weeks until the heat was off.

Crack wasn't around then, and I never saw anybody with heavy drugs, but in one of his books Kareem admitted to trying heroin. I once asked him why he had confessed. "I ain't playing no more," Kareem said, "so they can't do a motherfucking thing to me now. Besides, plenty of other guys knew what I was doing, and what happens if they write their own book and tell on me? Shit, if you ever write a book, Darryl, you got to tell some dirt on yourself. That's the only way your book is gonna sell."

Unlike Kareem, Micheal Ray Richardson couldn't hide the dirt while he was in the league. I played with him on the New Jersey Nets for three seasons in the mid-'80s and he was hands down the most talented player on the team. Sugar came to the Nets from Golden State with two big problems: Drugs and more drugs. He'd already been busted once and under the drug agreement with the players union, two more strikes against Sugar would mean permanent banishment from the league.

Sugar Ray would wear out Magic, tear up George Gervin like he was shredded wheat, and put fear into Isiah Thomas. Then Sugar would disappear for a week and show up again all fucked up. Had he been able to stay away from drugs, Sugar would have been one of the greatest players of all time.

Despite his drug problems, he was named to the NBA's All-Defense team twice and played in four All-Star games. If Sugar didn't have great range on his jumper, he could do everything else. And when Sugar got geared up to play defense he could put a box around the best guards in the league.

"I d-don't like white p-point guards," Sugar used to say. "None. Show me a little white p-point guard and I'm gonna tear his ass off."

So Sugar to used hump up and totally embarrass guys like John Stockton and Mark Price. And Sugar gave the same treatment to Isiah Thomas. "But, Sugar," I'd say, "Isiah's blacker than the inside of my ass."

"No m-matter," Sugar said. "He p-plays like a little white p-point guard."

No matter how brilliant a player he was, though, we believed the league was after Sugar's ass. I first suspected this early in the '83–84 season while Sugar and I were at a party at some girl's house after a ball game in Boston. I was just sitting around drinking a few beers with a local guy named Norman when Sugar went into the back room with one of the girls. Sugar was gone for about an hour and I was getting ready to head back to the hotel, so I said to Norman, "Do me a favor and go tell Sugar that it's time to leave."

So Norman went into the back room, came back and said, "Sugar and the girl he was with are gone, man. They went out the back way."

"Where'd they go?"

"The girl was taking him to someplace where they could score some coke."

Oh, shit.

Norman knew exactly where the drug store was, so we called for a cab and waited for it downstairs. As soon as the cab showed up, I knew something was suspicious. The driver was a black guy, clean-shaven, nice hair, dressed in an expensive suit and tie, and he was driving very cautiously, like he didn't know his way around the city.

All right, we got there and went inside this nightclub, and there was Sugar, flying high, dancing and carrying on with some girls like he didn't have a care in the world. "Sugar, how come you run off like that, man?"

"Fuck it, Ham. I got t-tired of that place, and now I'm t-tired of this place. Let's go back to the girl's house 'cause I'm ready to b-bust her pussy."

So we hailed a cab and got back to the house. I was happy enough drinking beer and bullshitting with Norman, but after another half hour I figured Sugar had enough time to do his thing. This time I went to get him myself and I started pounding on the door. "Sugar, come on. Let's go." Then Norman came over to say that Sugar and the girl had slipped out the back again.

Well, fuck him anyway. I had to get back to the hotel so I asked Norman to call me a cab. When the cab arrived, it was the same cab and the same driver as before. After a few blocks, the driver pulled over to the curb. Then he slid back the glass partition and said, "Where the fuck is Micheal Ray?"

"I don't know."

"When you see him, tell him we're gonna get him."

I started emptying my pockets. "You can search me, man. I'm clean."

"We're not interested in you. It's Richardson we're after, and we're gonna get him. It's only a question of when and where."

When I was finally dropped off at the hotel, I didn't bother to pay the fare because I knew he wasn't a real cab driver. He just drove away without asking for a dime.

I saw Sugar the next morning on the team bus, and I told him what happened. "They're watching you, Sugar. You got to be careful."

"Don't worry, Ham," he said. "They ain't real c–cops or nothing. It ain't a problem, b–believe me."

I never did find out who the driver was. He could have been with the local police but I always suspected he was hired by the league. Two weeks later, Sugar got caught.

Richardson wasn't the only one being watched. I know of a couple other guys who were tipped off and told to be careful. When Earl Cureton was with Detroit, he was invited to a party by one of the local jock-sniffers who always hang around pro athletes. Earl drove up to the house, but at the last minute decided not to go inside. The Pistons' coach, Scotty Robertson, came up to Earl the next day at practice and said, "You be careful what parties you go to, okay? All the guys you think are your buddies ain't really your buddies." Earl never knew for sure if Robertson was trying to tip him off about being under surveillance but, given the climate of the time, always suspected as much.

I also believe that I was being watched at various times in my career, and I have no doubt the Nets knew I was a part-time snorter. I always figured that after Sugar was caught he probably told management about the other snorters. One day I found a note in my locker advising me to "exercise some discipline." Even though there was no mention of drugs it was clear to me what the note meant. Every so often, somebody in the organization would ask me why I was spending so much time in a high-drug neighborhood. I'd say that I had a girlfriend living there and that seemed to satisfy them, but I got the message so I'd lay low for a while. I figured the only reasons why the Nets protected me were because I was popular with the media and because I was playing so well.

Another time, I had a teammate who had just gotten out of rehab, but I wasn't convinced his nose was clean. The team checked into a hotel and this guy called my room at three o'clock in the morning. "Hey, man," he said, "I got a joint down here, but there's no matches in my room. Why don't you bring some matches with you and we'll do up this doobie?" Back then, there weren't any no-smoking rooms, and every hotel room I'd ever been in had matches. So I was suspicious. It wouldn't have been the first or last time that a player on the edge was persuaded to set up a teammate. "No, man," I told him. "I'm all asleep here." Even though I turned him down, some of the other guys on the team started backing away from me. They thought the heat was on me and they didn't want to get burned.

When you pissed in a cup back in those days, you were only tested for cocaine and heroin. Marijuana was considered to be okay. But then Kareem and Robert Parish got popped for possession of weed, and other players were arrested by local police for driving a hundred miles an hour down a city street with a gun in the glove compartment and a joint on the seat. That's when the league started also testing for weed.

Now, why was the league going so hard after Micheal Ray? To make an example of him that would throw a scare into all the other guys who were using drugs. Sugar wasn't being featured in any of the league's advertising, and since he already had one strike against him, he was expendable. Another thing working here was that after his first drug rehab in 1982, Sugar was allowed back into the league and played so well that the sportswriters voted him the Comeback Player of the Year.

So guys around the league were thinking that getting caught by the league for drugs was no big deal.

9

Get Out of Town

During the summer of 1980, I mostly hung around the Midwest doing camps and playing in a summer league in Cleveland. In 1979, the Sixers had drafted Earl Cureton from Detroit Mercy College in the third round, and he didn't make the team. Earl was a great guy, he could run and he had a nice jump hook, but he couldn't hit a jumper to get into heaven. After the Sixers cut him, he went back home to Detroit and worked on his shooting. I ran into Earl again playing against him in Cleveland and we resumed our friendship. Next up on my summer itinerary was doing Terry Tyler's camp in Detroit, and then playing in Magic's Charity All-Star game there, so Earl invited me to stay with him at his mom's house as long as I was in town. Now, there are so many black people in Detroit that we sometimes call it "Chocolate City" and I really dug the place. I also hung around after my commitments were completed because Earl and I were having a ball, and because there were so many top-flight players living there—Terry Duerod, John Long, Phil Hubbard, Joe Kopicki and others—that the pickup games kept me in good shape.

Staying with Earl's family was also a very lively experience by itself. Earl's father worked hard all week and came home wrung-out and tired. He'd eat dinner, watch some TV, and then go off to bed. On Friday nights, however, he'd come home and give his wife some of his paycheck, then he'd go off and the family wouldn't see him again until Monday night.

Another reason why I stayed around was Mrs. Cureton's hospitality. She had me sleep upstairs in Earl's room while Earl slept on the living room couch. Before we all went to bed, Mrs. Cureton would say, "Darryl, what do you want for breakfast tomorrow?"

"Aw, Mrs. Cureton, I ain't had no biscuits in a long time."

So that's what she fixed up. Then the next day when me and Earl would get ready to go out and play ball, she'd say, "Darryl, what would you like for dinner tonight?"

"If you were to cook up some ham hocks and beans I would be mighty thankful."

This went on for three or four days.

One morning at 4 a.m., Earl came busting into where I was dead asleep in his room. Then he started shouting, "Wake up, you black bitch!"

"Huh?"

"Take your motherfucking ass and go home. My mother never cooks like that for me."

Then we heard his mother's voice calling from her bedroom down the hall, "Earl, you let that boy alone and let him go back to sleep."

"Yeah, Earl," I said. "Leave me alone." So he went back downstairs.

When I woke up, I packed my stuff and told Earl that I was sorry about the way things turned out.

"Yeah," he said. "You gotta go home, motherfucker. I can't let you come in here and take my mama away from me."

Well, Earl did make the Sixers that season and we were good buddies. We'd hang out, go eat together, go to the clubs. I'd tease him about his jumper, but he practiced and practiced until he developed a little short-range jumpie that was adequate enough to keep him in the league. Earl was one of the hardest-working guys in show business. And with World long gone, Earl made it easier for me to deal with my last two seasons in Philly.

On the road or at home, if I wasn't partying, I'd be watching movies. Westerns were my favorites, but I also liked sword-fighting movies with lots of sorcery and witchcraft. After watching and watching, I noticed something interesting. The king gets killed in every single movie. But not the duke. And the duke lives just as good as the king. He's fucking every night. He's got money and property and he lives a whole lot longer than the king. So I decided that I didn't have to out-drink, out-fuck, out-snort, out-smoke everybody. All I had to do was have fun. And that's another reason why me and Earl got along so well.

Even before the season started, I knew that me and Billy C. still weren't on the same page. One day in training camp, Billy thought I was loafing through some drills. He got pretty riled up, so we sat down on the scorer's table and he read me the riot act. Billy said that I was talented but undisciplined. How could a player who named his dunks, who talked about living on Lovetron and who smiled at pretty ladies in the stands during games really have his mind in the right place? Did I want to be just another bullshit player with unrealized potential? Or did I want to be a serious player who was respected throughout the league? He told me that my career was at stake. I just hung down my head and said, "You're right, Billy. From now on I'm gonna work hard all the time."

But I could never resist making mischief, so as soon as Billy got up to walk away, I stuck out my foot and tripped him. Both of us started laughing. And I think Billy became convinced right then that I was a lost cause. By his tight-assed standards, I probably was. But I always thought that NBA players were supposed to entertain the people who paid their hard-earned money to come out and watch us play a kid's game. If we can't play well, win more games than the other teams in the league and do it with flair, then the fans won't have a reason to come to the arena. And if the players aren't having fun playing, then how can the fans have fun watching?

Me and Billy had another confrontation that didn't end in laughter. We were the last ones in the locker room after I'd had a bad game and Billy was pissed. We were yapping at each other, then he said, "You'll play the way I want you to play, or I'll kick your ass!" That just sent me over the edge. I just balled up my fists and said, "Okay, Billy. Bring it on." But he saw the fight in me and left the room. Neither of us ever mentioned the incident.

Otherwise, the Sixers had a ton of fun that year, at least during the regular season. We tied with Boston for the most wins (62), which had to do with our skill level and intensity, but which also had to do with the fact that we'd made the NBA finals the season before. Since we were officially one of the league's elite teams, our playing schedule was adjusted accordingly. The bad teams were scheduled for long West Coast road trips that could last for 17 to 21 days. Being away from home for that long is a hardship and players get grouchy and pissed off with both their teammates and their opponents. Teams on long road trips inevitably get into fights somewhere along the line, and because of the increased fatigue factor they also suffer more injuries. But as one of the stronger teams, our West Coast games were played over the course of two short trips. At 25-16, we had the third best road record in the league (behind Boston and Milwaukee).

However, the most amazing statistic that season was that we led the NBA in team defense. Credit Bobby Jones, Caldwell Jones, Lionel Hollins and Mo Cheeks. Also, Billy was becoming a much better coach—more sure of himself, more organized and more savvy in getting the individual matchups to work in our favor.

Our offense got a boost from a talented rookie, Andrew Toney. Throughout his career (which was cut short by injuries) Andrew would always have trouble on defense, but from the get-go he could make the scoreboard light up like Fourth of July fireworks. He used to murder the Celtics, so much so that the media dubbed him "The Boston Strangler." The only problem was that Andrew was Billy's pet. Billy would often make excuses for Andrew's rookie mistakes, and any time somebody banged Andrew too hard in practice, Billy would intervene. Except for maybe Mo Cheeks, Andrew was the only dominant player drafted and developed during Billy's tenure with the Sixers. So perhaps Billy thought that Andrew was destined for the Hall of Fame and, in the absence of a championship, would be the outstanding legacy of his coaching career.

My own numbers (14 points and 7.2 rebounds) were off from last year, but I attributed that to the fact that my minutes were also down to 27 per game. I shot well enough (.607) to finish second to Artis Gilmore in field goal percentage, which only reinforced my feeling that I just didn't get enough shots. Yeah, my defense stepped up, I ran hard and I worked hard, but I still felt like an after-thought on offense.

Despite our 62-20 record the Sixers didn't have enough stuff to return to the finals. First we blanked Indiana in a mini-series, then we squeezed past Bob Lanier's big ass to beat the Bucks in seven games.

Up next were the Boston Celtics, and we jumped out to a 3-1 lead. Kevin McHale was a rookie who played like a veteran, while Robert Parish, Tiny Archibald, Cedric Maxwell, and Larry Bird just wouldn't give an inch. We couldn't come up with a big play when we needed one and the Celtics were rock-steady in the clutch. The Celtics won the last three games by a total of five points and went on to easily beat Houston to win the championship.

Damn! Another season, another disappointment. Nothing to do but work hard during the summer and go after it again.

I stayed around Philly in the off-season to keep myself in playing shape. I'd be a free agent after the 1981-82 season and, besides trying to win a ring, I was determined to have a banner year so I'd be offered another hefty contract. But the kicker was that I'd already played in exactly 400 regular season games without ever starting. Not even once! How, then, was I supposed to rack up the kind of numbers necessary to attract a long-term deal?

To add to my worries I had a girlfriend that summer named Lois. She had nice big hips like a horse, a little bitty waist and sizeable titties. Her parents were separated and her father was sickly so Lois would sometimes have to go take care of him. Okay. One night, Lois and I were sitting at home when three of her girlfriends drove up wanting to party. That's always all right with me, so we climbed into my Lincoln Continental and made stops at Whispers, Green Street and Kirby's, and we had a great time. Two nights later, Lois was out at her father's house, and the same girlfriends showed up wanting to party again. So that's what we did.

When I came back home at about three in the morning, I was drunker than Dean Martin. I was so fucked up that I had no business driving a bicycle. But I managed to get myself to the front door, only to find that the key didn't fit. I knew I was skunked, so I walked next door to look at the neighbor's house, I carefully inspected the mailbox, and I said, "Yeah, that's my house. How come the key don't work?" So I started beating on the front door. After a while, Lois came downstairs, peeked through a window that was beside the door, and said, "What you want?"

"What's wrong with you? Quit the bullshit and let me in my house."

"You were out with them 'ho's," she said. "Which one of them did you fuck?"

"You're crazy. They're your girlfriends. I didn't touch any of them."

"They're all 'ho's," she said then she went back up the stairs.

So there I was, sitting in the dark outside of my own house. I kept on getting angrier by the minute, until I picked up a lawn chair and tossed it through the picture window. CRASH! Then I stepped into the living room. By the time I got inside, Lois was there waiting for me and WHAM! She punched me right in the eye. I was off-balance and I fell backwards into the broken glass. I was bleeding in a hundred different places but I made a beeline for the phone. First I called Lois's mother to come get her, then I called the police. "Hello, officer? Yeah, I got a lady I need removed from my house."

While I was on the phone, Lois was hitting and kicking me. I let her do it because I knew if I hit her back I'd kill her and I'd spend the rest of my life in the joint. "You black motherfucker," she was screaming, "you won't even fight back."

The cop was Rich, a friend of mine, and he showed up just at the same time that Lois's mother did. By then, I'd shoved all of Lois's clothes into a suitcase. I grabbed the suitcase and threw it on to the lawn near where her mother was. "Take that 'ho' away from here," I said to the mother.

She threw the suitcase right back at me, saying, "She wasn't no 'ho' when she left home."

"Well, she's a 'ho' now."

"You made her one."

Then Rich stepped in. He was laughing his ass off, but he suddenly got serious and said, "Cut this out right now. And both of you ladies have to leave the premises."

So everybody finally left and I was still drunk. I was afraid to go upstairs and sleep because someone might just walk in through the broken window and steal everything they could carry. I sat in the living room all night, bleeding where I was cut by the glass, my eye swollen where Lois punched me and skeeters tearing my ass up. My only consolation was that it was the summertime. If it had been during the season, I would've been totally embarrassed by my teammates. "A girl did that to you?"

If something like that had happened these days, it would have been on the wire and the whole world would've known. Back then, the police and other public officials tried to protect athletes. As it was, I stayed home for about a week until my cuts healed, but I could hardly wait for the season to start so my life could get back to normal.

If Philadelphia was the City of Brotherly Love (except for Lois and her mama), then I was the brother that everybody in town loved the most. I've always been heavy into music, mostly soul and funk and some rap, and I had my own radio show on WDAN. *Tune in to 105, guaranteed to warm your thighs. This is Chocolate Thunder bringing you the general jive and the slow motion potion.* I'd talk some shit and play requests. "Thunder, could you play *Heat Wave*?" Yeah, baby, I'll play it just for you.

I also had my own column, "The Dunkateer," in the *Philadelphia Journal.* I'd answer questions that readers sent in and just have some fun. I even got to investigate the oldest joke in the world:

While the Sixers were in Los Angeles, like any good newspaperman, I decided to seek the truth. So when I saw the San Diego Chicken after the game I finally got the straight dope on one of the questions of the ages.

Why did the Chicken cross the road?

I should have known the answer was easy. The Chicken told me he wanted to help some fine hen on the other side hatch some eggs. And he said he didn't walk, but flew across the road. The Chicken is my kind of bird.

Every time I played well, the Sixers' owner, Harold Katz, would come over to me in the locker room and say, "Darryl, you *are* Philadelphia." I wouldn't find out until the end of the season what Katz was really thinking.

Meanwhile, Billy finally plugged me into the starting lineup, but then he made my promotion meaningless by cutting my playing time to 23 minutes per game. That's the primary number that concerns players—time on the floor. Time enough to develop a rhythm, time for the referees to at least theoretically learn your game, time to pile up significant numbers and help your team win. Sure, my reduced daylight was Billy's fault, and the refs' fault, but also my own fault for partying too strenuously and not working hard enough in practice.

By now, I had been around the league long enough to differentiate the players from the pretenders. In my opinion, the NBA's publicity machine often seemed to be working overtime to create gate attractions by promoting mediocre players as being authentic stars. David Thompson was a good example. He was a skinny, six-foot-four dude whose talent, as far as I could see, was limited to jumping to the moon and executing highlight dunks. John Drew was another one. The referees let Drew do more walking than your neighbor does when he takes Fido out for an airing. But Drew was the only player on the Hawks who could put the ball in the hole so the NBA made an All-Star out of him. When Butch Lee came out of Marquette, he was touted as being a future Hall of Famer, but he was a dud from the start and only lasted for two seasons. Add Kelly Tripucka to the list. He struck me as an over-rated white boy from Notre Dame who always worked hard and was protected by the referees. If you put Tripucka in a New York playground without the Big Whistle watching over him, I'd bet dozens of unknown black players would've busted his ass. What about Robert Parish? To me, this guy was an over-rated finesse player who was useless in the clutch and got bailed out time and again by Larry Bird.

And the NBA is still at it! Jason Williams is a wild-ass white boy who makes nothing but bad decisions with the ball and produces more turnovers than the Pillsbury Doughboy. Yet it wasn't so long ago that Williams was being promoted as the NBA's latest savior.

On the other hand, it seems to me there are plenty of players who are ignored by the NBA yet are considered to be all-stars by their peers. Dennis Johnson, for example, was the only guard who could keep Magic from flying down the court and creating early offense for the Lakers. Johnson had the strength and the length to turn Magic around and make him back his way into the attack zone. Who else fits this category? Nate Thurmond, Gus Gerard, and especially "Super" John Williamson. The prospect of playing against these guys would give you nightmares. But Williamson was so good and so nasty that most of the guys who had to defend him were afraid of him.

If the Sixers had a good season (58-24, second best in the league to the Celtics), my numbers looked mediocre (only 11 points and six rebounds per game). I was never a super-duper rebounder because, even though I had good hands and good hops, I wasn't a really quick jumper. So unless I got good position, quick leapers often beat me to the ball. Even so, if a center is supposed to average one rebound every three minutes, I was in the ballpark (one for 3.5). It was just one of those seasons where I couldn't get comfortable and couldn't develop any kind of consistency.

We were playing the Bullets in Washington just a few weeks before my 25th birthday when I got kicked hard in my right leg. Even though I finished the game, I knew my leg wasn't right. When the leg got worse, I sat out a couple of games. But sitting wasn't what management and the press wanted to see. They started making noises about how I was dogging it, and how other guys who got kicked went on playing and never complained. Nobody wanted to believe that I was really hurt.

So I guess I rushed back a little sooner than I should have. The leg felt stiff, but I played through the discomfort because I figured I was better off playing on one good leg than sitting around listening to everybody bitching at me.

About ten days after I'd been kicked, we were in New Jersey to play the Nets in a nationally televised game. Near the end of the first quarter, I got the ball in the pivot and made a sharp twisting move toward the basket when I heard a loud, sickening crack. It was my right leg breaking. Nobody touched me. The leg was just weak and it broke under pressure. Man, did that hurt. The pain moved up my leg, through my body and right into my head. I was lying there rolled up like a baby and grabbing at my leg.

While I was writhing helplessly on the floor, the trainer, Al Domenico, rushed out, took one look and told me that I was through for the day. Other than Al, nobody else came over to see what had happened or to try to help me out. Not my coach, not any of my teammates. Hell, if I had been Andrew Toney, Billy would have scooted out there on roller skates.

Sitting in the X-ray room at the local hospital, I remember thinking, "I'm not even 25. I should be at the top of my game and looking forward to another ten years in the league. I'm too young to have all this end. What the hell am I going to do now? Will I be able to run and jump like before? Will I be able to walk?"

When I got back to the Meadowlands Arena, the Sixers were already getting dressed in the locker room, and only a couple of them (Earl Cureton and Bobby Jones) came over to check me out. I was aware that professional athletes usually treat injured teammates like their injury is contagious, but I was so disgusted with everybody else that I didn't say much. It seemed like I was being quarantined and already forgotten, because the team bus left without me.

I was supposed to be through for the season, but I healed quicker than expected and came back in only eight weeks. In the playoffs, we beat the Celtics in a knock-'em-down-and-drag-'em-out seven-game series to once again qualify for the championship round. But the Lakers' dynasty was still at high tide and they swamped us in six games. I actually had a good series against Kareem, and just being able to play again was good for my peace of mind.

I was about to become a free agent when I was called in to speak to Harold Katz. I knew that if I signed with another team, the Sixers would get nothing for me, so it made sense for Katz to beg me to sign with him. I was afraid that his idea was sign me so that he could trade me. But I thought that declaring as a free agent would be a crapshoot. I might make a lot of money elsewhere but get stuck on a team that couldn't make the playoffs. Or I could wind up playing for a worse coach than Billy Cunningham. Besides, I liked living in Philly and I thought we had a great chance to finally win a championship. "You are Philly," Katz kept telling me, so I took a chance and resigned a five-year deal for three million. I figured whatever happened, I'd still have the big bucks.

I believe Katz never did like me. I often thought his daughter was sweet on me and that freaked him out. He must have hated the thought of any player ever messing with his daughter. Plus, he always wanted to be the biggest cheese in town and I was just too popular with the fans and the media. So two weeks after I re-upped with the Sixers I was traded to New Jersey for $700,000 and a number one draft choice (which turned out to be Leo "Who" Rautins). Later, when I sat down face-to-face with Joe Taub, the Nets' owner, he related exactly how the transaction had come about: After the playoffs, Taub called Katz to say, "Harold, would you ever consider trading Dawkins?"

Taub told me that Katz replied by saying he didn't want me

around his team any more. I wish I could say that race had nothing to do with Katz's opinion of me but I'm not sure that is true.

"Well, I want him," said Taub.

"All right," said Katz. "We'll work out a deal."

I could deal with racism. Growing up in the South, I'd dealt with it all my life. But even before I got to New Jersey, I had to face a bigger problem, one that I was totally unprepared to deal with.

It all came to light one day when I went shopping in the neighborhood supermarket where I had a credit account. The checker at the cash register wouldn't let me buy anything on credit and said my checks were also unacceptable. If I wanted the groceries I'd have to pay cash. It turned out that my check had bounced the previous month. In addition, the bank had warned the supermarket manager that my account was constantly overdrawn. It was humiliating—and all news to me.

Then I started hearing from other stores. My checks were bouncing everywhere. Next, the IRS claimed I had not paid my taxes for the past year, and my mother was worried that the government was going to to put a lien on the house I'd bought her.

I was under the impression that my bills were being paid by someone I'd hired some years earlier to help handle my affairs. I was to receive a personal allowance of $1,000 a week and my advisor would pay my taxes and the mortgages on both my mother's and my grandmother's houses. He was also responsible for investing my money. But I later discovered that investments he'd made on my behalf did not work out and I had been losing about $50,000 a year, leaving me unable to pay my bills.

So I fired the guy and hired a replacement, but a short time later my financial problems started up all over again. I found out that the new guy had also made some lousy investments on my behalf, including putting money in an African diamond mine and a movie about gigantic cockroaches devouring Fresno. And then the asshole wouldn't even return my phone calls. So I fired him pronto.

When the shit hit the fan, newspaper stories started claiming I was passing bad checks all over Florida, Philly and New Jersey. I was so distressed that my hair started falling out. I couldn't believe that people I'd trusted had let this happen to me. I remember thinking at the time that I wanted to go out and get a gun and shoot both of them, their wives, their kids and their dogs. Then I'd throw myself on the mercy of the court and plead temporary insanity.

Then a teammate recommended a financial advisor, Harvey LaKind, and with his help, things were eventually straightened out. We reviewed four years of tax returns and worked out a plan with the IRS to prevent a lien being placed on my Nets salary. We talked to the bank that held my mother's and grandmother's mortgages and convinced them not to foreclose. I caught up with the trail of bounced checks I had written and made good on them. The Nets management wasn't very sympathetic in our attempts to restructure our contract, but LaKind cut my personal allowance to $400 per week and everything slowly turned around. He arranged nice endorsement deals with PONY sneakers and Wilson basketballs. I did TV commercials for Pontiac and Friendly's, an ice cream restaurant chain. I was offered more speaking and personal-appearance opportunities than I could keep up with. But it took me several years to get straight.

I felt a little better when I realized that a lot of NBA players who had gone to college and earned their degrees (like Kareem) had said they'd also been swindled. And I resolved never to trust anyone with my money again.

After the dust had settled somewhat, there was even worse news from Florida: My grandmother had died.

On the sad drive back home, I couldn't help reliving some of the things she'd said and done: Like when I was 12 and I used to wash the dishes and clean the house while she napped. I loved her so much that it was a thrill to put on her house slippers and flop through my chores while she slept. One day, Chico walked in and started to tease me. "You big sissy, you're wearing a lady's slippers because you clean the house better than a lady."

I ran over to Grandma, whimpering, "Chico's picking on me. And I didn't do nothing to him."

Well, Grandma got up and said to Chico, "You better leave Darryl alone, boy, because he's gonna be the one that's gonna be taking care of everybody. Just you watch."

Grandma was a church-going Christian lady, but she wasn't shy about bedeviling anybody who needed it. Back in the day, the elderly ladies used to carry their money in their bras. They called it the Titty Citibank. Well, they were in church one Sunday morning and Sister Johnson started feeling the spirit come upon her. Oh, she was shivering and shaking and speaking in tongues. It was the job of the usher to come over and hold the women when they got happy so they wouldn't fall and hurt themselves. But when this particular usher grabbed Sister Johnson, he slipped his hand into her bra and stole her money—$44. The next Sunday the same thing happened to Grandma's sister Bea, and the usher took $50. So Grandma and my Great-Aunt Bea took to rocking on Grandma's porch, dipping snuff, and figuring out what to do about the thieving usher.

Come Sunday and Grandma made believe that she, too, was feeling the spirit. Sure enough, the usher came over, and while he was holding her steady, he reached into her bosom for her money. "This what you're looking for?" she said, and then she threw a fistful of snuff into his eyes. While the usher was sneezing and crying, the old ladies pushed him into a corner of the church and stuck him all over with their hatpins.

That was Grandma. She was the only one who could keep me down to earth, and I still miss her every day.

10

Net Gain = One Bullshit Coach

L arry Brown was my new coach and his training camp was even worse than Gene Shue's. Larry just ran us until our legs were dead, he'd give us Sunday morning off, and then Sunday night he'd run us ragged again. He called his favorite players by their names, and everybody else was "Kiddo." He'd say, "C'mon, Kiddo. Keep working hard. C'mon, Kiddo. Don't be such a quitter."

Larry had played under Dean Smith at North Carolina, so who were his favorites? The way I saw it, he liked Mike O'Koren from his alma mater, plus all the other guys from the Atlantic Coast Conference: Mike Gminski from Duke, and Albert King, Len Elmore and Buck Williams, who'd all played at Maryland. Of these, "Bucko" was the apparent favorite of favorites.

I was 25 when I joined the New Jersey Nets, and being a seven-year NBA veteran I knew what I had to do to be an impact player: Get into the pivot and go to work. I was good at my job and other teams were giving me the respect of doubling-down whenever I caught the ball. My jump shot was also well scouted, so whenever I went to the high-post, my defender would crowd me. And what did Larry do? To keep six-foot-eight Bucko happy, Larry plugged him into the pivot and hung seven-foot me out to dry on the high-post. Later on, after Larry left the Nets, this is how he explained the switch: "Darryl can catch it and pass it. It's a challenge for him, a chance to expand his understanding of offensive dynamics. Darryl is such a great target at the high post—so easy to find when the guards are under pressure, and it's so easy to initiate an offensive sequence with a guaranteed pass to the foul line. But Darryl did get to post up sometimes. Maybe he should have been inside more."

Like Gene Shue, Larry had been a guard in his active days and didn't know what to do with a true center. Meanwhile, I felt like I was out in the parking lot while the game was happening, and I was uncomfortable, confused, useless and all fucked up.

The only reason I remained relatively sane was that most of the other guys on the team were fun to be with:

Otis Birdsong grew up near Orlando so we knew each other from way back. He was a great guy who just couldn't keep from chasing women. Larry was frustrated with Otis because he was always just injured or else recovering from an injury, and he had a huge long-term contract that made him untradeable.

Albert King always played in his big brother's shadow. Albert was taller than Bernard, a better passer with more range on his shot, but the major difference was that Bernard was much stronger. It was my self-appointed job to give out nicknames, and since Albert had red eyes and knots on his face, I called him Crocodile.

Jeff Turner was a hard-nosed player who was white and left-handed. Jeff had a fairly decent jumper but not much overall talent, so a lot of the black players didn't respect his game.

Len Elmore was another player who had to work hard to cover a shortage of talent, but Len was one of the smartest players ever.

Mike O'Koren ranked up there with Bobby Jones on my personal list of loveable white boys. I surprised him one night when he invited some of the guys over to his mother's house for dinner. She served us what everybody said was a delicious Italian feast, but I can't enjoy any kind of food without my favorite condiment. "Hey, Mrs. O," I said. "Do you have any hot sauce?" Nope. So I reached into my coat pocket and pulled out my little traveling bottle of Tabasco. It's like American Express; I never leave home without it.

Mike Gminski was my backup, but he had some health problems so he was kind of weak and fragile. I'd start the game and bang the shit out of the other center, then Mike would come in and finesse them like a matador working a bull. Even though Mike was a terrific person and extremely intelligent, when he first came into the league the black guys put him in the same no-respect category as Jeff Turner. I remember one game when the Hawks' Bill Willoughby and me got into an unofficial dunking contest. BAM! Willow threw one down. BAM! Then I'd get an offensive rebound and slam it home. BAM! The guys on both teams were enjoying the spectacle and the point guards kept giving us the ball. BAM! BAM! Gminski was also in the game and as we ran downcourt he said to me, "Ham, this is no place for a no-jumping white boy!"

During practice, I would wear Mike's ass out and he had to develop a jump hook or else he never would've scored against me. That's the shot that made his career and finally earned the respect of the brothers around the league. In fact, lots of guys joked that Mike should've given me a piece of the big contract he eventually signed since it was me who made him an NBA player.

Before he was dealt to Cleveland, Sam Lacey was with the Nets in training camp. Both of his pinkie fingers had been broken so many times they were crooked and looked like little claws. The previous summer Sam had some surgery done to make his fingers normal, but he gave us a different version: "I met this bitch who was a health freak and she invited me up to her place for some hot sex. And she was hot, all right. When she started sucking my dick, I swear both my little fingers straightened out."

Darwin Cook was a hustling point guard who must've been eating some disgusting food because it seemed like he couldn't take ten steps without farting. I started calling him Skunky MacTavish and others picked it up, including the coaching staff.

Bill Blair was one of my favorite assistant coaches of all time. I loved his pre-game speeches: "All right, guys. I know y'all don't need a big ol' pep talk. The truth is that I don't know a whole lot about this game of basketball, and you guys don't know a whole lot, either. But I'll tell you what. If we put the ball in the hole more times than they do, and if we stop them more times than they stop us, we're gonna goddamn win tonight."

The other assistant was Mike Schuler. In my opinion, he was much harder on black players: He'd get all snotty and he'd look hard at any black guy who'd made a mistake and say, "We paid all that money for *him*?" And I seldom heard him criticize any of the white players. Of course I loved to bust Schuler's balls. "Hey, Pop," I'd say to him. "I'm gonna marry one of your daughters. That's right. I'm gonna be laying on your motherfucking couch, eating all your food and drinking all your booze." I could tell that got him mad because his whole face would turn red, but he never fucked with me.

Out-and-out racism was rare within the NBA community. It was a big deal in 1947 when Jackie Robinson broke the color line in major league baseball. Other players called him "nigger," pitchers threw at his head, and several teams threatened not to take the field if Robinson played. But in 1950, when Chuck Cooper and Earl Lloyd were the first blacks to play in the NBA, they were totally accepted by the white players. And, except for what Steve Mix told me about the divided locker room in Detroit, I never heard of any racial tension among NBA players.

It was the same with the coaches. They judged players by their talent, not their skin color. But one head coach lost all respect among many black players after reports spread around the league of an incident that allegedly occurred between this coach and a young black player. As it was told to me, the coach was overheard exhorting the player to become a better rebounder by comparing him to a gorilla and telling him to "climb up in that tree and go get those coconuts."

Larry Brown was from the Dean Smith school of head coaches so he never let his assistants do much. Larry's always had the reputation of being a great teacher, and I must admit he did help me develop my left hand (which was the only worthwhile thing he ever taught me). The unfortunate truth was that Larry saved most of his teaching time and most of his favors for his pets. He was constantly excusing Buck and Albert from practice. "You two guys worked hard in last night's game," Larry would say, "so you can take off. I'm going to make everybody else sweat their asses off."

Say what? Only two guys worked hard? Fuck that!

Larry was also said to be a tremendous motivator, but I never liked his tactics. He thought that he knew the right way of doing everything, from setting a pick to ordering in a restaurant. Whenever anybody did something just a little bit differently, whether the results were good or bad, Larry said we should've done it his way. He was like an old maid just nagging and bitching at us all the time.

We were playing in front of a small crowd one night in Milwaukee and me and Darwin Cook were setting up a pick-and-roll. My defender anticipated that I'd be rolling to the basket, so I made an adjustment and stepped to the foul line instead. I was wide open for a jump shot but Darwin had trouble with his dribble and the ball never got to me. For a moment the crowd was absolutely silent, and that's when Larry jumped up and yelled, "Roll, Darryl! Roll to the basket!" I just stopped playing and turned to face him. "No, no," I said. "I can't play with you screaming and hollering at me the whole goddamn night!" The players on the bench, and even the courtside fans, started laughing. That was one of the rare times when Larry backed down. "You're right, Kiddo," he said. "You're right."

If one of us was getting worn out by our opponent, Larry would talk to us during a break in the action. "Hey, Kiddo. C'mere, Kiddo. You're so much better than that guy, Kiddo, and you let him work you over? C'mon, Kiddo." So we'd go back on the court all fired up and bust the other guy's ass. Afterwards, Larry would come over and talk to us like we were nothing but lazy motherfuckers to begin with. "So, Kiddo. You finally did your job, huh?"

Yeah? Well, fuck you, too.

He'd also put us through grueling practices during the season. When the team was in Portland we had a three-and-a-half hour session. But we hated for Larry to give us a day off because the next day we knew he'd work us like runaway slaves. A number of Larry's players did not respect him, and it appeared to me that if you were too up-front about this, you were gone. That's what happened to Mickey Johnson.

Sometimes when the Meadowlands Arena wasn't available, we practiced at a place called APA Trucking in Newark. We came in there one day and the surface of the court was really slick. Mickey Johnson was a skinny, six-foot-ten small forward the Nets had just gotten from the Milwaukee Bucks. He was an okay rebounder and passer, a liability on defense, but Mickey could make a scoreboard flash like a pinball machine. (I called him "The Mad Hatter" because he showed up with a different one every day.) Mickey took one look at that court and started unlacing his sneakers. "I can't practice on that," he announced. "I'm 30 years old and I'm not gonna take the chance of slipping and getting an injury that might end my career."

All the rest of us were out there sliding around and trying to warm up. Larry pointed to us and said to Mickey, "Look, everybody else is practicing."

"Not me," Mickey said. "That fucking floor is too fucked up."

"Then you're out of here, Kiddo."

So Mickey sat and watched while we skated through a very cautious practice session. Two days later, we were in Houston and Mickey's hat-of-the-day was red with white letters that said "U.S.S. Johnson." When I asked him what it signified, Mickey said, "It means that any day now I'll be sailing away into the sunset."

In the first half of the game against the Rockets, Mickey made a nifty pass to Albert King, but the Crocodile fumbled the ball out of bounds. Next, Mickey dropped another nice pass right into Bucko's hands, but Bucko dribbled the ball off his foot. After missing a couple of shots himself, Mickey tossed one more pass to Albert, who fumbled it out of bounds again. So Larry put Mickey on the bench for the rest of the half.

During half-time, Larry usually had to say something about mistakes that everybody except his favorites had made. "Mickey," Larry said, "what the fuck are you doing out there?"

"I've been waiting for this shit! 'Cause it ain't me that's fucking up. It's your boys. I'm throwing them good goddamn passes and they're dropping them. And here you come, laying that bullshit on me! You little half-pint motherfucker, I'm gonna kick your ass!"

So Larry said, "Take off that fucking uniform right now!"

"No. The game ain't over and I'm gonna play some more."

Now Mickey and Larry squared off, getting ready to go at each other. The guys were saying, "No, no," and trying to separate them. That's when I started to think that I'd love to see Mickey and Larry duke it out. So I moved around the room pulling guys off Mickey, pulling guys off Larry, and clearing a space in the middle of the locker room for them to get it on. Larry liked the idea. "Yeah, let loose of him 'cause he ain't gonna do shit to nobody!"

I would've paid to see that fight, but the second half was about to start so the assistant coaches shooed the rest of us back onto the court. We were shooting around, trying to warm up real quick, and wondering what was what. Mickey weighed only 190 pounds, but he had long arms, and Larry had a bad hip, so we figured if push ever came to punch, Larry would wind up in a hospital. Then just before the second half got underway, Mickey came sashaying over to the bench still in his uniform. When I asked Mickey what happened, he said, "Man, the motherfucker told me he was gonna trade me, so I said that suits me fine. Then I told the motherfucker that as long as I'm still here, he better play me or I will kick his little ass!" Two days later, Mickey was traded to Golden State for Sugar Ray Richardson.

The following week, Golden State played us in New Jersey and we were up by 13 points at the half. Mickey had taken an elbow to his head a couple of games before that left him with 18 stitches. He was in uniform but didn't play at all in the first half. After the intermission, not only did Mickey play, he scored a shit-load of points, and led the Warriors to a dramatic comeback victory. After the game as both teams walked off the court, Mickey said to Larry, "I told you I'd be kicking your ass!"

When I first got to New Jersey, Larry said to me, "I'll never bullshit you, Kiddo." But when it came to protecting his favorites, Larry just couldn't help bullshitting. We were playing Washington and I was guarding Jeff Ruland while Buck Williams (at only six-foot-eight and 225 pounds) was guarding six-foot-ten, 260-pound Rick Mahorn. Ruland and Mahorn were both so big and mean that they were known as the "Bruise Brothers." This was Bucko's second year in the league so he was still trying to prove himself. After he dunked on Mahorn, Bucko strutted down court. Now, me and Mahorn knew each other from way back when Rick was in college, so I knew that Bucko was headed for trouble. To make matters worse, the next time there was a battle for a rebound, Bucko elbowed Mahorn in the nuts. *Uh oh!* Rick just spun around and started punching Bucko's lights out—BOP! BOP! BOP!—until I finally got close enough to wrap up Mahorn and settle him down.

Okay. A few days later, we were playing the Bullets again in New Jersey and Larry decided to change our defensive matchups. "Since you and Mahorn are so tight," he said to me, "you're gonna guard him. And Bucko, you've got Ruland." The trouble was that Ruland was also six-foot-ten, weighed close to 300 pounds and was even stronger than Mahorn.

"That won't work," I said to Larry. "Ruland is too big for Bucko to handle."

"You do the playing, Kiddo, and let me do the coaching."

Ruland got 11 points and eight rebounds in the first quarter so Larry said, "Now that you got Mahorn calmed down, Darryl, you get Ruland, and Bucko, you switch over to Mahorn." What Larry should've done was to sit Bucko on the bench and let Mike Gminski try to soft-shoe his way around Mahorn. And, as expected, with about two minutes left in a close game, Bucko tried to Bogart Mahorn and WHAM! WHAM! WHAM! Rick started kicking his ass again. This time, I stayed away.

After the game, Larry was all in my face. "What kind of fucking teammate are you not to go and help Bucko?"

"Larry," I said, "he's got to learn who he can fuck with and who he can't."

A few days later, we're playing in Cleveland and Bucko was guarding Lonnie Shelton, another powerhouse player. When Lonnie beat Bucko to the basket, Bucko got up under his legs and knocked Lonnie to the floor. "No, no," Lonnie said. "You shouldn't've done that." Somehow they got tangled up again and the next thing I saw was Bucko flat on his back and Lonnie was on top of him throwing punches. Bucko was kicking and scratching and trying to get up, so I grabbed Lonnie and pulled him away. Now me and Lonnie were pussy-hunting buddies so I was able to calm him down. But while I had Lonnie in a bear hug, Bucko was dancing around the edges and trying to hit his face. So I turned Lonnie loose and he beat Bucko's ass from one end of the court to the other.

Of course, Larry blamed everything on me. "You're telling all of your buddies to jump on Bucko."

"Larry," I said, "you don't know what the fuck you're talking about."

That entire season was a huge adjustment for me. I finished third in the league in field goal percentage (.599), but playing up on the high-post I was lucky to average 12 points. Even though I started

LOOKING FINE ... Even from a young age, I knew how to look good. At right, that's me at 12. Damn, I was fine even then. Later, once I started to make some money, I could go out in style. That's my brother Chico on the left, then me, then my other brother Mitchell and a friend.

MY CONTRACT SIGNING ... The Sixers
were sure happy to welcome me aboard on
May 31, 1975. From left, it's coach Gene Shue,
me, owner Irv Kosloff and GM Pat Williams.

(AP)

(AP

I'M EIGHTEEN ... My first publicity shot for the Sixers.

THE PUBLIC SPEAKER ...
Here I'm 22, and giving a
speech at a family reunion.

MY MOM ... Harriette
Yvonne Dawkins continues to
be a guiding influence in my
life. At right, that's the two of
us a few years back in West
Palm Beach, Florida. In the
photo below, my sister Shawn
hangs with Mom.

NOVEMBER 13, 1979 ... At left and below are photos of perhaps the defining moment of my career, when I shattered a backboard for the first time, at the Municipal Auditoriur in Kansas City. But, damn, do I ever love the photo on the right. You can see me and Bill Robinzine running for cover, plus the reactio of the Kings' Scott Wedman and the 76ers Julius Erving. I called the dunk "If You Ain't Groovin' Best Get Movin'- Chocolate Thunde Flyin'- Robinzine Cryin'- Teeth Shakin'- Gla Breakin'- Rump Roastin'- Bun Toastin'- Glass Still Flyin'- Wham-Bam-I-Am Jam!"

(both photos © Bettman/CORBIS/MAGMA)

(AP)

(AP)

(The SPORT Collection)

Less than a month later, I did the deed at The Spectrum in Philly. My sincere thanks to the folks who cleaned it all up!

NOBODY DOES IT BETTER ... I can't remember the specific name of this dunk, but it's obvious by the look on Clint Richardson's face that it was a damn fine one.

(The SPORT Collection)

RIDING THE PINE ... Despite my ability to perform in the big games, I too often found myself on the bench in Philly. The shaved-head and cool-facial-hair look is from 1977.

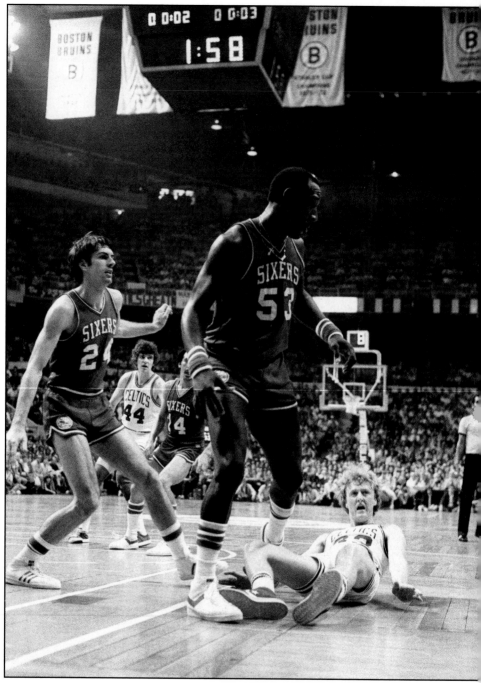

(© Bettman/CORBIS/MAGMA

BIRD DROPPING ... It didn't matter who got in my way, or how famous you were — you paid the price. Larry Bird learned this during the second game of the NBA semi-finals in April 1980. Bobby Jones (24) is doing the funky chicken dance behind me.

(© Bettman/CORBIS/MAGMA)

MAGICAL MOMENT ... I go up and over Magic Johnson during Game 2 of our NBA Championship series on May 7, 1980. Judging by Magic's pained look, and knowing the refs, they probably called a foul on me. Norm Nixon (10) can't believe my form.

THREE AGAINST ONE ...What can I say? It took three Celtics to guard me. Kevin McHale is in the air trying as Dennis Johnson and Cedric Maxwell watch in awe.

PIONEER ... Let's see, I'm flying through the air with my tongue out. Do you think a young Michael Jordan was a fan of mine? This shot from the 83–84 season shows Ray Williams trying unsuccessfully to stop me as Bernard King looks on in terror.

(The SPORT Collection)

LAST STOP ... The Pistons were my final NBA team.

(Claudio Scaccini)

ITALIAN-STYLE ... They couldn't stop me in Italy, either. I'm suited up for
Auxilium Torino during the '90-91 season in this photo.

(Claudio Scaccini)

KEEP YOUR EYE ON THE BALL ... I always loved grabbing rebounds, and my specialty was the defensive boards.

(Claudio Scaccini)

DUNKIN' DARRYL ... I always gave the Italian fans what they wanted to see,
even in Milan, where I spent the '91-92 season.

(DunkTV.com)

DUNK YOU VERY MUCH ...
My man Tim Stanfill and his web site
DunkTV.com named me one of the
Top 30 Dunkers of All-Time.

COACH OF THE CHAMPS ...
Winning the USBL Championship in
1999-2000 with the ValleyDawgs
definitely ranks among my proudest
moments.

(USBL/Dodge City Legend)

NOW LISTEN TO ME ... Hard as it may be to believe, I think that I've found my calling as a coach. I can teach, yell, console, complain and laugh all within a single game. Plus the fans dig my stylish clothes.

(All photos Tim Shaffer)

every game, the refs still treated me like a chump and I only got to play 26 minutes per game. No thanks to the refs I set a pair of all-time NBA records: Most personal fouls in one season, 379, and the third most personal-foul disqualifications in one season, 23. (A year later, I topped my mark with 386 personal fouls, a record which still stands.)

Also, playing in the Meadowlands was like playing in a morgue. I was dunking like I was eating donuts and coffee. I did the Go-Rilla Dunk where I swatted the ball through the hoop just like King Kong pawing at the airplanes while he was hanging on to the top of the Empire State Building. For an encore, I did the Dino De Laurentiis Dunk because he produced the remake of *King Kong*. I did the Rim Wrecker, the Look Out Below, even the Greyhound Bus Dunk where I went coast-to-coast. In Philly, I would've brought the house down, but in New Jersey all I got was some polite applause. *Damn! Maybe they'd been drinking too much swamp water.*

Even my own post-game drinking ritual needed some adjusting. After the games in Philly, we always had three or four cases of cold beer waiting in the locker room, and win or lose there'd be a mad dash for the brews. So after my first home game in New Jersey, I hustled over to the cooler, opened the door, and saw nothing but Cokes and 7-Ups and Dr. Peppers.

"Where's the beer?"

"Hey, Kiddo. No beer allowed in the locker room. My teams drink soda."

I was saved from non-alcoholic hydration by the trainer, Fritz Massman. Most trainers in the NBA were regarded as spies and drinking buddies for the coach. Besides taping ankles and putting ice on every injury he ever saw, that's what I figured Al Domenico did in Philly. But Fritz was his own man, one of the only trainers in the league the players could trust. And Fritz always had a bottle of vodka and some cranberry juice stashed in the trainer's room. So after games, that's where I always spent my cool-down time.

I loved Fritz because he reminded me of a frontier sawbones. In every hotel we stayed in on the road, the management would always put a fifth of vodka in Fritz's room. So I'd check into my room and go visit Fritz. "Darryl," he'd say, "you look tired. Here, have a swig of this."

With all of the goofy shit going on, we were 47-29 and bound for the playoffs, but then something even crazier happened. The team was playing well when Larry gave us two days off, a Sunday and a Monday. Oh, shit. We were heading out to Detroit for a game on Wednesday, and Larry was sure to run our asses off in Tuesday's practice.

Mike Weber was a reporter for the *Newark Star-Ledger* and he heard a rumor that Larry was in Kansas City and about to be interviewed for the coaching job at the University of Kansas. Somehow Weber found out the hotel and the room number where Larry was supposed to be staying, so he made a phone call.

"Hello?"

"Hello? May I speak to John Williams, please?"

"There's no John Williams here, but this is Larry Brown."

"Hi, Larry. This is Mike Weber from the *Star-Ledger.*"

BLAM! Larry hung up the phone in a hurry. But now the news was out.

Larry was back in New Jersey for Tuesday's practice and when he took it easy on us we knew something was up. The Nets' owner, Joe Taub, was pissed and called Larry in for a meeting, but Larry was still with the team as we arrived at the airport to board the plane to Detroit.

"Hey, coach," I said, real friendly-like.

"Oh, Kiddo. They're saying some bad things about me."

Then Taub came walking over and Larry left to talk with him. I didn't think much about it so I got on the plane. They'd talk about whatever then Larry would catch the plane at the last minute. But when we landed in Detroit and were waiting for our baggage, we all noticed that Larry wasn't around, so we asked Bill Blair what was what.

"I don't know if Larry's gonna be here," he said. "We'll have a meeting at the hotel and talk about it."

When we got to the meeting, Bill told us that, yes, Larry had been in Kansas City interviewing for the U. of Kansas job. Yes, he did get the job. And, yes, Taub had already fired him.

Then the door opened and Larry came in. He'd taken another flight and come to Detroit just to talk to us. "Hey, you guys, I screwed up. But I know you guys can turn this around and challenge for the championship."

Buck was really upset and he might've been crying, I couldn't tell for sure. But I did know that Larry was a positive father figure for Buck, teaching him how to dress like a professional and act like a professional. Albert King was also shook up.

Larry's last words to the team were, "Just go out there and do your thing and don't worry about what happens to me."

Bill Blair took over the team and we went 2-4 to close out the regular season. Without Larry yipping at me, I had a great playoff series in the first round against the Knicks. But Bucko and Albert were still hanging their heads and we were zipped in two games to end our season in the shit house.

The Sixers had used the $700,000 they got from New Jersey in the deal for me to sign Moses Malone. And they ripped through the playoffs, sweeping the Knicks, beating the Bucks in five games, then sweeping the Lakers to win the championship. Some guys in my position, traded from a team that went on to win a title, would've gotten all jealous and broken-hearted. Not me. I was so happy for Doc and Bobby Jones and Earl Cureton that I called each of them. "Hey, man, congratulations."

"Darryl, you should have been here with us," they said.

"That's all right. My time will come."

I was eagerly looking forward to a new season and, above all, a new coach. And as for Larry Brown, besides Bucko and Albert, who the fuck else was worried about what happened to him? The rest of us were glad to see him go. Shit, I would've driven him to the airport just to make sure he didn't miss his flight.

11

Stan the Man & The Sugar Blues

S tan Albeck was the Nets' new coach and I love him to this very day. When Stan was the head coach of the San Antonio Spurs, his center was seven-foot-two Artis Gilmore, a guy who needed a road map whenever he strayed more than five feet from the basket. So Stan had a completely different view of my role than Larry had. The first thing Stan said to me was, "Your outside jumper is now an antique. Put it up in the attic and forget it." Then he moved me back into the pivot and shifted Buck Williams away from the basket. The switch helped both me and Buck to become impact players.

That first season with Stan, I averaged 30 minutes and a career-high 16.8 points per game. And playing exclusively in the shadow of the basket, I also shot 464 free throws (which was 160 more than I'd ever attempted in a single season before). But Stan did much more for me than increase my personal production: He was the first coach I ever had who fully respected me.

For example, during a timeout Stan would ask me what I thought about a particular play. "Well, Coach, if we moved the guard over to here, then we'll force the big man to make the switch over here." And Stan followed my suggestion and the play worked. *All right!*

Here's another example: We were down by a point with only ten seconds left in a game against the Bulls, when Stan actually called my number for the last shot. "Darryl, you go down to the low-post, right here. And Sugar, I want you to dribble over to here, then dump the ball into Darryl and the game's ours." That was the first time in my

NBA career that a play was called for me to win or lose a ball game. While Stan was diagramming the play, Sugar Ray Richardson was standing in the huddle nodding his head and chewing on his bubble gum. "G-got it," Sugar said with his habitual stutter. "G-got it." But Sugar was rock-bottom crazy so nobody really knew exactly what it was that he got. Play resumed, so I ran down to my spot and watched Sugar dribble the ball to the top of the key just like he was supposed to do. But then Sugar shot the ball, and while it was still in the air, he said, "We win," then he ran off the court toward the locker room. Of course the ball just split the net. Well, the rest of us were jumping around and celebrating, and by the time we got to the locker room, Sugar was already coming out of the shower. "I told you s-stupid m-motherfuckers we win!"

Now, Stan had an easy way about him and he never got rattled no matter what—which wasn't easy to do with Sugar around. Whereas Billy Cunningham and Larry Brown would've been hopping mad, Stan just shook Sugar's hand and said, "Hell of a shot."

By now I'd been in the league for nine years, however, and I'd at least figured out how to tell the good coaches from the bad ones. Since most teams have a designated assistant in charge of X's and O's, the quality and effectiveness of an NBA coach is more about his personality that his basketball expertise. In general, the bad coaches are stubborn and arrogant. "My way or the highway" type of guys who never accept any explanations from the players. If a certain play misfires in a crucial situation, a bad coach will always blame a player: "The play didn't work because you didn't set the fucking pick!" A good coach will respect his players and ask their opinions: "Why didn't that play work?" That way, a player can respond with something constructive: "Hey, coach, I did set the pick but the guy came around the other side. You said to look for him around this side." Then the coach can come back with, "Well, you've got to go find him." This is the way of cooperation, which is always better for team chemistry than ego-driven, dismissive confrontations. Or to put it another way, bad coaches believe their own bullshit and good coaches don't.

Unfortunately, most NBA teams hire, and do not hire, coaches for the wrong reasons. Politics is more important than aptitude. Look at what happened to Paul Silas. He was an assistant with the Knicks, the

Nets, the Suns and the Hornets, and he only got the head job in Charlotte because he was the only one left standing when Dave Cowens, apparently having trouble handling young players, left the team during the '98-'99 season. Cowens expected his team to work as hard as he did when he played in the NBA, but the youngsters today aren't interested in busting their ass. And why had Paul been passed over all the years before this? No one ever knew for sure but people wondered if Pat Riley was spreading the word that when Paul was his assistant in New York, he didn't work hard. If so, that's bullshit. I played under Paul in New Jersey and nobody worked harder than he did.

There's got to be racism involved. Otherwise I don't understand how a guy like Chris Ford always winds up coaching in the league. His offenses were so simple I thought they could be run in Romper Room. When he was a player, Ford had very little talent but he worked hard. The only thing he knew how to do was to make his own players work hard. As far as I could tell, except for the fact that he's white, Chris Ford had no business coaching in the NBA. George Karl is another white dude who appears plugged into the good ol' boys network. Back when Karl was coaching Golden State, he wasn't happy with the way Joe Barry Carroll was playing. So Karl had the gall to go to Joe Barry's house and scream in his face. Not long after that, Al Attles fired Karl. In Seattle, Karl was reluctant to criticize Shawn Kemp and Gary Payton, and seemed to go after guys who wouldn't challenge him. Then in the 2001 playoffs, Karl said that the referees were favoring Philly in their playoff series against his Bucks because the NBA didn't want a small-market team like Milwaukee in the finals. If a black coach ever said anything like that, he'd be canned. I'm convinced that the only reason George Karl keeps getting jobs is because he went to North Carolina and is one of Dean Smith's boys.

Pat Riley is an excellent coach who always has his teams prepared. But Riley also works his players very hard. When some guys get traded to Miami, they say, "Uh oh. Playing for Riley will take about two years off my career."

I did like Jeff Van Gundy when he was with the New York Knicks because his eyes are sunk back in his head so nobody really knew what was on his mind. That's the way I'd like to be: Where I'm thinking one thing, but you're looking at me and thinking that we're both thinking something else. That said, I never cared for Van Gundy's offense. You can't have guys like Latrell Sprewell and Allan Houston going one-on-one for an entire season. Both of these guys are guard/forward types and aren't strong enough to put out the kind of physical effort Van Gundy's system required and still be effective by the time the playoffs roll around. Also, the Knicks liked to have Houston come off three picks before he got the ball, but that third pickee was a guard, so a simple switch nullified all of that movement.

One white coach who I'd be surprised to see ever get an NBA position is Rick Barry. He still thinks he's God gift to basketball and often seems to believe it's beneath him to go out of his way to be helpful.

On the flipside, Kareem Abdul-Jabbar has found it hard to get a coaching job because he was so nasty during his playing days. Like Barry, Kareem usually refused to do anything he didn't want to do. Watching Kareem over the years, I figured his mantra was, "You can't make me do shit."

Then you have a black guy like Alvin Gentry coaching the L.A. Clippers, despite the fact that wherever he's coached, he has problems getting along with players. The only explanation I can think of for Gentry continuing to find employment is that he must have a photograph of some NBA general manager fucking a sheep.

One of my favorite coaches is Phil Jackson. I do like his triangle offense, but to me, it's just a system that boils down to playing basketball the old-fashioned way. Everybody cutting and moving without the ball, maintaining good spacing, taking what the defense gives up, being unselfish, and when everything breaks down and the shot clock is set to explode, having a good one-on-one player who can create his own shot. What impresses me most about Phil is his ability to get inside his players' heads. He's a communicator and a motivator, but he also creates an environment that allows his players to communicate with, and to motivate, each other.

I feel a certain affinity for Phil. When he played with the Knicks in the 1970s, he had that hippie image that scared the NBA. But he learned his trade in the minor leagues, won his first-ever championship in the Continental Basketball Association and stayed true to himself, just waiting for somebody to take a chance on him. Of course, the Chicago Bulls did and Phil's teams have dominated the game ever since.

Then you have guys like K.C. Jones and Jimmy Rodgers, who were terrific assistant coaches but in my opinion lacked the forcefulness to succeed as head coaches. Bernie Bickerstaff fit into the same category, the main difference being that Bernie was able to survive as a head coach for much longer than his record seemed to warrant. It's the big money that pushes some assistants to jump into deep water before they've learned how to swim.

And some guys grow into their jobs—like Billy Cunningham. As a player, Billy was a winner so when he became a coach, losing would make him frantic. Eventually, Billy was able to say, "Well, we got beat because those guys played better than we did tonight." At the same time, being a coach for so long (eight years) wasn't particularly beneficial for Billy's well being. In my opinion, he's still a fun guy, but he's also totally weirded out, all twitchy and seems more nervous than ever. I think he misses coaching and he's got more money than he knows what to do with.

In general, I think that today's NBA head coaches are much better than they used to be, mainly because of the money they're now getting. Back when the players were making $5 million guaranteed and the coaches were only making $700,000 year-to-year, it was the coaches who were expendable. And what could a coach do 20 years ago to discipline an uncooperative player who was popular with the fans? Keep his ass nailed to the bench or even suspend him? Nope, because management wouldn't risk the fans' displeasure. What about fining the player? The maximum fine used to be $10,000, which not only was pocket-change to a player with a high-priced, long-term contract, but it was also a beneficial tax write-off. Nowadays, a head coach routinely makes anywhere from $2 million to $7 million per season and also has a multi-year contract. That's the source of the increased power the modern coaches have, and that's why most of them can afford not to be intimidated by their players. Also, because an increasing number of top draft picks are either teenagers or untested Europeans, management has accepted the fact they need considerable seasoning before they can be trusted with meaningful court time.

Some young players never seem to grow old and back in '83-'84, the Nets had another new player who I certainly could relate to: Bill Willoughby. Like me, he'd been drafted straight out of high school back in 1975. Willow was six-foot-eight, 205 pounds, a long-range shooter, and the highest jumper I've ever seen. He never handled the ball well enough to play small forward, and the Atlanta Hawks drafted Willow with the expectation that his body would fill out so he'd be able to play power forward. But as much as he ate, and as much as he lifted weights, Willow was always bone-thin. At the same time, NBA power forwards were getting bigger and stronger, so even with all his skills, Willow remained a player without a position. After two years with Atlanta, he'd played with Buffalo, Cleveland, Houston, and San Antonio. The 1983-84 season with the Nets would be Willow's last in the NBA.

Meanwhile, Willow was as animated and as fast-talking as if he was mainlining coffee. "I'm going in now any minute! Stan's gonna put me in any minute! Hey, Stan! Put me in! I'm ready! Fuck you, Stan! I'm growing old sitting here on the bench! Let me go, Stan! Just watch me, man! My shit's working!" He'd spend his spare time in practice creating new moves, and he'd be walking on every one of them. "Hey, man! Look at this one! You like it? Ain't it the shit?" But Willow could run like a big cat, so much so that you could hardly hear his feet when he touched the floor. And he was the only guy in the league who could shut down George Gervin.

Unlike most coaches, Stan genuinely enjoyed being around the players. When we were on the road, he'd come down to the hotel bar and buy drinks for whoever was there, and we'd all shoot the shit. And Stan could tell some funny stories. Like the time Wilt Chamberlain was the coach of the San Diego Conquistadors and Stan was an assistant. There was some girl that Wilt had hooked up with who was going to be in town for only one night. Wilt told Stan he would be arriving late for a game the team was playing that very same night, so Wilt taped a pre-game pep talk for Stan to play in the locker room. That had to be an all-time first.

Stan also had enough self-confidence to allow his assistants to establish themselves as important contributors in both games and practices: John Killilea (God rest his soul) was the staff's defensive specialist and we all liked and respected him. Killer had made his reputation as an assistant coach in Milwaukee, but he got pissed when he didn't get the credit for the Bucks' outstanding defense. He would make the rounds of the bars in Milwaukee complaining about this, which probably cost him his job. Still, Killer was always reminiscing about the good old days in Milwaukee, until I had to speak up. "Killer, that's all cool, but right now, whether we like it or not, we're in New fucking Jersey. So let's grapple with what the fuck we have here." Then Killer said, "Precisely," and we all had a good laugh.

But Killer's fatal flaw was the bottle. During a ball game, he'd have to run into the locker room every so often for a sip. "I know you need me on the bench, Stan, but I gotta pee real bad. I'll be right back." The other assistant coach was Herman Kull, who struck me as a know-nothing blowhard. He bought notebooks for all the players at the start of the season. "I want each of you to take a couple of minutes after each game," he said, "and write down how you played on both offense and defense, and what you thought about the team's spirit." We just laughed and tossed the notebooks into the nearest round file.

It was Stan who held us together. We couldn't bullshit him because he knew when a player was really tired, and also when a player was faking an injury. And if Stan worked us hard in practice, he didn't try to show how tough he was by wearing us out. "Look," he'd say, "it's a long season, so let's take care of business and get out of here in an hour. It's up to you guys how long we're gonna practice. If you start dicking around I'll keep you longer."

Stan's practices were the best I ever experienced. He was so well organized that there weren't any dead spots, and sometimes he'd liven things up with some shooting games played for our fine money. Or else he'd have the big guys post up the guards, and then the guards post up the big men. We stayed focused and we saved our legs.

We were erratic all season long, finishing 45-37, in fourth place in the Atlantic Division, and 17 games behind the Celtics, but we still looked forward to the playoffs with high hopes. As the season rushed to the wire, however, we'd been playing so hard that our legs were shot. Stan was hip to this but he liked to throw the responsibility back to his players.

There were only four games left in the regular season and during half-time of a close ball game in Milwaukee, Stan pulled up a chair and sat himself smack dab in the middle of the locker room. "I just want to know one goddamn thing," he said. "Is anybody in here tired? O'Koren, are you tired? Buck? Albert?"

Everybody was too macho to tell the truth, so they all said, "No." But I was never concerned with projecting any kind of bullshit image, so I finally spoke up: "Stan, I'm as tired as a two-dollar 'ho' on Sunday morning. And there's plenty other motherfuckers in this room who're also tired, but they're too scared to say it." Stan thanked me for having the balls to speak up, then he asked us to dig down and push ourselves for the second half. Well, we won that game, but we lost the next three.

Nobody likes going into the playoffs on a losing streak, so Stan was still upset when we got together to prepare for our first-round opponent—Philadelphia, the defending champs. Team owner Joe Taub was in the locker room with us and he nodded in total agreement when Stan said to us, "I'm gonna run your asses off in practice today." Sugar didn't like that. "F-fuck it, man. My motherfucking b-body is entirely wrecked and I ain't m-motherfucking p-practicing at all."

Now, Taub had a soft spot for Sugar and was committed to doing everything he could to help Sugar straighten out from his drug problems. Taub made sure to call Sugar every day to make sure he was cool. So when Sugar started complaining about being tired, Taub told Stan to cancel practice and go hard tomorrow, then he walked out of the room. This got Stan about as mad as I've ever seen him. When Taub was gone, Stan glared at Sugar and said, "There's a fucking asshole on every team, and you're it."

Sugar stood up, dropped his pants, turned away from Stan, bent over, opened up his cheeks, and said, "W-well, that makes t-two of us. 'C-cause if I'm an asshole you're one, t-too." The rest of us were screaming with laughter, but credit Stan for just chuckling, shaking his head and walking out of the room.

Throughout the whole season, Stan only overreacted one time: He'd love to diagram something on the blackboard then tap the chalk against the board to drive his point home. On defense, Stan's emphasis was always the same: "Do not let your man get into the fucking middle. Because once he gets there, he can pass right and he can pass left. No fucking middle." Tap-tap-tap.

The players were in the locker room one morning waiting for Stan to arrive and get a practice session underway. Kelvin Ransey was our starting point guard, a four-year NBA veteran in his first season with New Jersey. Kelvin and me played well together—we had a nice two-man game going, in to me, out to him, back in to me. Kelvin was a good Christian who later became a minister, but while we were waiting for Stan, the devil got into him. Kelvin went to the front of the room, started tapping the chalk, and saying, "No fucking middle. I'm telling you now, no fucking middle." Whoops! When Kelvin turned around to see what the rest of us were looking at, there was Stan standing in the doorway. Stan never said a word, but for the rest of the year, Kelvin's playing time just about vanished.

Why did Stan take shit from Sugar and not from Kelvin? Maybe it was that Sugar was famous for being nutty so his shenanigans were expected. Or maybe Stan didn't like being personally mocked by somebody who was supposed to be such a solid citizen. I only knew for certain that coaches were a different species than players were.

For me, the highlight of the whole season was beating Philly three games to two in the first round. They had the same cast of characters that won the title the year before—Doc, Mo Cheeks, Moses Malone, Andrew Toney, Bobby Jones, Billy Cunningham and Harold Katz. The referees kept me in foul trouble, but Mike Gminski was terrific and held the fort until I could come back in late in each game to wreak some havoc.

Take that, motherfuckers!

Milwaukee was up next, with Junior Bridgeman, Sidney Moncrief and Marques Johnson. Bob Lanier was playing his last season, and his ass was even bigger. The first game in Milwaukee I scored 32 points. Even sports writer Pete Vecsey, who'd been on my case for years, wrote that I'd finally left Lovetron, landed on Earth, and justified my entire career. The most amazing thing about this game was that I shot 14 free throws, by far the most I've ever had. I just made up my mind to take everything hard to the basket and the referees gave me some calls. The most gratifying type of respect is when you're respected by people who don't like you.

It was a gangbusters series, and the Bucks beat us by one point in the sixth game when the referees counted a shot that Moncrief took after the shot clock expired. I think Joe Taub would probably have protested the game if it wouldn't have cost him a bundle to do it.

So there I was, a nine-year NBA veteran at 27 and at the top of my game. Little did I know that I'd never even come close to playing a full season again.

12

Meanwhile, Back in the Hood

My troubles began even before the 1984-85 season got underway. I was living within my means, paying back the IRS and taking care of my family. Then I got some phone calls from the U.S. Post Office and the New York Attorney General's office. It seemed that my money was being invested with a stockbroker who was giving kickbacks to Harvey LaKind, the guy I'd hired to oversee my affairs.

Government officials had gotten involved when a torn envelope showed up in the post office. Inside was a $5,000 check made out to me but with my name crudely crossed out and another name substituted. As the investigation deepened, it was discovered that I wasn't alone. Several pro athletes, including NBA players, bowlers, boxers and a hockey player, who were all using the same advisor, had lost a ton of money. At the end of it all, LaKind was convicted of fraud and conspiracy to defraud, but the money I'd lost was gone for good.

I was able to get my mind off my latest problems when the Nets made an overseas trip just before training camp. I'd never been out of the country before and I really didn't want to go. Mike Gminski said he wasn't going because he didn't want to play any basketball during his vacation, so I said, "Yeah, that goes for me, too." Then Lou Schaffel, the Nets' general manager, said that the trip was mandatory and I'd be heavily fined if I stayed home. What about Gminski? Well, he was excused for "personal reasons." Uh huh. It was business as usual. Just another shovelful of the same old racial bullshit. I couldn't afford to pay the fine, so as a minor protest I left a few days late. Most of the guys brought their wives along—Darwin Cook, Otis Birdsong, Buck Williams, Kelvin Ransey, even Sugar. Stan came with his wife, so did Fritz Massman and Lou Schaffel. The only single guys were me, Mike O'Koren and a non-roster player from Nigeria named Yomi Sangodeyi, who was auditioning for a spot in training camp.

Our first stop was Israel and the schedule was tight. We played Maccabi, one of the professional teams in Tel Aviv, and since we had to leave at seven the next morning, everybody went back to the hotel to eat and then pack. But I wanted to see some of the local sights, so I slicked up and went to the main desk to get a cab. All of a sudden, Yomi showed up. "Yo, Chocolate," he said. "I go with you."

"Let's go get it, then."

"You know why I like you?" Yomi asked. "Because of what my name Sangodeyi means in English. It means 'Thunder'."

The cab driver took us to a lively little beer garden about 20 minutes from the hotel. There were a whole bunch of beautiful girls there who loved to dance and drink and fuck, so we all had a ball. And me and Yomi were drinking and drinking, and gradually the place started to clear out, and we were still drinking. Then we noticed that the sun was coming up. Oh, shit! We called a cab at 5:30 but it didn't get there for another hour. And the girls wanted to ride with us back to the hotel.

When we all pulled up to the bus, everybody was already on board and Schaffel gave us dirty looks as we said good-bye to the girls. "We were getting ready to leave without you," Schaffel said. Otis's wife had been kind enough to pack our stuff and have it loaded on the bus. We were headed for the airport and a flight to Rome, so everybody was dressed very conservatively as proper representatives of the NBA. Not me. I was still kind of woozy from the drinking I'd done and I was wearing jeans, a colorful shirt, sandals and a big straw hat. When I climbed into the bus it was exactly seven o'clock, but Schaffel kept glaring at me like I was a criminal.

"You know what?" I said loud enough for Schaffel to hear. "I went out last night and did some serious drinking and some serious fucking. And you know why? 'Cause unlike the rest of you mother-fuckers, I'm not married."

Yomi was just as fucked up as I was, so he also had to have his say.

"I was with Thunder, and you know what? It was all worth it for one night with Thunder."

Everybody was laughing and rolling on the floor except for Schaffel. He was so pissed that he wouldn't let his wife laugh.

We landed safely in Rome, but Yomi wasn't allowed in the country because there was some political bullshit going on between Italy and Nigeria, so he had to stay in the airport for two days. His parting words were, "Now you got to thunder for two!"

There was barely room for one in my hotel room. I could open the front door and the window, turn on the TV, and take a piss without getting out of bed. Everything in Europe was undersized. The people. The basketball courts. The referees. Everything but me.

We did some sightseeing and saw several paintings and sculptures by Michelangelo. Whew! But I was more impressed with the works of Leonardo da Vinci. This cat was definitely ahead of his time. He made detailed drawings of a helicopter and other flying machines hundreds of years before the Wright brothers. This was a guy who could have come up with all kinds of good stuff to make basketball more fun: The da Vinci helicopter sneakers. Leonardo's Go- Up- And- Never- Have- To- Come- Down- Hello- Air- Controllers- 360°- Upside- Down- Funka- Dunk. Of all the other sights we saw in Rome, I identified most with the Coliseum. It had great sight lines, but the floor needed work. Sort of like an Italian Boston Garden.

Europe was incredibly beautiful and incredibly strange. Whenever and wherever I turned on the tap, the water came out brown. The food was terrible every place except Italy, and the people dumped their garbage out of their windows and into the streets. I had no trouble finding a good place to eat in Rome. Not far from the hotel, a restaurant called The Cowboy served fried chicken. So I unholstered my bottle of hot sauce, ordered a batch for myself and an even bigger portion to go. Then I found a taxicab and paid the driver a huge tip to take the fried chicken over to the airport and make sure that it got to Yomi.

The next morning we were scheduled to take a bus tour to see some castle. Now, I'm always ready for an adventure, but I'd much rather find one on my own than have a bus and a guide take me there. So I said, "Y'all go and see the motherfucking castle and the moats and the ghosts and shit. I'm gonna find a cold bottle of beer and see what I can see by myself."

"But Darryl. We're gonna be gone about four hours."

"Then you'd best be on your way."

So I just found a place that had Heineken on ice and I walked around saying *ciao* to everybody. I loved the little old ladies who looked like they'd been wearing their widow's weeds for 50 years. They peered up at me and had to shade their eyes from the sun, then they'd cross themselves and scurry away. *Arrivederci*.

While I was walking around, I saw a beautiful black girl who looked familiar. Damn! It was the singer Amii Stewart. So I went over and started talking, then she invited me over to her apartment to play some backgammon and eat fried chicken with her and her boyfriend. And we had ourselves a great time.

When the guys came back from the castle, they were too exhausted to speak. We had a game that night and since I was the only player with fresh legs, I was putting on a show: Dribbling behind my back and fastbreaking and dunking and clowning at every opportunity, while the fans cheered me on. Then a pint-sized referee miscalled a foul on me so I picked him up and held him in my arms like he was a baby. He tried to twist and kick his way free, but I didn't let him loose until we got to the scorer's table. Then I set him down gently on top of the table and planted a big smooching kiss on his cheek. Naturally, the fans went crazy.

Our last stop was Varese in Northern Italy and from there we flew back home. As we approached Newark International Airport, Sugar said, "I love the m-motherfucking U.S.A. Soon as we l-land, I'm g-gonna kiss the motherfucking ground." And that's exactly what he did.

Once the season started, Sugar was better than ever. He averaged a career high 20.1 ppg and finished sixth in the league with 8.2 assists. With Sugar back in gear, we thought we'd be able to build on last year's playoff win against the Sixers and have a kick-ass season. But Otis Birdsong (our leading scorer at 20.6) was in and out of the line-up with a variety of injuries, then Albert King (who was contributing 12.8 ppg off the bench) also got hurt and missed half the season.

Meanwhile, my back was killing me. The pain was sharp and constant, and no exercises or massage or pills seemed to help. I tried to play though the pain, but my game was stiff and half-assed. Eventually the team doctors came up with this diagnosis: "Excruciating and debilitating back pain caused by a smaller-than-normal bony canal surrounding the spinal cord and some small bone chips causing irritation of the sciatic nerve."

Just before Thanksgiving, I checked into New Jersey's University Hospital in Newark, where I spent 44 of the most difficult days I have ever experienced. In addition to the nerve irritation, I had hurt some soft tissue that, by itself, took five weeks to heal. I spent some time in traction, was restricted to my bed for my entire stay there, and also received some high-voltage electrical stimulation and ultrasound treatment. I was given muscle relaxants and anti-inflammatory medication. After a few weeks, the doctors put me on a gradual and carefully supervised exercise program. But even though I was mostly flat on my ass, I still managed to get into trouble.

While I was in traction, word got back to me that a coach I barely knew was telling people that he had visited me in the hospital. That was bullshit to start with. I never played for this guy and I never even met him, so why would he come to visit me in a hospital? But there was even more bullshit to come: He said that he saw me laying on my back with a plate balanced on my chest, and on the plate was a big mound of cocaine. Say what? Exactly why that motherfucker would spread such ridiculous lies about me was a mystery I've never solved.

I never had much to do with the other coaches in the league. I wasn't a big fan of Don Nelson's until one night when we were playing the Bucks in Milwaukee. I was squatting in front of the scorer's table waiting to come into the game and Nellie happened to be standing nearby. "You know what?" Nellie asked me.

"What?"

"You guys are kicking our ass, the beer's cold in the locker room and I gotta get the fuck out of here."

So he shouted to the nearest referee, "Hey, you fucking asshole! That was a terrible call!" BOP! The ref gave him a technical foul, but Nellie wasn't through. "You're still a fucking asshole and that was still a terrible call!" BOP! The second tech meant that Nellie was banished from the bench. Before he left, Nellie winked at me and said, "See you later."

The only other opposing coach I'd ever said anything to during a game was Hubie Brown back when he was coaching the Atlanta Hawks. All I knew about Hubie was that he screamed and hollered at his players and acted like an old washerwomen. I was having a good game against Steve Hayes so Hubie sent Tree Rollins in to try and quiet me down. As I ran past the Hawks bench, I said to Hubie, "He can't guard me either." And that was that.

Lying on my back, so immobile and helpless, I had plenty of time to think about where I'd been, where I was and where I was headed. I used to think that I was bulletproof. Sure, I'd been scared when my leg broke in Philly, but an injured back seemed much more serious. I thought, Damn! This shit could end my whole trip! I went through a period where I was angry and resentful. Why had this happened to me? Then gradually, I began to think about my family and my church. About how my life had always been blessed with so much love and inspiration. I also thought about how many places I'd already seen and how successful I'd already been. If my run was done, then I still had plenty to be thankful for. Nothing can humble an athlete like a major injury.

A lot of guys placed on the injured list have this kind of attitude: "Fuck! I'm hurt and I can't play. But I'm going to party my ass off." Then they go off on a two-week party binge. But once I was up and walking again, what I tried to do was to bring a more critical eye to the ball games. What makes a player a superstar? I'd sit in the stands and watch some games where a guy averaging 20 points would stink up the court, missing easy shots, fumbling passes, committing stupid fouls. Then comes the end-game and he'd make a clutch shot to put his team over the top. The conclusion I came to was that superstars work hard every night even when their game is in the shitter. They just keep busting it until, maybe, they'd find themselves in the middle of a play that could redeem their poor performance and decide the outcome. It was a lesson that I knew before in a half-assed way, but I resolved that when (and if) my back ever healed I'd always do 48 the hard way.

Sitting there and watching the games, I also saw another aspect of life in the NBA that I'd never seen before: How good players survive on bad teams. Up until then, I'd never played on a losing team, but I saw World playing for a pathetic Cleveland team that would finish with only 36 wins. Also guys like Herb Williams with Indiana (22 wins) and Walter Davis with Phoenix (36 wins). "The motherfucking season lasts forever," World said. "It's the longest, most painful year of my life." And how did World get by? "You know what?" he said. "I just go out there and get mine. I play to keep my stats up. Because if you go to a bad team and your numbers take a dive, then people around the league say that you must've been a bullshit player to begin with. But if you're still scoring your 25, then the good teams all want to make a trade for you."

On the other hand, I remember that Hubie Brown always used to say, "Be careful of guys who score a lot of points on bad teams." What Hubie meant was that if a guy like that moves to a good team, he's no longer the only player who can find the basket. So when he isn't the focus of the offense, there's nothing else he knows how to do and he can easily disappear. That's why I think that even outstanding point-makers on inferior teams have to play hard at both ends. Look at Ron Harper—he was a big-time scorer on some shitty teams in Cleveland and with the Clippers in L.A. But then he signed with the Bulls in 1994 and found himself playing with MJ and Scottie Pippen. So from one season to the next Harp's scoring went from 20 points to six, but he emphasized defense and executing the offense and he wound up with a handful of rings.

Okay, but what if a player's not a scorer? Then he's got to be a good guy and have a great work ethic. Bump and bang with the toughest guy on the other team. Be eager to step up and take whatever big shots are available. That way, everybody will think that he'll be a much better player and an easy fit with a good team. "If you're a competitive player stuck on a sad-ass team," World said, "the idea is to find a way to get the fuck out of there."

Anyway, the traction was only partially effective, but when I was unhitched, I tried to finish out the season. For all the good I did the Nets I should've stayed in bed. I ended up averaging only 13.5 points and 4.6 rebounds in 39 games. We finished the regular season at 42-40 before getting swept in the first round of the playoffs by the Detroit Pistons. My only consolation was Stan Albeck's plan for the future. He said that he'd finally realized I could do more than he was asking me to do. Next season, I was going to handle the ball more and get more shots. Stan would even create some baseline isolation plays for me. Thanks, Stan, for reviving my spirits and for continuing to believe in me.

So guess what happened next—Stan got canned!

I certainly had a lot to think about during the summer of 1985. My financial losses. My aching back. My new coach, Dave Wohl, who I didn't particularly care for. My entire future. To keep myself from obsessing on my own problems, I spent some time in Florida, did some camps and hung with some of my basketball buddies. And it worked. Staying busy and moving around kept me distracted. At the same time I was able to take a larger view of the black NBA experience, and I didn't like everything I saw.

My biggest concern was the black players' attitudes toward their old neighborhoods. After most white players succeed in the NBA they try to give something back to the communities where they grew up. They'll pay for a basketball court to be built, or they'll do a camp to raise funds for a recreation center, or something along those lines. And black players? With very few exceptions, the only time they go back to their neighborhoods is either to buy drugs or to hunt pussy.

There's absolutely no reason why black guys can't go back to the hood with a positive mindset and words of encouragement: "You guys can make it out of here, too. You just gotta work hard, do your thing, and ignore all the street shit." Instead, the standard black attitude is, "Hey, look at me, everybody, I made it and I made it big. I ain't gonna be here if I don't want to be here. But you motherfuckers are here because you have to be here."

Having an NBA player cop the indigenous pussy also creates enormous problems because the guys in the community watch all the young girls growing up and they have their own plans for them. "Yeah, she's only 13 now and she's real fine. In a few more years I can get her." The sons of bitches just sit there knowing that a young girl's family has no money so they'll sometimes drop $10 on her just so she'll be grateful. Then she's 18, she's beautiful, and the neighborhood guys are getting ready to make their move on her. Uh oh! Here comes the NBA star cruising back into town and he also remembers the girl. The difference is that now he's driving a Mercedes or a Rolls Royce and he's got major league cash in his pocket. So he says, "Hey, baby. You ever been to Bermuda? No? Pack your bag and I'll come pick you up."

They go to Bermuda, fuck their brains out, and the problem starts when the player brings her back to the hood and then goes on his merry way. Naturally, the girl will be bragging all over the place. Oh, she was in Bermuda with so-and-so and he treated her like a queen. Here's the jewelry he bought her, the clothes, maybe even the fur coat. Meanwhile the neighborhood pussy sharks are saying, "I've been watching and waiting on that girl and that motherfucker just comes along and scoops her up. I ought to bust him in his motherfucking mouth." But it's not cool to fuck with somebody who's still got that NBA glow. So the sharks go after the girl instead.

They'll spread rumors to the other girls in the neighborhood. "Hey, you know what that bitch said about you? She said you sucked everybody's dick on the team. Yeah, she said you suck dick every morning before you eat breakfast."

Now there's trouble. The "Bermuda bitch" gets beaten like a step-daughter who just peed her bed. Sometimes she'll even get her face slashed with a razor. "Yeah, bitch, let's see how pretty you are now. Let's see if any motherfucker's gonna take you to Bermuda now. Bitch, the only place you're going is to the dog pound." All because instead of doing something good, the black guys are creeping back to their old neighborhood looking to show off.

There are some black guys, like Kevin Johnson and Charles Barkley, who do go back and get some beneficial stuff done for the kids. But for most of the other black players it's all about how many houses they have. How many cars. How many computers. How many women. How many boys are in their posse. And the more money these young brothers make the crazier they get. They're young, black millionaires and they don't know what to do with their lives. They want to walk around like gangsters with gun-packing body-guards. "I'm bad, motherfucker, and you ain't shit." They drive their Mercedes into the neighborhood late at night and park in front of the house where everybody in the community knows there are drugs for sale. And that's when Mr. Big Time NBA Star really fucks up. Because blacks are the most jealous people alive and sooner or later somebody's bound to turn him in.

Back in Florida I often heard it said that black people were a lot like crabs. When you see a bunch of crabs caught in a bucket, there'll be one busting his ass trying to climb his way out. Then just when he gets near the top and he's got one claw over the edge, another crab will reach up and pull him back down. That's the way black people are.

But it doesn't have to be that way forever. So just be cool, brothers. Be humble. Be respectful. Be gracious. Be thankful for your blessings and be glad to share as much as possible of what you've been given. Above all, go back home and do something to help the kids feel good about themselves.

13

A World of Trouble

D ave Wohl was my fifth coach in 11 seasons and, from my perspective, probably the worst. He'd been a backup point guard for
a few years, the last being in 1977-78 with the Nets, and like most
guards-turned-coach his game plan didn't emphasize big men. The players' nickname for Wohl was "The Little Commandant" because he was
such a hardass. We'd play five games in six days and on the seventh day,
when we needed a 24-hour vacation from basketball, Wohl would force
us to watch game tapes for several hours. One time our cross-country
flight into L.A. was delayed four hours and he still made us practice. Just
like with Larry Brown, Wohl believed that his way was the only way.
Wohl was never interested in discussing anything with his players—he
delivered lectures instead—and he walked around like his shit didn't stink.

I suspected Wohl had sucked around Joe Taub and told him what
a shitty job Stan Albeck was doing, and that that was probably why he
got the Nets job.

But I have to give Wohl credit for one strategic move he made:
Starting Gminski and using me as a sixth man off the bench. This meant
that the refs couldn't hit me with quick fouls at the start of a game that
would tie my hands the rest of the way. I actually prospered in this
role, averaging 15.3 points in only 24 minutes per game. Because I
knew I was going to play in crunch-time, I could sit on the bench and
watch how the game developed and then scout how I could be most
effective when my turn came. I was also in the best physical shape of
my career because of all the rehab work I'd done in the off-season.

The only other good thing Wohl did was to hire Paul Silas as one of his assistants. Paul was a black man who played in the NBA from 1964 to 1980. He was "only" six-foot-seven and 230 pounds, but during his career I'd banged heads with Paul on the boards and he was always a tough customer. Because honesty was Paul's only policy, he didn't hesitate to analyze exactly what Wohl's problem was: He thought Wohl needed to get laid but the problem was going to be finding someone who would fuck him.

Paul had a gorgeous young daughter so I rudely busted his chops at every opportunity. "Paul, I want to be your son-in-law. Your daughter's so beautiful that I can't wait to tear that pussy up."

"Boy," he'd say, "you got nothing to do with that girl." And he'd laugh and call me a "sick motherfucker."

Paul was my teacher and the coach I went to for advice on how to play certain players who were giving me a hard time. Wohl, I just ignored as much as possible.

The team started out playing pretty good ball, but then two catastrophes put the season in the shithouse. The first problem involved (who else?) Sugar. It all happened during a Christmas party the Nets gave for everybody in the organization. After successfully completing his rehab, Sugar was back on the straight-and-narrow, so Joe Taub rewarded him with a lucrative two-year contract. Sugar had just bought his wife a Mercedes convertible and both of them were in a festive mood. I was also feeling good because I had just started going out with Kelly Barnes, a beautiful light-skinned girl.

After the party was officially over, the plan was for the players to go over to the Sheraton Hotel in nearby Aspen Heights and start another party. I wasn't planning to join them because it was snowing like we were at the North Pole, so Kelly and me were eager to get back to my house and do some hot and heavy mattress-bouncing. Then just before everybody else was about to leave for the Sheraton, Lou Schaffel said, "Darryl, are you going over to the hotel?"

"I got this girl, Lou, you know? And we want to spend some time together."

"I understand," he said, "but this is very important. Please, you got to go over there and keep an eye on Sugar."

"All right," I said. "I'll stop by for a little while."

When we got to the Sheraton, I checked out what Sugar was up to. He was drinking and laughing and dancing with his wife and just having fun. Being so fresh out of his rehab, Sugar wasn't supposed to be drinking, but he seemed to be totally under control.

Bobby Cattage had come back from playing in Europe and was the Nets' third big man off the bench. He was a home boy from Louisiana and a down to earth kind of guy. So I went up to him and said, "Bobby, I gotta go, man. This girl I'm with is real hot. Schaffel wants me to keep tabs on Sugar, but I can't stay."

"No problem, Ham. I got Sugar's back for you."

"Thanks, Bobby."

So me and Kelly left.

When I got to practice the next morning, Bobby rushed up to me, saying, "Ham, I gotta talk to you."

"Hold on one minute," I said. Then I called out, "Hey, anybody seen Sugar?"

"Ham," Bobby said. "I gotta tell you something."

"Where the fuck is Sugar?"

"That's what I'm trying to tell you. Last night at the Sheraton, I turned away from him for about a minute, right? And when I turned back around he was gone. So I ran outside and I saw him drive off with some white girl that nobody's ever seen around here before. And you know how much it was snowing, right? And there's Sugar driving off in his wife's car with the top down. And nobody's heard from him since."

Oh, shit!

Later that same day, Sugar called the Nets office. "I b-been kidnapped," he said. "If I d-don't come up with $5,000, they say they're g-gonna hurt me bad." Then he screamed and hung up the phone.

Now, I knew that Sugar was a tough motherfucker. I figured he'd either kill somebody or get himself killed before he'd let himself be taken hostage. So I guessed he was back on the pipe.

Sugar stayed missing for a week, and when he finally showed up, he told me what had happened. "This f-fine looking white bitch came up to me when my w-wife went to the ladies room. I ain't never seen this bitch before, b-but she was fine as she could be. Then she said to me, 'S-sugar, I got some hot pussy for you, baby. Come go with me, we'll take a c-couple of hits off the pipe, and then I'll fuck you like you never been f-fucked before.' So I went with her to some motel and everything she s-said was true. The shit was top-notch and the p-pussy was red hot. When I woke up the next morning, it was already t-too late to get to p-practice, so I said, 'Fuck it.' Then me and her was smoking and f-fucking again. The next time I woke up the b-bitch was gone, so I holed up there smoking all the shit she left there for m-me. When they came to g-get me, I was still fucked up."

I, like a lot of NBA players at the time, have always believed that the NBA probably sent the white girl to get Micheal Ray. This latest bust was Sugar's third strike, which meant permanent banishment from the league. If it was a sting, it worked, because a lot of guys dropped the pipe right then.

Bobby Cattage felt guilty for letting Sugar down, and so did I. Until I realized that it was only a matter of time before Sugar started chasing the pipe again and nobody could have watched him 24-7.

As it turned out, Sugar landed on his feet. He eventually cleaned up, then he went to play ball over in Italy and, later, France. Last I heard, he was still playing with a French team at age 46.

Meanwhile, the season was humming right along. We were hurting without Sugar, but Otis stayed healthy and the Nets picked up Ray Williams from San Antonio so we still had some pop in the backcourt. And me and Kelly were fucking so much that I could hardly shoot the ball, but I was rebounding like I was on welfare and the ball was made of gold. Even Wohl said, "I don't know what you're doing differently, Darryl, but you sure have improved your rebounding." Then in early March, my back started hurting again, so I had to go back into a rehab program. Even so, Wohl wanted me to travel with the team. I tried to convince him that it made no sense for me to be riding in planes, sleeping in undersized hotel beds and possibly re-injuring my back. Also, if I was on the road then what about my rehab? I really don't know what was on Wohl's mind. Maybe he thought that on my own I'd do nothing but party.

Imagine my surprise when Wohl called me at 1 a.m., just before the team was scheduled to leave on a long road trip. "All right," he said. "You don't have to travel with us. But you do have to go to your rehab every day and work hard. Maybe you'll be ready for the play-offs." I think it was Fritz Massman who convinced Wohl to change his tune.

A couple of weeks later, the Nets' playoff drive was starting to stall, so I tried to make a comeback to give the team a boost. I would be feeling fine before a game and have high hopes that I could play effectively, but after five minutes of game-time I had to retreat to the bench. The doctors said that I'd definitely be facing surgery in the off-season. *Oh, shit!*

We finished the regular season at 39-43, the first time any pro team I'd ever played on was under .500. We still managed to squeeze into the playoffs and prepared to face off against Milwaukee. Bob Lanier was retired and Alton Lister was in the middle, but with Sidney Moncrief, Terry Cummings, Paul Pressey, Ricky Pierce and Craig Hodges, the Bucks were still a tough outfit. Knowing what we were up against, I told Wohl my back was feeling better and I wanted to give it another shot. The doctors huddled and gave their approval. I had a romantic notion that just like Willis Reed did for the Knicks against the Lakers in Game Six of the 1970 championship series, I would limp out on to the court and inspire my teammates to victory. But Wohl kept me on the bench for the first game and we lost 119-107.

I did play 17 minutes in Game Two, scoring 10 points and grabbing three rebounds, but I was unable to psyche my teammates and the Bucks didn't seem to care if I was playing or not. They beat us 111-97. At this point, the doctors pulled the plug and I was a spectator again as the Bucks closed out the mini-series by beating us in New Jersey.

In May I underwent successful surgery at the Hospital for Joint Diseases in New York, but it wasn't easy because I was too big for the operating table. A couple of days later, I caused another ruckus. I was still under heavy medication and sleeping most of the time. Even when I was awake I was still in a daze. Well, one night I was having a dream about the Flintstones where I was riding Dino in the Flintstone Derby. I was whooping and hollering in my sleep loud enough to wake up just about every other patient on my floor.

"Dino! Don't stop, Dino!"

One of the nurses came running into my room and shook me

awake. "It's okay, Mr. Dawkins, you're just having a bad dream."

"Bad dream? Hell, no. I was winning the race. Now let me go back to sleep, I got some pari-mutuel tickets to cash."

I recovered a lot faster than the doctors expected. What did the trick was remembering what my grandmother had once told me. "Lessons and blessings come in many disguises."

Now I had another round of daily rehab—walking, then running on treadmills, climbing stairs, doing toe lifts and walking around on my heels. But aside from being pain-free, there were some other glad tidings that perked up my spirits. Kelly and I were married in September, and for a while we were as happy as we could be.

This was my father's advice about getting married: "Your mama can't pick a wife for you, and I sure as hell can't pick one. You could've had this girl or that girl, a Chinese girl, a white girl, a black girl, or one of them Puerto Rican girls running around New York. But you got what you got. Just remember that you gotta live your own life and you can't let your new wife keep you from doing it."

All right, soon enough it was time to play basketball. I was in terrific shape and hyped to have a great season. Too bad Dave Wohl hadn't changed a hair. He more or less let me be, but it was infuriating to see how Wohl treated the Nets' latest number one draft choice, Dwayne "Pearl" Washington.

Like Wohl, Pearl was a point guard, and despite his characteristic laid-back look, he always played hard. Pearl's specialty was the running game and he was an incredible passer in a broken field. He had a stumpy little body, but he could outrun everybody else on the team. Half-court was more difficult for him because Pearl couldn't shoot his way out of a paper bag. But Wohl seemed to think that Pearl's biggest problem was the guys he hung with, most notably Run-DMC. Wohl didn't like rappers one bit. So, even though Pearl did everything Wohl asked of him, Wohl oiled that kid day after day after day. He had Pearl come to the gym 30 minutes before practice and stay 30 minutes after practice, just to make the kid run extra windsprints.

One day, Pearl's brother, a tough guy, had a few words with Wohl and from then on Wohl left Pearl alone. But because of Wohl's abuse, Pearl had already lost his passion for the game and he was out of the league three years later.

I started off the season moving cautiously. After the first six games, my average was 9.5 points in only 17 minutes per game. Then I slipped while taking a shower at home and re-injured my back. Another round of surgery was required and I was done for the season.

(I didn't miss much because the Nets turned out to be a bullshit team and finished the season at 24-58.)

The second operation took place in Lenox Hill, a hospital that I highly recommend. That's because the night before the surgery I was allowed to eat a pile of Chinese food and to drink a martini. But this time, my recovery was slow and painful.

To compound my discomfort, Kelly and me were having serious problems. The honeymoon was over by January. That's when Kelly started asking me to buy her everything she saw. She wanted a car, so I bought her one. She wanted a fur coat, so I bought her one. A diamond necklace. A new wardrobe. No matter how many things I got for her, there was always something more. A leather sofa. A gigantic TV.

Hey, slow down, girl!

Then she said, "My mama wants a new car and a fur coat and…"

"Hold on, Kelly. I didn't marry your mama."

"Nigger, if you can't take care of me and my family, then you ain't shit."

So she stormed out the door and went home to her parents' house in Philly. When she came back a few days later she was all lovey-dovey again, but it wasn't long before she started on the same bullshit. Her mother wanted this, her father wanted that. "No," I insisted. "Like I already told you, I'm married to you, not to your family." This sparked another argument and she began to punch me and kick me. That was it! "Get the fuck out of here, bitch!"

She was happy enough to leave, but then she came back pounding on the front door only a few minutes later. I had fastened the security chain so that she couldn't open the door all the way. "You better let me back in my own motherfucking house!"

We screamed at each other for a while longer, then I slammed the door shut just as she was moving forward. BAM! The door accidentally smacked her in the face. So she called the police and pressed charges against me.

We were both in the courtroom a couple of weeks later, when she had a change of heart. "I'll drop the charges, Darryl, because I love you and I want to live with you."

"I love you, too, baby, and it breaks my heart the way we're battling each other. Okay, let's try it again."

She moved back in, but it was no good. The loving feelings we once had gradually slipped away and we both had to face the fact that our marriage was over. Kelly left again after a few weeks and she was out running around, doing her thing, and I was doing the same. One day she came by the house to pick up some of her clothes and I told her to get her shit and get the fuck out in a hurry. That's when she came at me with a knife. We started tussling and rumbling and I was trying to keep from getting cut to pieces, so I reached over to knock the knife out of her hand. Damn! But I missed and fractured her nose. She ran straight home and told her parents that I had straight out punched her.

So her father called, saying he was going to come over and get the rest of Kelly's stuff. I feared there might be trouble, so I called up my stepbrother Rusty Dawkins. Now, I understand that I haven't mentioned Rusty before and there's a good reason for this: Rusty was so bad that I didn't go near him except for an emergency. And when I told him what the situation was, Rusty came over from Philly with his girlfriend Caroline. The idea was to have a couple of eye-witnesses in case Kelly's family was planning to do something crazy like shoot me or burn the house down. Well, it worked. Kelly and her parents did a lot of woofing and made a lot of threats, but they got her stuff out of there with no further incidents.

When September rolled around, I flat out told the Nets that I wasn't coming into their training camp and that I wanted to be traded. A few days later I was dealt to Cleveland for Keith Lee, a six-foot-ten benchwarmer from Memphis who only lasted three seasons in the NBA. Good enough. Lenny Wilkens was the Cavaliers' coach and I was looking forward to playing for him. So I packed my bags, went to sleep and dreamed of playing in Cleveland.

The next morning I got a phone call from the Cavaliers telling me that me and Mel Turpin had been traded to Utah. Now I was pissed off for two reasons:

1) Mel Turpin was my favorite opposing center. Whenever I had three or four bad games in a row and I was down in the dumps, all I had to do to feel better was consult the schedule and see when we were playing Cleveland. Turpin had good skills, but he should have been driving a truck for Mister Softee. If I hit him once, he'd spend the rest of the game avoiding me. There was nothing like going against Turpin to get me back on track. But if we played on the same team, then I'd miss out on four or five highlight games.

2) Chocolate Thunder in Salt Lake City, Utah? Where the Mormons believed that blacks were descended from the devil? Fuck that. So I told the Jazz that I was retired.

Well, Jim Lampariello was the new president of the Nets and he made a beeline for my house. There were beer cans, food wrappers and empty pizza boxes all over the place, but Lampariello waded through all of it and got right to the point. "In order for the Nets to get Keith Lee, you have to report to Utah."

"I don't want to play anymore, man. I'm sick of all the bullshit and the politics and everything to do with the NBA. I'm done."

But Lampariello sweet-talked me for a couple of hours and finally convinced me to go ahead and report to training camp in Utah.

Fat Frank Layden was Utah's coach, a blubbery white guy who thought he was the funniest man in the history of Western Civilization. To prove his high opinion of himself, the Jazz public relations department distributed a collection of his best gags to the media. I weighed over 300 pounds and I was in terrible shape. But I pushed myself every day and Layden said that he liked my skills, my smarts and my work ethic.

I also learned that if the Mormon founders discriminated against blacks, their women sure didn't. There were beautiful white ladies practically standing in line to give their pussies to the black players. When I first got there, I stayed at Karl Malone's house until I could get set up at a hotel. Then at a club called Champs, I met a tall, gorgeous model, Shakira, who couldn't take her hands off of me. That's when I moved out of Karl's house, so me and Shakira could have some privacy. What I didn't know was that Karl had been dating her. After we were together for a few days, Shakira apparently called Malone and said, "I don't need you any more. I got a real man now. In fact, he's one of your teammates. And Thunder's got it all over you."

Shakira told me about the phone call later, but I was unaware of it when I arrived at practice the next morning. I still didn't know about the connection between them until Karl said to me, "I need you to leave my bitches alone or I'll knock you on your fat ass."

"What're you talking about, man?"

"That bitch, Shakira, she ain't no good, man. You leave her alone."

"Fuck you, Karl," I snapped. "I'll fuck anybody I want to fuck. And if you want some of me, I'll kick your ass up a hill and down the other side."

Layden happened to overhear this little conversation. He didn't seem too happy about it, and I suspect that was the beginning of the end for me in Utah.

I felt that Karl Malone only cared about himself and had no sense of decency.

I did like John Stockton a whole lot. He never backed down, never took a game off, and, best of all, he'd pass to anybody who was open.

Thurl Bailey was the team's second-leading scorer (behind Malone). Bailey should've worn night-vision glasses, because his head was all the way up Karl Malone's ass. "Yes, Karl. You're right, Karl." Darrell Griffith was a high-jumping, rim-shivering guard who'd been with the Jazz for seven years, and we used to hang out on the road. "Ham," he said, "don't send out your laundry because they're gonna get rid of you. Karl doesn't like you, and the media here thinks you're funnier than Layden. When Layden tries to be funny, everybody tries to be polite so they do little chuckles. But you make them mother-fuckers bust out laughing. I know it sounds crazy, but Frank doesn't like being upstaged like that."

When the season started, I mostly sat on the bench and picked up splinters in my ass. "You're outta here," Griffith kept saying.

I had been in Utah for about a month when Kelly called. "Take me back, Darryl. I love you, baby. I want to come out there and be with you because you're my husband. My parents want me to stay home, but I love you too much to stay away."

"I love you, too, Kelly. I swear that I do. But I can't take you back because I know what you're doing. You only want to come back to me long enough to sue me."

"No, no, Darryl. That ain't it. We can make this thing work."

She begged for a while, but I held fast. Then she said, "That's all right, nigger. I'm still gonna sue your black ass."

A few days later, me and Shakira split so I hooked up with a really short girl who had just turned 21. I mean she was petite, but she was also hot. Then I heard that assistant coach Jerry Sloan had said I was fucking a minor. So I asked Sloan straight up, "Why are you spreading bullshit rumors about me and an under-aged girl?" Of course he denied any such thing.

The next morning I was traded to Detroit. *Fuck that! And fuck the NBA!* I went home to New Jersey and tried to figure out what to do next.

A couple of days later, I was watching the evening news when I saw my picture on the screen and something about "Darryl Dawkins' estranged wife committed suicide." I was stoned at the time, so I thought I was dreaming, and I went to sleep.

The phone rang early the next morning. It was my stepbrother Rusty saying that Kelly had indeed killed herself. She'd been at her mother's house in Philly and swallowed too many sleeping pills.

Oh, shit! I was devastated and started bawling like a baby. I couldn't be by myself so I went over to Philly and stayed with Rusty and his wife. Somehow, Kelly's brother got Rusty's phone number and called before I got there. Rusty told me Kelly's brother blamed me for her death and we feared he might be out to get me. So Rusty arranged for two armed bodyguards to accompany me when I went to the funeral parlor.

Kelly's mother always saw my side of whatever problems I'd had with Kelly, and she called begging me to come to the funeral. "She's gone, Darryl. She's gone." And we cried together for a while. When I went to view the body at the funeral home, the bodyguards cleared my path and also watched my back. I just walked over to the casket, looked at Kelly, then left quick before I started crying again.

A few hours after that, I was preparing myself for the funeral, but I started to break down. My chest seemed to swell up and I couldn't breathe. Rusty was even more scared than I was and he rushed me to a hospital. The doctor said I was having an anxiety attack, so he told me not to attend the funeral.

When I got back home, there was a threatening message on my phone machine from a voice I didn't recognize: "If you ever show up in Philly again, we're gonna blow your motherfucking brains out."

At the same time, I got several calls from my mother and all of my brothers and sisters. They all said that it wasn't my fault and there was nothing I could have done to prevent Kelly's suicide. But I didn't really believe them. I felt that I could have prevented it by taking her back.

My father also called. "Look, man, you're too big and strong to fall, so you have to get through this shit. You can't be tripping on this every day for the rest of your life. Later on you can look back at this, but for now you got to put it in the past."

I was totally fucked up. I stayed in my house with the shades drawn and for about two weeks I didn't shower or shave. I was all smelly and funky as a Skid Row bum. When my beard grew out it was gray and black and I was shocked when I caught a glimpse of myself in a mirror because I looked older than my father.

Maybe my father was right. Maybe I needed something to distract me just to make the time pass. The only option I could think of was to play basketball, so I called the Pistons and made arrangements to join them in Detroit.

I'd always liked the way Chuck Daly was able to blend white and black basketball, so I thought I could lose myself in the game while I swallowed my grief. It didn't work out the way I hoped because everywhere I went I heard people muttering about how I had killed my wife. My only recourse was to play harder.

Fortunately, I was easily distracted by my new teammates, who were some of the wackiest motherfuckers I'd ever seen.

I found Isiah Thomas to be nothing but selfish: If he was having a bad game, he'd just keep on shooting until his game came around. Guys sat on the bench and whenever Isiah missed his first two or three shots, they'd say, "Uh oh. Nobody's gonna get passed the ball until the little motherfucker hits about five in a row."

In Detroit it was apparently Isiah, not Daly, who ran the show. If Isiah didn't like something Daly said or did, I figured the little shit would just go to the owner and get everything changed to suit himself. Isiah would come across to the public all sweet and soft-spoken and cute, but he was a nasty character.

Everybody also knew that Dennis Rodman's elevator didn't stop at the top floor. He'd come over to me about a dozen times every day saying the same thing, "Hey, don't you feel well?"

"Yeah, motherfucker, and I'd feel a whole lot better if you'd stop asking me the same stupid question." Then ten minutes later, here he'd come again with the same silly bullshit.

I was about four inches bigger than Rodman and probably 60 pounds heavier, but one day at practice he decided that he was going to guard me. So he was scratching at me and holding me and fouling me every time I tried to move. I proceeded to knock the fuck out of him. As hard as I hit him, he just kept coming back for more. Crazy as Rodman was, I knew there'd come a time when I'd have to smack his face.

Bill Laimbeer was another goofball. In the past, I'd known him to be a cheap-shot artist, but now that he was on my side he was only being "aggressive." And Laimbeer gave me a hearty welcome: "I'm glad you're on my team, Dawk, because I'm tired of fucking with you."

One night I was getting dressed in the locker room after a ball game, when Laimbeer had a question for me. "How come when black guys get dressed they always put their socks, shoes and drawers on first?"

"Because if you're in the wrong house at the wrong time, and the husband is putting his key into the front door, then you got to be ready to run."

But it was no good. I couldn't concentrate on basketball and I couldn't forget the pain. After a couple of weeks, I left the team and went home swearing that I'd never play basketball again.

14

Ciao, Y'All

K elly was gone, but I still wasn't finished dealing with her family and I had to hire a lawyer to try to clean up the loose ends. The family said they didn't know anything about the car I bought for her. They didn't have it, didn't know where it was, didn't know what I was talking about. I just bit the bullet and finished up the payments. There was also a question of the three-carat engagement ring, which Kelly's family also swore was not in their possession. They said that Kelly had given it back to me when we first broke up.

I sat around for about nine months doing an occasional line of coke and eating a lot of chocolate cake. I did some TV commercials and with my deferred money from New Jersey I was doing okay. One thing I didn't do was touch a basketball. During that time I also met another girl, Robbin Thornton, who had been a cheerleader for the Nets and was now a high school teacher. We started dating and we hit it off real good. Good enough to get married in September of 1988.

Then I got the itch to play again. Detroit owned my rights, so I called general manager Jack McCloskey, told him that I weighed 303 pounds, that I was willing to go on a strict diet and that I wanted to come into the Pistons' training camp. Jack said neither of us had anything to lose so it was okay with him.

The first day of training camp was rough. I couldn't jump high enough to dunk, but I still felt good about playing. The second day, a Piston player passed on the latest NBA rumor: "They say you've been sleeping with a crack pipe and that you're a big cocaine hitter. They say you're all strung out on drugs. That's why I expected to see you all thin and emaciated and throwing up all over the place. Now I can see that the rumors are nothing but bullshit."

And who was the "they" that was spreading all the rumors? I always suspected it was someone from the Nets.

I was getting into game shape quicker than anybody expected. By the time the exhibition games rolled around, I was almost there. I got 13 points and 10 rebounds against Washington. Next up was a pre-season game against the L. A. Clippers and I was dunking all over Benoit Benjamin and knocking his shit into the bleachers. By now my jumper was also falling. Bill Laimbeer was impressed: "Yeah, big fella. You're killing people out there. We're glad to have you."

Then we played Dallas and my opposite number was seven-foot-two James Donaldson, a bona fide All-Star. BAM! I was spinning and dunking and rebounding and blocking shots and running the court just like the old days. Now Chuck was impressed: "That's the kind of stuff that'll keep you around."

Then three days before the season started, the word was that William Bedford had finished his drug rehab and was ready to play. Bedford was a skinny seven-footer who didn't like contact and couldn't play dead, but for some reason McCloskey thought he was a player. According to the Detroit newspapers, the Pistons had too many big men and I was the likeliest candidate to walk the plank. Then Chuck said, "I'm gonna make a bold decision, Darryl. I like the way your game's coming around, so I'm gonna keep you."

All right!

Chuck put me in a few games backing up James Edwards and I was getting better every time I played. My popularity was also on the rise: The Pistons' fans screamed my name and went nuts whenever I dunked. Isiah gave me funny looks when the crowd yelled, "DARR-YL! DARR-YL!, but I paid him no mind. I got the word through an overseas agent that a team in Spain wanted to bring me over there for a whole pile of money, but Chuck kept encouraging me so I decided to stay with the Pistons.

We were in Denver when one of the guys on the team told me that Isiah thought I was overshadowing him and that he was pulling strings to run me off the team. Coincidently, the media began saying that I didn't get along with any of my teammates and that I was a troublemaker. Fennis Dembo had the balls to tell a sportswriter that the rumors were absolutely false. So the Pistons cut him and kept me! But I knew I was on borrowed time. A few days later, the Pistons signed a guard, John Long, and finally put me on waivers.

I went home to New Jersey and took stock of where I was and where I might be headed. I was 32 and I'd already played in the league for 14 years. The Pistons had guaranteed my contract for the entire season, so I didn't have to worry about money for a while. The more I thought about my situation, the more I realized that I'd had my fill of the NBA. Maybe it was time for me to quit. I had faith that the Lord would provide something worthwhile for me to do with the rest of my life. A couple of days later, the Washington Bullets called and offered me $50,000 to finish the season with them, but I turned them down. I had the feeling that something new and exciting was in store for me.

About a week later, I got a call from an agent named Steve Zucker. "Darryl," he said, "there's a team in Torino, Italy, that wants you. They're trying to round up enough money to make you a good offer. What do you think?"

Well, I certainly enjoyed my brief time in Italy with the Nets, and the Italian fans sure did take to me. "I don't know," I said. "I'll have to think about this."

The next night my phone rang. "Hello, Dawkins? I am Pepe di Stefano from Torino and I have money for you. I will come there and speak to you man-to-man."

So I flew into Chicago to meet Pepe at Zucker's office and this was the deal: "We give you $50,000 American to come now for one month and practice with the team. You don't play this year. You play next year. We give you a house. We give you a car. We treat you like a person." It sounded interesting, so I accepted.

My plan was to check it out for the month by myself. Robbin had been teaching for eight years and was on the verge of getting tenured, so I thought it would be best for her to keep her job just in case the scene was a bust in Torino. But she wanted to come along, and when the school wouldn't give her a leave of absence she just quit. And off we went.

Everything was set up just the way Pepe had promised. The new car, the house in the country. The refrigerator was stocked with juice, milk, bread, and a ham. They even supplied us with one of the most luxurious items in Italy—toilet paper.

Right after we settled in I wanted to make myself a sandwich for lunch. I loved the Italian meats and cheeses, the prosciutto ham and the provolone, but I couldn't find soft bread for a sandwich in any of the grocery stores and bakeries. Instead of nice soft Wonder Bread, all of the Italian bread was hard and dry. I had to mash the stuff down to make a proper sandwich.

So I asked Pepe what to do. "You must get up early," he said. Six o'clock the latest. Go to a bakery and ask for *panni casetta*. *Panni* means bread, and *casetta* is the little pan it's made in."

All right. *Panni casetta*. Little pans of crusty white bread, perfect for what I needed. Then I found out that if I came into the bakery at seven o'clock it was already too late. Most of the good bread was sold and I had to battle the old ladies for what was left. That's because in Italian families it's bad luck to run out of bread. I could identify easily with that particular superstition because black people had a similar one: Bad luck was sure to strike if a black family ever ran out of salt.

So I practiced with the team and went to all of the games. Even though I was dressed in civvies and stuck on the bench, the fans would scream my name: "Dawkins! Dawkins! Next year, Dawkins!"

For a while, practicing with the team was an exercise in frustration because I couldn't hit a turnaround jump shot. CLANG! Off the rim. SPLAT! Off the backboard. It felt like the normal dimensions of a basketball court were just a little off and I couldn't find my comfort zone. Then I realized that the trapezoid foul lane was messing with my depth perception. Once I scoped that out, I was back to where I wanted to be.

There was also a problem with the backboards. Not only were they thin, but there was no padding along the bottom. I had to curtail any overly rambunctious dunkings to avoid getting all cut up.

The coach was Dino Guarieri, an Italian-American who was born in Seattle and had married an Italian woman. He was in his mid-fifties and he spoke English fluently but very slowly and in a breathy, guttural tone like Marlon Brando in *The Godfather*. This is the way Dino introduced me to the other players: "We have here Dawkins, the old man, so don't treat him like a baby. Treat him like a man. Go ahead. Bust his ass. Break his neck. If you can."

And Dino had a personal warning for me: "Torino is called the Triangle City because it's near Rome and Florence. But Torino is also the city of the devil. I have here a story to show what I mean. One night me and my wife, Tosca, we go to hotel in mountains for our, how-do-you-say? Spark, weekend of the flame. So we go in the room and we fuck. I fuck good for an old man. I fuck, fuck, fuck, fuck. When we are finished, I hear sounds from room next door. 'Oh! Oh!' My wife, she say, 'Someone is being hurt.' I say, 'No, they fuck just like us.' It started again. 'Oh! Oh!' All night they do this. I think, hey, they fuck as good as me and Tosca. Then I hear them talking. 'What time do we leave tomorrow?' Another voice say, 'We leave at seven.' Mother of God, it's two men! The next morning I go down to check the register. There's a Bob and a Georgio in the room. Be careful in Torino, Dawkins. Things not what they seem here."

How could I not like my new coach?

The other American on the team was Joe Kopicki, a six-foot-nine shooter from Earl Cureton's old school, Detroit Mercy, who had played parts of three seasons for the Washington Bullets and the Denver Nuggets. Joe was kind of flabby, he ran with a waddle and he wasn't built like a ballplayer. The Torino fans called him "The Fat Dove," but Joe could stand in the corner and make eight of ten shots.

Nino Pellacini was a pretty good rebounder with big hands and good hops. The Torino fans would shout, "Jump, Nino, jump! Jump for us!" And because he could jump like a black guy, they called him "Black Nino." After every home game, the Torino media would pick a player of the game and the reward would be a free meal someplace. Kopicki would have 30 points and 10 rebounds to Nino's ten points and six rebounds, and guess who'd get picked. "Oh, magnifico, Nino!"

Our shooting guard, Ricky Morandotti, was an NBA-caliber shooter, but he only had one move to the basket. He dribbled with his right hand and just before he shot he stuck out his left leg. His defender either had to get out of the way or get kicked in the stomach. And the referees never called the move a charge.

Abio Alexandro was our point guard. He was very young and he wasn't afraid of anything except playing poorly and having to sit on the bench.

I liked being in Italy very much. The food was great, I didn't run out of hot sauce, the people were friendly and they loved basketball. So after my month was up, I let Zucker negotiate a new contract for the 1989-90 season. I ended up making $600,000.

Me and Robbin came back home to Jersey, made a trip to Florida and just hung around until it was time to return to Torino. We were both glad to be back and I was almost looking forward to my first Italian training camp. Turned out that as much as I liked Dino, some of his pre-season practice routines were ridiculous.

There were several rubber tires suspended from the ceiling and I had to run through them while holding a basketball. There was also what we called the "sissy run," a hip-swishing, ass-wiggling 40-yard dash. But the worst drill was having to run around a track with a rope tied around my waist and a tire tied to the other end of the rope. Dino swore that this increased foot speed, but I knew it was bullshit.

Once the season began I also had to adjust to a different style of play. The Italiano fast break called for the point guard to push the ball upcourt, then pull it back out and wait for his teammates to catch up. Taking it straight to the basket wasn't considered appropriate. I'd be throwing bull's-eye outlet passes and Abio wouldn't go with it. "No, no, no," he said. "We must pull the ball out. If not, coach get mad. This is how we play in Italy."

"Fuck that," I said. "If you score the coach ain't gonna say shit." So maybe once every week, Abio would fast break right to the basket.

The Italian players on Torino got anywhere from $60,000 to $150,000 for the season. They were scrappers and scratchers, so me and Joe had to do all of the scoring and rebounding. I shot 77% from the field and was good for about 22 points and seven rebounds every game. The local players never resented us, but whenever we got a big lead they'd get all cocky and arrogant and forget about passing us the ball.

Most of the Italian teams played zone defenses, but their idea of defense was to grab hold of an opponent's jersey and not let him move. Your shirt could be sticking way the hell out and the refs would never call a foul.

The refs also took getting used to. If I caught a pass and made a simple head fake without moving my feet, the refs called walking. But if I dribbled, I could do whatever I wanted—from taking two extra steps when I pulled the ball up, to coming to a jump stop then taking a couple of small shuffles.

One night we played at home against Sassari and their center was a six-foot-ten muscular American named Floyd Johnson, who'd been playing in Italy for 11 years. He literally jumped on my back while I was going up for a shot and the ref called a foul on him. Johnson turned and said this to the ref: "That was a terrible fucking call, you little grease ball motherfucker! I hate your motherfucking ass!" The ref didn't even blink and the game resumed.

A week later, we were playing in Sassari, and there was the same ref that Johnson had cussed out. When I blocked one of Johnson's shots, the refs called the foul on me. "That's a bullshit call," I said. And the ref turned to me and said, "Be careful, Dawkins."

English was their second language, but they felt dumb trying to speak it. Just like I did with Italian. And the only time an American got to the free-throw line was when he was fouled by another American. An Italian player could hit me with a crowbar and there wouldn't be a call. But if an American happened to be in the neighborhood when an Italian missed a shot, TWEET! I figured it was their country and their game so they were entitled to make their own rules.

Italy is the only place where I've seen a referee call a game. We were playing in Pisa and they had Leon Douglas and Joe Binion so they were supposed to beat us. But with two minutes left in the game, we were up by four points. The fans started hissing and throwing some hard, heavy coins at the referees. Then they started throwing rolls of toilet paper. Next came the bigger, heavier coins. One of the refs said to me, "The game, she is over. Your team win, Dawkins." And all of us ran to the locker rooms before the fans could storm the court. I think that was the most courageous action I've ever seen from a referee.

So I was playing and having a great time.

Because I was very committed to making my marriage work, I didn't fool around on the road at all. I didn't do any drugs either, because if an American got busted for dope he'd be banned from playing in Italy for the rest of his life. It was such easy money over there that I didn't want to jeopardize my career.

Speaking for myself, I didn't experience much racism in Italy. In fact, only two incidents come to mind. The only time I was ever called a nigger was in Forli when a lady stood up during a game and shouted it out. The fans in the area just ran her out of the gym. The second time was in a butcher store during my second year in Torino. By that time I was fairly fluent in Italian, good enough to ask the butcher for beefsteak cut in a certain way. There was an old woman standing on line in back of me and she said to the butcher in Italian, "He's a stupid black. He don't know anything. My hair is gray. You should wait on me before him." The butcher's eyes opened wide because I had just spoken to him in Italian and he didn't know what to say. But I did. I turned to her and said in my best Italian, "Your mama sucks dick." She got on her horse and got out of there quick. But it all ended happily. The old woman bought a season's ticket, became a big basketball fan, and invited me to her house for a wonderful meal.

The fans at the games were the most rowdy I've ever seen. When an opposing player scored a basket, they stood up and shouted, "*Va fon gulla*," which means "Fuck you!" And they loved to fight against the fans who were rooting for the visiting team. One time the Torino fans were battling in the stands with fans from Milan and the police dispatched a 40-man riot squad to break it up. The cops had their shields and their clubs and they were whipping heads left and right—until the fans of both teams turned on the cops, took away their equipment and sent them scurrying from the arena.

The fans in Livorno were the nastiest of them all. There was a woman in the stands who had a baby in her arms. When I passed by, she pulled the blanket back and, I swear, the baby gave me the finger. Every time we had to go to the locker room, the fans would hang over the railings to spit at us and throw garbage. We had to wear towels on our heads to protect ourselves. But Nino Pellacini came up with a better idea. Because the basic theory of Italian basketball is that the best defense is a good offense, as we walked through the stands he just reached up and slapped the faces of the fans who were leaning over and throwing stuff. That was the end of that problem. But, after every game in Livorno, win or lose, the only way we could safely get to our bus was to ride there in a police paddy wagon.

My second season in Torino, I even broke a backboard. It was a home game and I was running the break with Joe Kopicki. He threw me a perfect lob pass and I couldn't resist. WHAMMO! CRASHO! What was most amazing about this one was that the fans immediately ran onto the court and grabbed handfuls of the shattered glass. They were fighting each other for the pieces. There was blood all over the place. It was absolutely nuts. Like rats tearing at a dead body. That's why, as long as I was in Italy, I made sure never to even come close to tearing down another rim.

I was a major celebrity in Torino, especially once they found out that I spoke Italian. I was on all of the local TV shows and I was the player the sportswriters interviewed after every game. People would follow me around when I went shopping in the grocery store. Whatever I put in my shopping cart, they put in theirs. Before I got to Torino, the basketball games drew 1,400 fans. By the time I left, they were drawing 4,000.

Naturally, the competition in Europe didn't approach the NBA, but it was good enough to keep my chops up. Also, since our practice sessions were easy and we only played two games a week, there wasn't as much wear and tear on my body. When I was asked to return to Torino for a second season, I couldn't sign the contract fast enough.

I loved playing with Joe Kopicki. He was The Fat Dove and I was the slow old man, but we knew how to play together. That second season we beat some of the best teams in Italy: Milan with Bob McAdoo, Scavalini with Darren Daye, Messina with Michael Young and Charles Shackleford. And we moved from the A-2 division up to A-1.

I was still only 34, but I knew my limitations. I could go to my favorite spot in the pivot and score. I could overpower any of the Italian big men. I could still knock down the jumper and I could still dunk with flair. Torino wanted me back for a third year, but since it was one of the smaller cities they were short of money. If it wasn't economically feasible for me to return to Torino, then I wanted to play in Bologna because they had plenty of lira and because their Italian players were the best in the country.

By then I had hooked up with an agent named Warren LeGarie, who specialized in European teams. LeGarie had so much stuff going on that he agreed to represent me for nothing. LeGarie had a sweet deal worked out for me with a team in Spain, but I didn't want to go there. I spoke Italian, I knew what was going on in Italy and how I was going to be treated. I had my sights set on Bologna when LeGarie presented me with a $600,000 offer from Milan that also included an apartment and a car. He told me that I wouldn't get screwed in Milan because the owners had lots of money. LeGarie also represented the coach in Milan, Mike D'Antoni, so he swore that I'd also have the best coach in all of Italy. It was take it now, or take a chance on Bologna. So I signed with Milan.

In Torino I lived in a nice house out in the country, and because it was such a small place I knew just about all of the fans. But Milan was a major league city. My apartment was plush: Marble floors, a big-screen TV, three bedrooms and a decent kitchen. But it was on the 12th floor of a high-rise. Man, I wasn't happy there for even a minute. I want to live on the ground floor. Even when I check into a hotel, that's where I want my room to be. The apartment had a luxurious balcony that I ventured out to maybe three times the whole season.

As much as I disliked Milan, I liked D'Antoni even less. He was another sawed-off ex-guard who didn't know how to maximize the capabilities of a low-post player. At the start D'Antoni said the right things: I was going to get the ball in the low post exactly where I wanted it. I'd be the team's primary scorer. Etcetera. The way it turned out, though, was that every time we lost a game it was my fault. If I had anything less than 20 points and 20 rebounds, then I was stealing the owner's money. I guess D'Antoni was worried about covering his own ass.

Anyway, we played well enough to qualify for the European Cup in Istanbul. For me, the highlight of the season happened before the tournament even began. I was walking to my room when I heard someone saying "Daddy! Daddy!" It was my daughter, Dara. Her mother was working for TWA and had arranged for Dara to come to Istanbul as a surprise for me. We had a great time strolling around the open-air markets and just getting reacquainted.

I'm so proud of my daughter. She was born with only 30% hearing in one ear and 20% in the other, but she learned to read lips and also to communicate in sign language. She went to regular school all her life and always had good grades. These days, Dara is 22 and at

Temple University. She wants to be a veterinarian and I know she'll succeed. Spending that time with Dara also made me appreciate her mother more. Penny never got married, but she's made a good life for herself. The only problem between us was that when we got together we were both too young to really know what we were doing and what we really wanted. Like our daughter, Penny is a sweetheart.

We lost in the semi-finals to a really good team from Yugoslavia, Partizan Belgrade, that included future NBA players Zeljko Rebraca, Predrag Danilovic and Aleksandar Djordjevic. I was double-teamed every time I touched the ball, and I finished with 21 points and 19 rebounds, while the other front-court starters (Antonello Riva and Ricky Pittis) shot 4-15 and 3-17. NBA commissioner David Stern was at the game and on the bus going back to the hotel, he said, "Darryl, the team didn't lose because of you. You couldn't have done any more than you did."

The next morning, the owner of the team told me that we would've won if I had played better. I wanted to smack his face, but I realized that he was only repeating what D'Antoni had said to him.

After the season, I wanted nothing more to do with Milan, so LeGarie hooked me up with a team in Forli for the '92-'93 season at just about the same money. The best I can say about Forli was that it wasn't far from Bologna, which had a McDonald's. Back in the States I only ate at Mickey D's in an emergency, but in Italy it was worth driving an hour and 20 minutes for a hamburger and fries. There was a line of 50 people at every cash register, so we even had to wait another half hour to get served.

Switzerland was also close to Forli and we could get all kinds of goodies there, from barbecue to American cookies. Italian cakes were too hard for my taste, so we'd also buy some Duncan Hines cake mixes. Getting the kind of food I was used to was a continuing problem.

Come Thanksgiving, Robbin wanted to make a turkey. When we went to the butcher shop, the turkey had the head, the feet and the feathers still on. So I asked my teammates what was going on. Many years ago, Italian butchers used to skin cats and sell them as chicken or rabbits. Nowadays, the chickens and turkey are sold *au natural* so the customer knows exactly what he's buying. Robbin was so turned off by having to decapitate and pluck the turkey that she couldn't eat it.

Robbin was even more freaked out when a friend took us to a restaurant and she was served some meat that she couldn't identify. "Not bad," she said. "Tastes something like chicken." When they told her it was rabbit, she spit it all out. That's because she was a city girl. Eating rabbit was a delicacy for poor country folks.

In Forli I ate some roast pigeon that I liked. And a horse steak that was cooked up like filet mignon also tasted good. As long as I didn't run out of hot sauce, I could enjoy whatever they put on my plate.

I had a teammate there who had a much harder time than I did with the local food. His name was Adrian Caldwell, who'd already played parts of two NBA seasons and would play two more after he left Italy. Adrian was a rebounding fool, but he was even more of a country bumpkin than I ever was. Instead of getting used to pasta and the local fare, he had his wife cook him some soul food that he would take on the road. Fried fish, black-eyed peas, smothered chicken. After a day or so, that stuff would start to stink. But Adrian didn't care. "I'd rather eat good food that's rotten," he'd say.

When I first started playing in Forli, there was an Italian player who just would not pass me the ball. If I was standing by my lonesome under the basket, the pass would still go elsewhere. After a while, I asked the little runt what his problem was. "It's no my problem," he said. "It's your problem. You must prove you appreciate the way I play by giving me the money." After that, the more lira I gave him, the more passes I received.

Joe Kopicki was still with the team, but when he suffered an injury they brought in six-foot-ten Johnny Rogers for a tryout. Rogers had played two years in the NBA (for Sacramento and Cleveland) and he played like a guard. The only time I saw that motherfucker under the boards was when he inbounded the ball. The only rebounds he'd get were off a missed free throw, or else a three-point shot that bounced high off the rim and wound up near the foul line. I mean if he had three rebounds in a game, that meant he was doing some work. On defense, he couldn't guard a telephone pole without getting faked off his feet.

After a few games, the Torino newspapers reported that Rogers was on the verge of being cut because he wasn't helping the team. Well, the kid came to me all worried about having to go home without making any real money. I kind of liked him, so I concocted a private strategy for our next game. "You go stand in the corner, and when the defense double-teams me I'll look to pass to you before I'll try to score or look for anybody else."

And that's just what happened. Rogers scored 41 points to my 18. After the game, the media crowded around him in the locker room. "Johnny," they said. "You played great tonight, but what's wrong with Dawkins?"

"I don't know," Rogers said. "He wasn't running or hustling. He wasn't rebounding and he certainly wasn't scoring."

Oh, shit. From then on, Rogers was on his own. He wound up getting cut even before Kopicki was ready to play.

All in all, I had a very productive season and maintained the numbers I had produced in Torino. But as soon as I got back to New Jersey, there was bad news heading my way: My father died two weeks before his 61st birthday.

He had a blood infection, cancer and severe arthritis, so he died in a lot of pain. The reason he was so sick was that he had been called to be a preacher and he'd run away from his calling. When you don't do what God wants you to do, then you'll die in misery.

Being human, instead of going to the Lord in prayer, I went first to the liquor cabinet for a bottle of vodka. And I sat in the same chair for a day and a half trying to drink away my sorrow.

I simply adored my father. The fact that he chased women and drank didn't matter to me. And as I sat there I couldn't help remembering some of the funny things he did and said. Like one time when he came over to New Jersey to see me play. I was dating one of the Nets' cheerleaders and she had a sister who was thick and kind of heavy. When Big Daddy saw the sister he got right down on his knees and said, "Lord, you're gonna give me the one with the big ankles for my birthday." When I told him that he couldn't get a girl that way, he just smiled and said, "I know the Man."

My father was the funniest man ever. We were planning to go out to a fancy dinner one Friday night, so I told him to dress accordingly. "Yeah," he said. "I don't want to make you look bad so I'll wear one of my old suits."

Right after Kelly committed suicide, my father also said this to me: "One sure thing about Frank Dawkins ... When I die, people are gonna say that I damn sure knew how to live. So you got to make yourself happy, son, because nobody else out there is trying to make you happy."

Long before he was gone, my father had planned and paid for his funeral. He also left money for four people to accompany his remains from New York down to West Palm Beach because he wanted to be buried there beside his father. He even spoke to me about some of the details: "Let them morticians do me up here in New York. Shoot me full of joy juice so that I look good. Do not by any means bury me in New York. That's 'cause so many people die in New York that they bury people on top of other people. I want to wear my blue suit for traveling. When I get down to Florida change my ass into a white suit." Those were his exact words.

My brother Mitchell, who had become a minister, came up from Florida to arrange for Pop's clothes and to say some prayers over his remains. And I couldn't believe how good he looked, like he was just sleeping in the casket. Then me and Mitchell went back to New Jersey. We were under the impression that in two days' time we'd be flying down to Florida along with the body. But that's not what happened.

Several years back, Big Daddy had remarried a young girl who had been a high school classmate of mine. They eventually had a little girl named Bianca. Well, while me and Mitchell was waiting and doing our own private grieving, unbeknownst to us Daddy's wife was changing the funeral plans. Instead of flying the body to West Palm Beach she had Daddy buried in a local graveyard. We didn't find out any of this until it was too late. She was the wife and had the legal right to do what she wanted done. But we were furious with her and we still are.

To cap it off, we knew that Daddy had been careful when he made out his will. He told us that he wanted to leave his gold rings and his other jewelry so that each of us got some. He also said that every one of his children was going to get $5,000. But apparently Daddy had been persuaded to change his will so that none of his children got a thing. We never pursued this because, except for the sentimental value of the rings, none of his worldly possessions really meant much compared to his spirit that still lives on inside of us. But it was a hurting time.

And the living have to keep on living.

So I went back to Forli for another year and I was looking forward to playing there for another few seasons. So what if I was 37? I was still strong enough and smart enough to get my 20-20 every game. Trouble was that the owners of the Italian teams went to war with each other. Just like every other war in the history of the world this one was about M-O-N-E-*motherfucking*-Y! The outcome was that they reduced the salaries of the American players. The highest paid American in Italy would only make $150,000, and I wasn't going to live in a foreign country for that kind of money. So me and Robbin went back to New Jersey.

I was all ready to finally retire for good until some friends started saying that I should still be playing. Look at some of the old stiffs still getting paid to be backup centers in the NBA. Guys like Danny Schayes and Herb Williams and Charles Jones. Shit, Tree Rollins was two years older than me. So I signed up to play for the Sioux Falls Skyforce in the Continental Basketball Association. The pay was good—$3,000 a week—but I didn't like the coach.

Flip Saunders played with Kevin McHale back at the University of Minnesota, and their friendship sure went a long way. During training camp, Saunders had us running like we were a track team. When we were finished running we'd go lift weights. That was okay with me because I knew I had to get into shape, and I was willing to bust my ass to get there. But Saunders also had basketball drills that nobody had ever seen before except the guys who had already played for him. All right, that was cool, too. Innovation is good in a coach. Trouble was that Saunders never explained to the newcomers exactly what was going on in these drills. *What the fuck am I supposed to do now? Zig? Zag? Or drop my drawers?*

Saunders also had a habit of sniffing the air hard. It reminded me of someone who wished there was a plate of coke sitting up under his nose. Now, I know that later on McHale became the general manager of the Minnesota Timberwolves and brought his buddy on board to coach the team. But from what I could see, Saunders couldn't coach a stagecoach if they gave him the horse and the whip. Needless to say

I wasn't looking forward to the season.

Right before the season started, I got a call from the Harlem Globetrotters. They offered me $2,500 a week to play on a four-month tour of South America. I would be the first NBA graduate ever to play for the Globetrotters.

Yeah, hombre. South America, here I come.

15

Hell Must Have Frozen Over

W hile I was growing up, I was aware of the great history of the Harlem Globetrotters: The team was originally founded by a little five-foot tall white guy named Abe Saperstein back in 1926. It was an all-black team that barnstormed the country from their home base in Chicago. At the start, the Globetrotters played it straight and won over 90% of the 150 to 175 games they played every year. But since the games were often lopsided, Saperstein decided to have the players spice up the action. The Globetrotters' first showman was Inman Jackson, whose trick was to roll the ball up one arm, across his shoulders and down the other arm. In 1948 and 1949, the Globetrotters defeated George Mikan and his NBA champion Minneapolis Lakers to stake their claim as the world's greatest basketball team.

Saperstein was a shrewd businessman and he knew that if the lily-white NBA started signing too many black players then his Globetrotters wouldn't be such a unique gate attraction. So Saperstein made a deal—if the pros limited the number of blacks they signed, the Globetrotters would play preliminary contests to regular-season NBA games. This was the status quo until the late 1950s when more and more black players began appearing on NBA rosters. Saperstein was pissed and started his own pro league in 1961, the American Basketball League, which only lasted for a season and a half.

Saperstein died in 1966, but the Globetrotters played on. Through the years, a variety of big-name black athletes have been Globetrotters, including Wilt Chamberlain, baseball pitcher Bob Gibson, and Goose

Tatum, the Clown Prince of Basketball. About once every month, a TV show called *The Wide World of Sports* would feature a Globetrotter game, and I never missed a one. I grew up just loving the Globetrotters, and that was one reason I signed to play with them. Unfortunately, I found out that the Globetrotters treated their players like niggers.

Now, $2,500 a week sounds like a pile of money. But by the time the organization deducted taxes, medical insurance plus several other fees that I couldn't even keep track of, my paycheck dwindled to about $1,500. Other guys who made less than me were working for a pittance. That's why several players had to borrow money in advance of their future salaries. Playing for the Globetrotters was like working for the company store. Even so, the organization was constantly bringing in new players to replace the established players who were becoming too popular and therefore too expensive.

The team was run by Mannie Jackson, a former vice-president with Honeywell Inc. who paid $6 million for the team in 1993 to become its first African-American owner. Mannie worked us like slaves: There were times when we played a game at 11 a.m., rode on a bus for five or six hours, then played another game at eight that night. One time we rode the bus from ten o'clock at night to seven in the morning to catch a plane for a six-hour flight. When we landed we had a 60-minute dinner break before we played a ball game. The buses we used were downsized for school children and were never air-conditioned. They were sometimes so old and rickety that they'd break down when they hit a bump in the road. I don't know how many times we sat on the side of the road for two or three hours when the temperature was over a hundred degrees just waiting for a bus to be repaired.

The Washington Generals, our traveling opposition, followed us in their own separate bus that was even more beat up than ours. There were three black players on the Generals and the rest of them were white, but we were all niggers, so we went out to eat and drink together.

Just about everybody moaned about the way we were treated. "Man, I ain't playing no more for no $400." So I encouraged the guys to take their complaints straight to Mannie Jackson's greedy face. But how did they act whenever Jackson came around? "Hey, Mr. Boss

Man. How you doing?" That's when I called them chickenshit motherfuckers. They'd hang their heads and swear they were going to speak
up to him the next time. Then the same ass-kissing stuff would happen again.

Now, Jackson had a shit load of money. In addition to raking in
the bucks for the Globetrotter games, he has served as a director with
several Fortune 500 companies. Jackson's policy was to shun players
who had an agent. He would make only one offer directly to a player and would seldom negotiate.

Though they were afraid to rock the boat, most of the guys were
fun to be with. The notable exceptions were Paul Gaffney and Sweet
Lou Dunbar, who were Jackson's pets. Of the rest, Bill Harley went by
the name of Super Charlie and he'd been a Globetrotter for 21 years.
Charlie could drink all night long, but as soon as the lights went on he
was straight as an arrow.

One of the coaches was another ex- Globetrotter, Tex Harrison.
When I grow up, I want to be as funny as Tex. "Dammit, boy," he'd
say to me. "The more I teach you the dumber I get."

I was ready to be one of the funny guys who cracked jokes and
clowned around because I was that way naturally. But Jackson had
other plans for me: I was mainly the designated dunker. My other job
was to go to the sideline and fetch a trampoline whenever Eli 'The Fly'
Akin went into his dribbling routine. I had to put the trampoline
under the basket just so, and Eli would dribble up to it, take a good
bounce and wind up sitting on the rim. Then he'd jump down, I'd
catch him, and carry him to the bench. Ha ha. Jackson said he'd give
me a chance to do some funny routines, but it never happened.

When we played in Lima, Peru, the hotel had a casino downstairs
and everything was cool. The food was tasty, the beds were soft and
the women were willing. Then we went to some Godforsaken village
in Uruguay and stayed at a hotel that the Salvation Army wouldn't
even use to house the homeless. Not only were the sinks and toilets
flooded, but there were no screens on the windows. The mosquitoes
were so big there that they wouldn't even bite us. They'd just fly in,
kick us, then fly back out. We also played on concrete courts that
pounded our feet into pancakes, and where the showers were filthier
than a prison bathroom during a riot in Cell Block F.

After three months I was sick of the phony basketball and Jackson's penny-pinching ways. When the tour moved on to Canada, I told Jackson that I wanted to go home. "I need at least a short leave of absence."

"I can't authorize anything like that," he said. "You have to stay with the team for the duration of your contract."

"Then let's say our good-byes right now, 'cause I'm packing my stuff, then I'm gone."

"All right," Jackson said. "You can have a four-day leave."

Once I got back to New Jersey, I was there to stay. Five days later, there was an item in the newspaper saying that Jackson had suspended me from the Globetrotters for an "indefinite period" because of my disruptive behavior.

I immediately called Jackson and said, "You're the only one who disrupted anything. All you're doing is trying to make yourself look good."

"I paid you everything I owed you, Darryl. I always acted in good faith."

"Bullshit. I'll tell you what you always did: Promise everybody everything and give them nothing." Then I hung up. And that was the end of my short and unhappy career as one of the Clown Princes of Basketball. The only positive aspect of my time with them is that during our games I'd never seen so many children so happy.

Now I was 38, and the same questions were staring at me again: What do I do now? Give inspirational speeches? Do commercials? Did I want to (*gasp!*) coach? Or did I still want to play basketball? Then I started getting calls from NBA teams. Portland, Milwaukee, Philadelphia, New Jersey and Boston were all interested in bringing me in for a tryout. I was still in decent shape, so I gave it a shot.

Even though I couldn't really get my chops up, I had a really good workout in Boston and they were interested. The coach was M. L. Carr and he said I was a little overweight, but I still had my skills. He'd let me know their decision in a few days. Meanwhile, I went back home and worked hard to trim down. When Carr called back he said they were going a different route and couldn't bring me in. But he was encouraging enough to make me feel I could still compete in the NBA.

Next up was Milwaukee and, once again, despite my lack of enthusiasm, I had another good workout. They put me head-to-head against Ralph Sampson and I ate his lunch. When Mike Dunleavy called back, he said he wanted to sign me but the owner of the team nixed the possibility. I also had a good workout in Portland, but they turned me down, too. Mike Fratello was impressed when he put me through my paces in Cleveland and so was the general manager, Wayne Embry. "We'd love to have you here," said Embry, "but we just let Larry Nance go and if we brought in another 38-year-old player, the media would roast us."

That was it. I remembered something George McGinnis once told me: "There will come a time when playing basketball won't be fun for you anymore. When that happens, you've got to walk away from it. Just let it go." I had a pretty good career and I had enough money to last for a while, so I promised myself that my latest retirement would be my last.

I was cool with where I was, and just like before the Globetrotters called, I felt good about putting my future in God's hands. I didn't reckon, however, on having serious marital troubles.

When I first married Robbin, she was very adventurous. Yeah, she wanted to go out and have fun wherever it was to be had. But now all she wanted to do was sit in the house. The only time she walked out the front door was either to visit with her friends in New York, or to hang out with her mother in Philly. Either way, she'd stay out until way past midnight. Left on my own, I got back into sniffing cocaine. Nothing excessive, just enough to give me a lift.

Now, we'd been married for several years and I always wanted to have another child. Trouble was that Robbin had a mean streak, and I was reluctant to have a child with her. Slowly, painfully, we grew more distant. Everybody always says how much fun it is to fall in love, but no-fucking-body ever talks about the hell of falling out of love. I'd seen so many ugly sides of Robbin that I couldn't think of her as being beautiful anymore.

Then Robbin said that she wanted a career for herself. She wanted to become a beautician. Since the basketball season in Italy was relatively short, we still were in New Jersey for most of the year, so I spent

$10,000 to put her through beautician's school. I bought her an Explorer so she could get to and from school in bad weather. I supported her all the way and I was proud to be at her graduation. And what did she do as soon as she got her diploma? Went out and got another job teaching at Freehold Boro High School.

Ten thousand bucks out the window!

One night I got a call from Nick Antonelli, who lived three towns over in Marlboro. Now, Nick was my unofficial godfather. Nick had befriended me, steered me toward good people and away from bad ones, got me some speaking engagements and always gave me good advice.

At the time, Nick was coaching a team of ten-year-old girls that included his daughter, Lexis, and he asked if I would help him out. I was happy to oblige. I never asked for money, but it was a wonderful experience for me. In those days, there was no WNBA and girls played strictly for the fun of playing. I loved their enthusiasm, their unselfishness and their ability to focus.

While I was working with Nick, I was contacted by a lady named Donna Chicarelli, who had a 14-year-old daughter named Candice. "Would you be interested in training my daughter?" Donna asked me. "I can give you $50 for each session." "Sure." Candice was big and strong, but unsure of herself on the court. In a way, she reminded me of myself when I was her age. (After I worked with Candy she not only made her high school team but became its best player.)

One thing led to another and during the summer I moved into another voluntary position—helping a guy named Pete Navarro coach an AAU team of 15-year-old girls. What a blast! There were no knuckleheads, no attitudes and no bullshit. Just a bunch of kids who wanted to play and wanted to learn.

All the while, Robbin and I had come to accept that our marriage was fading fast and we even began discussing a divorce. Then one day she came home from school and said, "I just took the job of coaching the freshman girls basketball team and I want you to help me out."

We weren't on very good terms with each other, so I said, "Hell, no."

"How come you're helping all these other coaches and you won't help me?"

Now she had me feeling guilty, but I was also stubborn. "You'll figure out what to do on your own."

A couple of weeks later, me and Robbin went out to dinner. We were still talking divorce, but we still cared about each other, too. After we had a couple of drinks, both of us were feeling nice and cozy together. All right. Time for some jelly roll! But when we got to bed, Robbin moved all the way over to the other side. "What's wrong?" I asked.

"If you can't help me, then I can't help you."

Oh, shit! There I was with my dick as hard as petrified wood, trying to go to sleep, and thinking that something drastic had to be done.

The next day when Robbin got home from school, I was sitting on the couch wearing my sneakers and my workout clothes. "I'm going with you to practice," I said. "Just to take a look."

It was a mess. The girls were playing out of position with the taller ones handling the ball and the smaller ones near the basket. There was no offensive or defensive scheme. Right away one of the girls came up to me and said, "Mr. Dawkins, will you help us?" My heart went out to them and I couldn't refuse. So I concentrated on putting them in the proper spots and working through some basic skills drills. The next day they had a scrimmage with another school and they got trounced, 59-17. Afterward, I said to them: "I'm not going to be part of a situation like this. I'll help you but you're going to have to do whatever I say. If not, you're going to be the laughingstock of the school." And they all agreed to go along with whatever program I had in mind.

These were 15-year-old girls and they were a great bunch of kids. A little black girl named Shikenya had long arms and could dribble the ball and play defense. Gina was boy crazy—she'd be running laps around the court and as soon as she saw some boys walking around, she'd just run over to them. A pretty white girl named Champ was a straight-A honor roll student. Lacey came from a poor family of 11 children, but she could run and jump and make layups. Mandy was six-foot-one and wore a men's size 11 sneaker, and she became my special project.

Robbin wanted to cut Mandy, but doing that would have devastated the kid's feelings, so I insisted she be kept on the team. When I first started working with Mandy on catching passes, the ball would bust her in the face. She couldn't dribble two times in a row without getting her legs tangled, but she worked hard.

After I got to know them, I told them what their roles on the team would be. Mandy and Lacey were the rebounders. Champ and a girl named Kerry were the shooters. "Shikenya, you're going to guard the other team's best scorer. You're going to trail her wherever she goes. When she goes to the bathroom, you're going to be there to hand her the toilet paper."

The school's athletic director came to practice one day. "I'm thrilled that you're making such a wonderful contribution to our program, Darryl. But we can't pay you anything."

"I'm not asking to get paid. I'm just here to help out my wife."

"Oh, thank you. If there's anything I can do for you, please let me know."

(There was, but that came later on.)

Robbin was also thrilled to death. She knew she was in over her head, so she just sat back and let me take over.

Before the first game, I gave the perfect pep talk. "For the past couple of weeks you all've been beating and banging on each other in practice. Now there's some fresh meat out there for you. All you have to do is go out there and play hard and play smart." They played unbelievably good, and we won by 20 points.

The girls kept playing hard, losing by four or five, losing by 13 to the best school in the area, so they started believing in themselves. That was half the battle won right there. One game came down to the last few seconds: The score was tied and the other team had a chance to win the game when Mandy blocked a shot, then she took off full-speed down the court. Shikenya came up with the ball and threw a long full-court pass to Mandy. Nobody expected Mandy to catch the ball, but she did. Then she laid it right through the basket. We were up by two with three seconds left and the other team had used all its timeouts. Game over, right? Nope. Mandy came running over to the bench. "Coach!" she said. "I'm so excited that I gotta go pee right now! I mean right now!" So I had to call a timeout while Mandy ran a fastbreak into the bathroom. We won the game, but nobody could figure out why I stopped the clock.

Before long, we had a little bit of an offense. One play was

"Chocolate," another was "Thunder." And we had a little junior press. We finished the season at 11-4 and had ourselves a great time of it.

After the season, I ran basketball clinics twice a week at the Boys and Girls Club. About 20 girls showed up on a regular basis, working on their reverse dribbles, their defensive slides and all kinds of footwork. I didn't know that coaching could be so much fun.

The next year, Robbin went back to her old school, Monmouth Regional High School, and I went with her. We had the same setup there: On paper Robbin was the head coach and I was the assistant, but I did everything. At Monmouth, we had a 22-6 season.

Meanwhile, I was doing some speaking engagements and some basketball camps, so I had enough money to buy groceries, pay my mortgage and my bills. But there wasn't a lot available for luxuries. Then the IRS audited my latest tax returns. Even though I'd been living in Italy, they said that I owed five years of state taxes. *Say what?* If I was living and earning money in Italy, why should I have to pay taxes in New Jersey? It didn't seem either logical or righteous, but I had no choice except to ante up. Things were so bad that the bank foreclosed the mortgage on my house. As my financial situation worsened, so did my relationship with Robbin and we finally split.

The divorce talks heated up. I wanted to get out of our marriage with my shirt on, but I didn't expect that to happen. Then Robbin said that a lawyer friend advised her to remove all her belongings from the house. I didn't object because I had to admit that I still had some feelings for Robbin and I didn't want anything around that would remind me of her. So I said, "Yeah, take it all. Take everything you want."

Robbin came over with her sister and another friend and they just about picked the house clean. They took everything except a big-screen TV, a couch and a chair. Then she moved in with her mother and sued me for divorce.

A few weeks later, I was feeling like the world's biggest loser, when the phone rang. It was John Spencer, the basketball agent for all of the Asian countries. "I've got a clinic and a game set up in Hong Kong," Spencer said. "Adrian Dantley was supposed to go but he canceled out at the last minute. I need somebody to fill in. You've just got to do one clinic and play in one game. I can give you $6,000, a first-class plane ticket and expenses while you're there."

Money from heaven.

When I got to Hong Kong, I helped run the clinic and I saw who else was in on the gig. Alex English and Kiki Vandeweghe were playing for the other team, along with some Chinese players. My team was coached by Bill Klucas and included Michael Cooper, Spud Webb and some Hong Kong players. There was a lot of money wagered on the outcome, and each of the winners would get a $500 bonus. Now, the Chinese were much better than the Hong Kong players so we were supposed to lose the game.

All the former NBA guys hung around together whenever we could, and Alex had a question for me: "I hear you're coaching high school girls and that you're winning a lot of games. Would you ever consider coaching guys?"

"Never, because I know that sooner or later I'd have to bust one of them in the mouth."

"Well," Alex said, "I'm the commissioner of a one-year-old new pro league called the International Basketball Association, and the team up in Winnipeg needs a coach. How about if it's you?"

"Who coached there last year?"

"Bill Klucas."

"Stop right there," I said. "I don't want to steal somebody else's job."

Then Klucas piped up. "No, Darryl. It's all right. Me and the Winnipeg owners have an understanding. I don't want to go back and they don't want me back."

"I don't know, man. I'm happy coaching the girls."

"Why don't you give it a try?" Klucas said. "The people in Winnipeg may be assholes, but they're still good people."

We tabled the conversation and got ready to play the game.

Klucas was a hellfire-and-brimstone type of coach. We were down by 14 at the end of the first quarter and I only had two touches because the hometown Hong Kong guard was firing up long-range jumpers. In the huddle, Klucas went nuts. "You little son of a bitch!" Klucas said to the guard. "You're playing with Darryl Dawkins, the biggest man in Asia, and you're shooting like you're all by yourself out there. I don't care if your whole fucking family and everybody that you ever met is here, let that seat fit your ass, you little shit!" Of course we came back to win the game. I hit a three-pointer, I shot my free throws underhanded, I sat up in the stands with two women on my knees, I dunked the ball up-down-and-sideways, and I gave the fans a show. The win also put an extra $500 in my pocket, plus a watch and another $500 for being voted the game's MVP.

Just before we left, Alex made one last plea. "Come on, Dawk. Go see about that job in Winnipeg."

"Nah, man. I'm not into that."

When I got back home, there was a message on my phone machine saying that "Manitoba" had called. *Who? I don't know any motherfucker named Manitoba. Must be the wrong number.*

The phone rang the next day. "This is Sam Katz from Winnipeg up in Manitoba, Canada. Alex English gave me your number." Katz was one of the team's owners and when he tried to sell me on the coach's job, I was all set to turn him down. "Before you say no, Darryl, let us send you a plane ticket so you can come up here and look around. If you like it, you'll take the job. If you don't, you don't. Either way, it's worth a trip."

All right.

When I got there, they put me in an old hotel that had obviously been modernized, but the whole place seemed very spooky. I swear that things were moving around in my room all night long. Just as I was falling asleep, I felt that somebody was on top of me. I thought maybe I had already fallen asleep and had a bad dream, but no. I was awake and alone in the room, yet I had the sensation that there was some kind of invisible body pressing me down into the bed. The only remedy was to get up and read my Bible. I found out later on that the entire hotel was rumored to be haunted by ghosts.

Katz and Rob Berkowits, the Winnipeg Cyclone director of operations, showed me around town. It seemed like a nice place with good restaurants and a lively nightlife. The arena where the team played was also first-class. So we struck a deal: Just under $3,000 a month for a season that stretched from November to April. Plus a car and a room in any other hotel than the haunted one.

D. Dawkins, professional coach. That's me.

16

Off to the Races

Since my house in New Jersey had been foreclosed, I was fortunate to be able to rent an apartment in a house owned by a friend, Dave Keyes, in South Belmar, NJ, near Asbury Park. I had already signed with Winnipeg for the upcoming season, so I was just cruising around the neighborhood half-heartedly looking for a summer gig. One day at the mall I ran into Jim Jennings, a local businessman. "Hey, Darryl. Me and a partner of mine own a team in the United States Basketball League. The team is called the Jersey ShoreCats and the season lasts from early June to the end of July. Why don't you come over and see us play?" Okay.

Well, I saw Rick Barry coach the team, and there seemed to be a lot of antagonism between him and his players. Afterwards, Jennings pulled me aside and asked if I'd like to coach the ShoreCats the following summer. "I can promise you that Rick Barry will definitely not be back," Jennings said, "because we don't want him here. We'll pay you $650 a week, plus a car and a hotel room. And I'd love you to keep your winter coaching job in Winnipeg because that'll make it easy for you to bring some of your players along with you."

The Jersey Shore wasn't far from my old stomping grounds in Philly, and I also needed the money, so I didn't have to think twice. "Hell, yeah."

"That settles it," Jennings said. "Next season, you're going to coach the ShoreCats."

Coaching all year round would certainly accelerate my development, but I still needed a game plan. Fortunately, I'd played for several noteworthy coaches in my pro career, so I had lots of do's and don'ts to pick from.

From Gene Shue, I learned that my players would have to be in great shape. Also that if I had a point guard who was willing and able to push the ball, as well as two other guys who would run with him, then my team would always be competitive. From Chuck Daly, I learned to be open-minded and not to be afraid of trying something new. From Stan Albeck, I learned that a coach has to communicate with his players. A play won't work just because a coach says it will. It'll only work if the players are comfortable running it. I learned from Paul Silas and Bill Blair that dignity and honesty go a long way toward earning the players' respect. From Billy Cunningham, Larry Brown and Dave Wohl, I took what not to do.

I wanted to be known as a players' coach, someone who could understand when a guy was tired, or hungover, or fucked over and couldn't be pushed past a certain point. I didn't care about gaining a reputation as a tactician. I'd rather get along with my players and work with them to find a way to win. I didn't want to break my players' spirits, so when a guy was playing badly, I was going to wait until he did something good before I took him out of a game.

By the time I got to Winnipeg, I had a ready answer when a local sportswriter asked about my basketball philosophy. "We're going to do one of five things—run, run, run, run, or run. That means the only time we're going to walk the ball downcourt is when we're taking time off the clock. Otherwise, we're going to run from the opening tip to the final buzzer."

What usually happens when somebody scores is that the scoring team wants to hold a mini-celebration, while the defenders want to hang their heads. But that's the best time to snatch the ball from the net, even before it hits the floor, and throw a pass to somebody who's already running full speed downcourt. I figured that every time the other guys scored a jumper, we were going to get a layup. I wanted teams that faced us to know they were going to have to play the entire game. I had devised about seven set plays to use when we were forced to play half-court, otherwise we were off to the races.

By playing an all-out running style, the outcome of a ball game would all come down to will power. Would our opponent have the physical and mental resources to stay with us?

My squad was a rag-tag bunch, but they fit my specifications: They let me whip them into better physical condition than they ever thought they could achieve. They understood that everybody would play but that nobody would play more than 30-or-so minutes per game. Even the big men could run and finish. And their hearts were as big as basketballs.

Kwan Johnson could play both guard spots and small forward, and he certainly had raw NBA talent. Sean Tyson from Clemson was part black, part Cherokee, and tough all over. Andrell Hoard was another talented guard. Monte O'Quinn was a distant cousin of mine and a good rebounder. Kaylon Coleman was from Chicago; he was six-foot-two and really didn't have a discernible position. But he was as ferocious as a pitbull so I just turned him loose.

Even while we were still in training camp, everybody around the league was disrespecting us. Bill Klucas was coaching in Rochester, Minnesota, and this is what he was saying: "Those poor bastards up in Winnipeg. If they only knew what they've gotten themselves into. If Dawkins couldn't control himself when he was a player, how can he control a team?" Other coaches were saying that my team was bound to be a joke since I was never serious about anything. Even the Canadian newspapers expected me to flop. One writer said that letting Darryl Dawkins coach was like letting a rapist into a whorehouse.

Meanwhile, I liked Canada, especially the women. Before I left New Jersey I was living with a Puerto Rican woman, Stella, who was bringing up two kids, hers and her sister's. After my marriage to Robbin turned sour I swore that I'd never fall in love again, but I was starting to feel that I could love Stella. She had been very supportive when I was trying to make up my mind about taking the Winnipeg job. I was afraid that my going to Canada for six months would mess up our relationship. "If we're meant to be together," she said, "then we'll survive." My point is that even though the Canadian girls were beautiful, smart, independent and open-hearted, I remained faithful to Stella.

In fact, my whole team was in the Palomino Club one night (Monday was hip-hop, the rest of the week was C&W) and there were girls everywhere. I saw one of the players sitting up at a table like he was a sheik with a harem—one girl was buying his food, another was buying his liquor, another gave him her car keys. "That's just the way Canadian girls are," he said. "You can have the same deal if you want it, Coach."

"Not me. I got a girlfriend back home."

When I went to the bathroom for a pit stop, I heard a loud noise coming from inside one of the stalls. BOOM! BOOM! BOOM! I took a peek and saw one of my players in there working over some girl. "Hey, man," I said. "Are you crazy?"

"You want some of this, Coach?"

"No, no, no."

Then the girl said, "Come on in here, Coach. I'm like the most unbelievable piece of ass you'll ever have."

So it wasn't easy keeping Ham Dick undercover.

Even the hotel setup was top-notch. I had a one-bedroom suite that included a small sitting area, as well as a kitchen with a microwave and refrigerator. It was like a little apartment. The players had almost the same arrangement, except their suites came with two bedrooms and they doubled-up. Depending on their experience and their previous accomplishments, their weekly salaries ranged from $350 to $700, which I thought was a good deal.

Earl Barris and Sam Katz were the co-owners and they treated me like family. I was always welcome at their houses and I'd be there often discussing ball games and roster moves. If I wanted to bring in a new player, they'd work out the specifics and bring the player in without complaining about the cost. Through it all, my gratitude to them for giving me a chance never diminished. They were typical of the people who lived in Winnipeg—so friendly and good-natured that they'd rather hurt themselves than do harm to someone else.

We lost our first game of the season against Wisconsin, then we traveled down to Minnesota to play Klucas's team, the Rochester Skeeters. The word had already spread around the league that my team was going to run-and-stun. I spent a few minutes with Klucas while our teams were loosening up. "I'll tell you what, Darryl," he said, "you gotta learn how to control those boys because they'll run right over you." Even after we ran his team out of the gym, Klucas wasn't convinced. "Mark my words, Darryl. Playing that style isn't gonna get you anywhere." In any case, we kept on winning.

I discovered, not entirely to my own surprise, that I had a talent for coaching professional athletes. I could jump and jive with them and still keep them playing hard. I put a certain level of competition into most of our drills and running routines to make the players think they were having a good time. And I never played favorites because I'd seen first-hand under Larry Brown how much damage that can do to a team. The guys who played the hardest played the longest, whether their shots were falling or not.

I think it was precisely my even-handedness with the players that enabled me to hold the team together. No team can prevent hostile cliques from forming around certain players, and we were no different. The guys from Chicago hated the guys from Detroit, and vice versa. Nobody liked the guys from New York because they swore that they knew everything. I didn't care if a player was from New Hampshire— if a teammate was open, that's where the ball had to go.

As much as I've always despised referees, I would not let my players fuss with them. The players' job was to play. Dealing with the asshole referees was part of my job. So even in practice I would not let them speak to the guys I brought in to officiate our scrimmages. If one player so much as complained too loudly, I stopped the scrimmage and had everybody run ten sprints. If it happened again, they'd run some more.

I also had an unusual rule about participating in practice. Every player had one free pass to come to practice and not suit up. It's a long season and sometimes guys are hung over or fucked out or whatever. I warned them to pick their day off wisely. "Don't use it if you're just feeling lazy and half-assed, because when you really need it you won't have it."

Off the court, I never set a curfew, even on the road. "But if you ever get into trouble," I told them, "then I'm gonna kick your ass off the team." This was a potent threat because most of the guys lived in shitty conditions in bad neighborhoods. Places where there was a lot of shooting and cutting and stabbing. Meanwhile, they had nice living quarters in Winnipeg. They had spare change in their pockets and all the pussy they could handle. So they did not want to leave.

In truth, there were maybe five or six players in the entire league who had the talent to some day play in the NBA. Plus maybe another two dozen who fantasized that they were NBA-bound. And that's cool, because everybody's got to have a dream. But the players who impressed me the most were the players who just *had* to play. The hungry guys who'd play for practically nothing. "Coach," they'd say, "let me guard that big motherfucker."

"But he's six inches bigger than you."

"Put me on him, Coach. I can keep him from putting the ball on the floor."

These were the guys who came up with every loose ball, never gave up no matter what the score, and even loved to practice. I played with and against plenty of guys like that in the NBA: World B. Free and George Gervin had to play. Dave Cowens had so much anger and aggression building up inside of him that he would've exploded if he couldn't have played. Jo Jo White had so much basketball intelligence that he just had to express himself on the court. As crazy and wild as Wali Jones was, he was another gym rat. Paul Silas. Rick Mahorn. Charles Barkley. And me, too.

There were also a bunch of NBA players who, in my opinion, never loved playing basketball. Elmore Smith, for example, was big, strong, and usually carried a bottle of Jack Daniels with him everywhere he went. Elmore played because of the money, but if his heart had been in the game he would have re-written the record books. Bill Laimbeer's parents were rich and I figured he played only to prove he could make money on his own. David Robinson had some juice when he first came into the league, but he's been on cruise-control for years. Horace Grant is a power forward forced to play center, so he gets beat up like a punching bag. It seems to me that Grant is mostly in it for the money anyway, but playing every night against bigger and stronger players seems to have stolen whatever's left of his desire to play basketball. Dwight Jones was another center-fied power forward who seemed to lose his heart for the game. Tommy Burleson played only because he was seven-foot-five. Who else didn't look hungry to me? Bill Cartwright. Tom LaGarde. Benoit Benjamin. Dinner Bell Mel Turpin. To me, these were the guys who didn't really give a fuck. You'd dunk in Joe Barry Carroll's face and say, "Yo mama," and he'd say, "That's all right, you got that one." Then you'd dunk on him again and he'd say, "Damn, I can't do nothing with you tonight."

Geoff Crompton was a special case. This guy was six-foot-eleven and at least 350 pounds and he loved to eat and drink. He'd come into a bar, order a case of Molson beer and chug-a-lug the whole thing. He used to bring a big bagful of burgers with him to bed and wake up at three in the morning to wolf them down. Crompton could gain 15 pounds over a weekend. He played only to make enough money to feed himself.

And if I loved to play, I soon found out that I also loved to coach.

For so many years black players had trouble getting coaching jobs in the NBA because the scouting report was that the brothers could only run, jump, dunk and shoot. We could do everything except think. But when guys like Bill Russell, Lenny Wilkens and Al Attles successfully moved from the court to the bench, they changed everybody's perceptions. And I soon learned that thinking was a big part of the job.

There were actually two games happening at the same time: One on the floor and one in the opposing coaches' heads. Besides trying to get their players to out-play the other guy's players, the two coaches are always trying to out-coach each other. "Oh, he's sending this guy into the game. Okay, I'll bring that guy in to step up the pace. Then he'll have to bring the other guy back in and his players will lose their rhythm." One of my favorite ploys was to play two point guards at the same time. This would usually cause my opposite number to throw two big guards in to post up my little guards. But because I was now so quick in the backcourt it was easy to run down and double-team the low post. And with two ballhandlers playing together my team would be flying up and down the court.

Once an athlete learns to compete he never forgets how to do it, so I loved the man-to-man competition between the coaches. My chops were up and I was having a great time.

About midway through the season, the team was in Bismarck, North Dakota, when I got a call from my lawyer. "Hey, Darryl, Robbin filed for divorce while you were in Canada and since you didn't show for the proceedings, you could be in some trouble. You better get down here and straighten this out." So I had to leave my team, fly to New Jersey and put together $1,500 to get a lawyer.

That's when I learned about Robbin's deposition. According to her, I was a drug addict, I routinely physically abused her and I couldn't be "trusted" around the girls I'd coached (which I took as her way of saying that I was trying to fuck them).

All of this bullshit was easy to refute: First off, even in my wild days in Philly, I never put doing drugs ahead of taking care of business. Secondly, I only had two physical confrontations with Robbin: Once when I got so mad that I grabbed and shook her, and once when, to avoid slapping her, I slammed my hand onto a table and broke a knuckle. Thirdly, her suspicions about me and the girls was just her way to hurt me and ruin my career. When word of these charges got out, a couple of the girls' mothers offered to come forward on my behalf.

At first, I couldn't believe that Robbin would resort to such tactics. Especially not after I had taken such good care of her, helped out her family, put her through beauticians' school and gotten her involved in going to church. It was the same old routine of blacks trying to bring down other blacks who were successful. And the question that I finally had to face was this: Why was this so?

Because my life experiences had been so vivid and so educational, I was now able to figure out an answer: I think it has to do with a basic lack of personal power. Because of the racism in this country, blacks have less to say about how their own lives are run than white people do. I don't think I need to list all the ways racism disempowers black people, but when people are helpless in so many day-to-day ways, they become angry and resentful. And what available targets are there for the blacks' anger? Their bosses? The local police? The Supreme Court? Of course not. The only outlet for their anger is each other. Black-on-black anger leads to black-on-black crime, also black-on-black envy and scheming and lying. And which group of blacks has the least power? Women.

Knowing this allowed me to understand and forgive Robbin's attacks.

In the final stages of the divorce proceedings, the judge said that, instead of having the lawyers doing all the talking, he wanted the participation of the people involved. So he sent us into a room with our lawyers and we were able to reach a settlement. The judge was never required to make a ruling and, finally, we were divorced.

PHEW! I felt like I had dumped a load of bricks from off my shoulders. As I was leaving the courthouse, Robbin came up and said, "Darryl, you want to go across the street and have a drink?"

Hell, no. I was suffering from emotional relief and emotional distress at the same time, and I needed to get back to Winnipeg ASAP.

Because the team kept winning and winning, even Klucas had to change his tune. "You know what?" he said to me after we kicked his ass again. "A lot of coaches can't make that all-out running game work, but you can. Don't you change it, Darryl. Keep doing what you're doing."

My players stayed in line and we were just running through the league when Sean Tyson tried to buck me. One of my guards, Lou Davis, was hurt so my assistant coach, Darren Sanderlin, had to scrimmage with the team. Darren had played in the CBA so he knew how to conduct himself out there, but Sean was dissatisfied with the way Darren was playing. "He won't pass me the ball the way I want it!" Sean screamed. "Pass me the fucking ball right!"

This went on for a while, so I had to step in. "Why don't you shut the fuck up?" I said to Sean. His reaction was to swell up like he was about to come at me. "Tyce," I warned him, "you better get away from me with that shit."

Our next game was in Bismarck and Sean couldn't find the handle on the ball. A pass went off his fingers and out of bounds. Then he dribbled off his foot. Then he fumbled another pass. He kept getting hotter and hotter, until he hollered at a teammate, "Can't you throw a fucking pass the right way?" I immediately took Sean out of the game, and as he approached the bench he kicked over a couple of chairs.

Meanwhile, the game was still happening and Bismarck grabbed three consecutive offensive rebounds. That brought Sean running right over to me, saying, "I'm the best fucking rebounder on the team and you got me sitting on the bench!"

We were down by seven at the half. In the locker room Sean was sitting in a corner just panting like a dog in the sun. So I walked over to him, took off my jacket, rolled up my sleeves and said, "Come on, Tyce. Get up. Let's get this shit over with. Come on, son."

He started sobbing. "I'm sorry, Coach. I just want to win."

"No, no. That's too easy. Either you're gonna get your ass beat, or you're gonna beat my ass. But I'm not taking any more of your bull-shit. Let's go."

"I'm sorry, Coach. I just want to win."

All right. Now it was time to sit down and talk. "You can't be so disrespectful, son, to your teammates or to me. If you don't respect anybody else, how can you expect anybody to respect you?"

Well, Sean went out for the second half, rebounded like a maniac and we won a tough game on the road. That was the one and only time that any of my players gave me any shit.

I was surprised by how much these young kids didn't know about being a professional athlete. They had no idea how to mentally pre-pare themselves for a ball game. Instead of focusing and getting into a warrior's mind set, they just bopped on to the court before a game and started bullshitting and yoohooing with guys on the other team. "Hey, how you doing, man? How's your mother?"

I had to freak all over them for this. "How can you be buddy-buddy with someone whose ass you're gonna try and whup in anoth-er ten minutes? You think he really gives a shit about your mommy? And why do you give a shit about his? Game time ain't the time for that kissy face bullshit. Save it for later when I can't see it."

I also made sure that we all prayed together before and after each game. And we did our praying in the privacy of our locker room. I really have to question the sincerity of those players in the NBA who come to center court and pray in public after a game is over. Same thing with football players who drop to their knees and pray after they score a touchdown. These guys are just making sure that everybody knows how holy they are. Some of them are even trying to prove something to their families: "Yeah, Grandma, I'm thankful, just like you told me to be." It's always good to pray, but stuff like that is too showy. The most sincere praying is done in private. Any preacher will tell you that you've got to steal away to talk to God.

Somebody somewhere must have done a heap of praying for me because I was named the IBA's Co-Coach of the Year, along with Kevin Mackey of the Mansfield Hawks. I wonder what Billy Cunningham thought about that.

After finishing the season at 22-12, we headed into the playoffs as the top-seeded team in our division. We opened up a best-of-three series in Billings, Montana, and lost the opening game. The IBA had a rule that all the teams in the playoffs had to travel by bus. Nobody was allowed to fly. So we suffered through a 16-hour bus trip back to Winnipeg, only to find out that the Billings team had taken a plane! The league fined the owner of the Billings team, but I was still pissed because they were well rested. Even so, we played with heart and hustle to win Game Two and even the series. The deciding game was the next day so I told my players to go straight home. And we came up big again.

With just a few seconds left in Game Three, a little nine-year-old boy who was a devoted Cyclone fans walked up behind the Billings bench. "You see?" he said. "Real men ride the bus."

Next up were Mackey's Mansfield Hawks. Kevin had done a great job years earlier with Cleveland State but had gotten involved with drugs and had been bouncing around the minor leagues ever since. We lost at Mansfield after I got booted by a jackass referee but won the next game at Winnipeg despite some lousy calls by a hometown ref. Throughout the season, winning on our home court was difficult only because the folks in Winnipeg are so friendly that the local refs seemed to favor the visitors. Anyway, we lost the third game all by ourselves to end my first season as a professional coach.

By then, I knew that I had finally found my calling. Coaching and teaching young men, giving them the benefit of all my experience, helping them to avoid the mistakes that I made. Like my brother Mitchell said, coaching was my "ministry."

17

Alphabet Soup (Xs & Os in the IBA, USBL & ABA)

I was looking forward to applying what I'd learned in the IBA to my new team in the summer league. But when I got back to New Jersey, I was surprised to read in the newspaper that Rick Barry had been re-signed to coach the ShoreCats! *What kind of shit is this?* So I called up Jim Jennings. "I was just as surprised," Jennings said, "because we never expected Barry to return after the bad season he had last summer. But, hold on, Darryl. I'm also part-owner of another USBL team up in Allentown, Pennsylvania, the ValleyDawgs. The coaching job is open there if you want it."

All right. So they fixed me up with a car, a hotel room, even a radio show. Jennings' partner in the ValleyDawgs venture was John Walson Jr., who owned the biggest cable TV company in the Lehigh Valley. Mike Sweet was the general manager and Chick Craig the scout, and through a free-agent draft they stocked my roster. Trouble was that these players were not well suited to my game plan. After winning only two of our first six games, Jennings told the media that I was about to be fired. The main reason he gave was that I was too easy on the players.

When I finally cornered Jennings, he said, "Well, Darryl, the organization wants to move in a different direction, so we're thinking about letting you go."

"No problem. Just give me the money you owe me. And while I'm still here, I'd like to know exactly what you don't like about me."

Jennings said that he wanted to see certain guys playing more and

203

certain guys playing less. I asked him if he wanted to coach the team, and he said, "No." Eventually, Jennings agreed to keep me around for a couple of games before making a final decision.

Just before our next home game I was approached by Sam Unera, a friend of Walson's and part owner of the team. "You're not going anywhere," Sam said. "Jennings can't fire you." Then Sam and I sat down, went over the list of available players and highlighted the guys I thought would best fit my system.

Well, the team went on a rampage and won 13 in a row. Now Jennings was falling all over me. He gave me a $500 bonus, and also the team's credit card. "I know that the players stay in dumpy hotels on the road," he said. "I want you to use the credit card and put yourself in a good hotel. You're doing a great job, Darryl. I always knew you could do it."

That's when I knew for sure that Jennings was a bullshitter.

I liked the level of competition in the USBL and the expertise of the coaches, but the referees were horseshit homers. One ref made a horrible call against us in Kansas with the score tied and three seconds left in the game, so I said to him in a very calm way, "That wasn't a good call." He said, "You didn't like that one? Watch this one." Then he called a technical on me. As a player from the home team approached the foul line for the resulting free throw, the ref handed him the ball and said, "I made the call, now you gotta make the shot and win the game." There was also an incident where one of my players was ejected from a game. He trashed the dressing room and told me he lost it because the ref had said to him: "Nigger, get on out of here." I understand that referees are a necessary evil, but these guys were sucking the devil's dick.

There were also some odd practices that the league condoned. Kids would come running up to me after games wanting me to sign official "Darryl Dawkins USBL Coach" cards that they bought at the concession stands. So I spoke to one of the league bigwigs: "I never gave the USBL permission to use my likeness. Don't you think I should get part of the money you're making on this?"

"No, no. You're part of the league, so I'm sure that what we're doing is legal."

I was just as sure that it wasn't, but it wasn't worth the time or money hiring a lawyer to get what was coming to me.

Anyway, we led the league in attendance and had a very successful season. All the while, I was learning more and more about how to coach. I began making better adjustments during a game and my timeouts were more fruitful. Once again, remembering what not to do from my days with Larry Brown, I made sure to give my assistant coach as much responsibility as possible. That's one of the reasons why I had Darren Sanderlin do all of the scouting. It was a way to show that I trusted him and valued his judgment. The other reason had to do with my own superstitions. Throughout my entire coaching career, whenever I went to see a future opponent play, watched them on TV, or even looked at a game tape, they always beat us the next time we played. That's happened 100% of the time.

So my pre-game routine was simple. Darren would do his scouting thing, then I'd have the final word. Now, I'm not interested in trying to out-coach my opposite number because I realize that it's the players' skills, energy and willpower that determines who's going to win. My job is to give them a system that works for them and then to help get their chops up. So my pep talks all had the same theme: "If we play the kind of ball we're capable of playing, we'll win."

Another of Darren's jobs was to drive the van, and during the playoffs in Kansas City he saved us all a lot of trouble. The whole team was coming back from celebrating a victory at a local club and most of us were drunk. But Darren was the designated driver, and besides, he wasn't much of a drinker anyway. He was driving us back to the hotel when a cop pulled the van over. "You were speeding," the cop said to Darren. "I know that you just came from the club, so my guess is that you've been drinking. If you're drunk, I'm gonna have to arrest you."

"No, Mr. Officer," Darren said. "I'm not drunk. Here, let me prove it to you." Then he got out of the van, went over to the side of the road and did a back flip. "If I was drunk could I do that?'

The cop laughed and let us slide.

The USBL playoffs were a single-elimination tournament among the top eight teams. We won our first game, then lost the second. Yet by every measure except winning a championship, it was another good season for me.

All right. My divorce was behind me, I no longer felt so guilty about losing my home and I had a new career, so I wasn't feeling like a loser any more. While it was true that coaching minor league basketball wasn't a very secure profession, I still felt confident that as long as I was healthy and as long as I was willing to put my future in God's hands, I would prosper. Along the way, I would also be able to help some young men become better players and, more importantly, better people.

I was anxious to spend the rest of the summer doing some necessary R & R, but the difficulties I've always had in my relationships with women wouldn't go away.

I wasn't getting along with Stella. She had a real hot temper and she often found something to be jealous about, so we were getting into fights just about every time we went out. If she was pissed at me she didn't want to dance, but then she didn't want me to dance with this girl or that girl. She even attacked me in the parking lot of some club. "I told you not to dance with that bitch." As drunk as I was, it was all I could do to just stand there and block her punches.

We had another battle at a cookout hosted by some Italian friends of Nick Antonelli, my godfather. Since I spoke such good Italian I was chatting with some of the girls. Nothing serious, just "You look good" and cracking some jokes. Suddenly Stella got real angry. Anything she couldn't understand was a reason for a fight. "What the fuck are you saying about me, nigger?" And I finally realized that I was more in love with her kids than I was with her. I enjoyed taking them shopping and to amusement parks, but after the kids were put to bed me and Stella had nothing to say to each other. It got to the point where I hated getting into bed with her. So our relationship just fell apart.

When I got back to Winnipeg for the 1999-2000 season, I made a conscious decision that I was through dating women of color. White women respected me for who I was, not what I could do for them. And I've never had a white woman call me "nigger."

For my second tour of duty in Winnipeg, I got a $100 per week raise and I set my sights on winning the championship. But things were spooked from the start. I had anticipated that Kwan Johnson would once again be the heart of the team, but he was playing professionally in the Philippines. Likewise, several other players were unavailable. Without my handpicked players, I couldn't get my running game to fire on all cylinders. We finished the season at 15–21, and under the circumstances I felt good about the job I did.

At the same time, I had learned my lesson about trying to play full-court with half-court players, so I was determined to assume more control of the ValleyDawgs' roster in the summer. Over the winter there had been an important change in the team ownership: Jim Jennings was bought out by Sam Unera. Sam was my guardian angel and he made sure that I got the players I required.

One of the more interesting players on the team was Dominick Young from Fresno State. I had noticed him in the NBA's pre-draft camp in Chicago. He was a five-foot-nine point guard and even though he wasn't in the best of shape he was still outrunning and outshooting everybody. I called him "Psycho" because he came to practice on even the hottest days wearing a silver-colored fire-resistant hood. Dominick also had a friend who, according to some of the players, was selling her pussy around Allentown for $500 a pop and giving Dominick $300. But Dominick took to my system like he was born wearing track shoes.

The previous summer I had cut a player named Ronnie Fields from Chicago. A few years back, Ronnie had declared his eligibility for the NBA draft when he was a high school senior, but nobody picked him. He was still very immature and I had to let him go because he wouldn't work hard. The second year, however, Ronnie was ready to play. Kwan Johnson was back from the Philippines and I was happy to have him onboard.

We had another good season and were primed for the single-elimination playoffs in Salinas, Kansas. But that's when Dominick was subpoenaed to testify in a point-shaving investigation back in California. According to newspaper reports at the time, the FBI and a federal grand jury were investigating allegations of point shaving at Dominick's alma mater, Fresno State. Dominick steadfastly denied any involvement in point shaving and the investigation did not result in any charges, but we entered the playoff tournament without our starting point guard, the one player who put the zoom in our running game. Not surprisingly, we lost our first game and we had to go back home.

The USBL's All-Star Game was scheduled for the day after the championship game and I was asked to be one of the coaches. So I stayed behind while Mike Sweet went back with the players.

On the first leg of the flight home, from Salinas to Chicago, two of my players, Kwan Johnson and Lonnie Harrell, started drinking. They bought a *Playboy* magazine during the stopover and took it with them on the flight to Allentown. According to Mike Sweet, the guys had been drinking but they weren't drunk, loud or unruly. There was also a nearby passenger who was taunting them with racist remarks. Anyway, Kwan and Lonnie were waving the magazine in the air, so a flight attendant told them to put the magazine away and quiet down. "You're just jealous," one of the guys said, "because your picture isn't in here." The stewardess complained to the pilot and Kwan and Lonnie were put off the plane in Harrisburg, about 90 miles from Allentown.

The next day, newspapers all over the country reported that Coach Dawkins and two of his players were rowdy and insulting on a non-stop flight from Chicago to Allentown. The story also said that the plane had to make an emergency stop in Harrisburg to kick us off. I was pissed. If I *had* been on the plane, Kwan and Lonnie would've been as quiet as church mice. That's when I started to wonder if I wanted to continue coaching in the USBL.

Another consideration was that a brand new pro league was being established, the American Basketball Association 2000, and I was offered the chance to coach a team in Tampa for $80,000!

The biggest problem in Tampa was lack of money. The owners were Ron Shaffer and Gary Elbogan, who were in the real estate business in Phoenix, and Clyde Perlee. In addition to the team in Tampa, they also owned ABA2000 franchises in Kansas City and Memphis. The players that I wanted in Tampa had to pay their own way into town. When they did show up, the players were quartered in a seedy hotel that catered to prostitutes, which, for some of them, was quite acceptable.

The team went through two general managers in the first season. The second general manager was fired and replaced by Deb Belinsky, whose original job was to do advertising for all three teams. I knew the wheels were about to fall off the entire league, but I also felt duty bound to honor my contract. I was making appearances at the

Chamber of Commerce, the Rotary Club, the Knights of Columbus and everywhere else, so even before the season started I was burning out in a hurry.

Our opening game was set for New Year's Eve! With no advertising anywhere and no schedules posted, we were lucky to draw the 300 fans who did show up. We lost that game and our next one as well. Shaffer and Elbogan were frantic. Then we won the next two and the owners were as happy as if they'd just won an NBA championship.

The only good thing about my brief tenure in the ABA2000 was that my family could come over and see some of the games. I also had plenty of time to go to Orlando and visit with them. That's when I decided to start paying a tithe to my brother Mitchell's church, and to this day, I send 10% of all my earnings there.

I thought I'd seen bad officiating elsewhere, but the ABA2000 version was a living nightmare. These fuckers were so bad that you could shoot them dead and they'd still get up and make a bad call.

In truth, most of the players on the ThunderDawgs had more dawg in them than thunder. On offense, they didn't want to run, on defense they didn't want to press. They just wanted to laze around and play one-on-one. They complained to the owners that the only reason we were practicing so late was that I like to sleep all day. They said that I worked them too hard in practice and that my game plans were no good. This was the first and only time that I didn't like most of my players and they didn't like me.

I was already halfway out the door when I spoke to another coach in the league who had been a highly respected coach at several powerhouse college programs. "I'm getting out of here, Darryl, because the people who run this league are half-assed. I want out before my reputation is ruined and I suggest that you do the same thing."

Things came to a head when I was required to fly (all seven feet of me in coach!) from Tampa to L.A. for a press conference. That's when Shaffer and Elbogan gave me the standard bullshit that coaches have to hear when they're fired: "We want to go in a different direction." *Yeah, I've got a different direction they can go! Up each other's assholes!*

"That's fine with me. You owe me $30,000, but just give me

$20,000 and I'm gone."

I was still trying to get my money when Art Blackwell bought the Tampa team. He's a black guy who owns a business development consulting company and casinos in Detroit. But hard as I tried, I was not able to get Blackwell to pay me. My arrangement with the previous owners had been a handshake deal so, without a signed contract, I was out of luck.

The ABA2000 was a doozie, all right, and I couldn't wait to get back to the relative sanity of the USBL.

18

The Paper Chase

After my wretched experience in the ABA2000, coming back to the Lehigh Valley quickly got me revved up again. Even before my third USBL season began I'd come to realize that I loved everything about coaching—from the practice sessions to the traveling, from the community work with the kids to the appearances at trade shows. Being an ambassador for the ValleyDawgs was just as much fun as working with the team.

How far can I take this fascination with coaching? Well, I understand that many factors are working against any possibility of me ever becoming even an assistant coach in the NBA. I'm positive that most of the people who make the hiring decisions still think of me as an undisciplined, rambunctious person. The truth is that I'm still a free spirit, and the adventures of Chocolate Thunder are still unfolding. But my past has also made it possible for me to communicate freely with today's hip-hop hoopers. And make no mistake, today's players are a different breed.

For starters, too many of them feel that the game owes them something and that the entire universe revolves around them. Back in the day, I always felt incredibly blessed to be doing something I enjoyed and getting top-dollar for doing it. Meanwhile, most Americans hated their jobs, felt frustrated with their lives and had to put up with all kinds of shit just to pay their bills. Playing in the NBA is one of the ultimate blessings in a young man's life and should not be taken lightly.

I blame most of the modern-day players' narcissistic behavior on David Stern's philosophy of marketing individual players. Today's NBA player wears gold chains around his neck that are worth more than most civilians earn in a year. Mr. NBA hotshot also has diamonds stuck in his ears, yet he still walks around mad at everybody who won't kiss his ass. These guys don't even have time to sign autographs for kids. "I ain't got time for you. And back away from my goddamn car before I have to bust your ass."

Even worse, these guys today absolutely hate contact. When somebody so much as touches them, they'll flop on the floor and whine to the refs. I can't stand it when an otherwise self-respecting NBA player sucks up to the referees.

For sure, the players are quicker these days and everybody can handle the ball the way only guards used to. They're also more talented than we were. But they don't work nearly as hard as we did, and that's why they get more injuries.

Even so, there are certain players who do have my respect. Allen Iverson, for one. He's just about the hardest-working player I've ever seen. He's not afraid of challenging the big men and putting his body at risk, all for the sake of winning.

I also like the way Iverson conducts himself off the court, though I don't like the subject matter of that rap CD he put out which denigrates women and homosexuals. But I believe that the NBA has no business criticizing his right to rap. Hey, I went through the same damn thing. Long before rappers became well known, me, World, and a woman named LadyBee Behiya had a rap called *Yeh-She-Shaw* that we performed in clubs all over Philly.

I'm in the house, yeh-she-shaw.
What's it all about?
So you bring the butter, and I'll bring the salt.
If you don't freak, then it ain't my fault.
Yeh-she-shaw.

But the Sixers made us stop. They said that we had to concentrate full-time on basketball.

I think the NBA looks at guys like Tupac Shakur and Biggie Smalls, gangsta rappers who got killed, and they're afraid that something might happen to Iverson. The league might have thought those concerns were coming true last summer when Iverson was arrested after allegedly making threats while carrying a gun. I'm more afraid that some 300-pound center is going to get a good angle on Iverson and blast him to smithereens. Shit, that's what guys like Dave Cowens, Bob Lanier and I would've done to any sawed-off guard who constantly challenged us where we lived.

Shaq is another player I like, and I have no doubt that when he was growing up, he watched me very carefully. I used to wear a Superman T-shirt all the time, and Shaq's got the Superman logos tattooed on his arm. He also has the same power move that I had: Lower that left shoulder and plow into the middle. The only difference is that the refs would make charging calls against me, but Shaq is the league's number one guy so the refs let him get away with all kinds of mayhem. NBA action has become so oriented toward corporations that fathers can hardly afford to take their kids to a game. "If you make the honor roll, Junior, then I'll take you to see Shaq and the Lakers." Now if Shaq is sitting on the bench because of early foul trouble, Junior's going to be very unhappy. And Dad will also be unhappy because he's just spent way over $200 (for tickets, parking, gas, tolls, a couple of hot dogs and sodas, a Lakers T-shirt, a Lakers hat, and a program) to hear his kids piss and moan.

So Shaq's got to play.

I also like the talents of Vince Carter and Tracy McGrady. I've seen enough intelligence in Carter's game to believe that he really knows how to play. Their challenges are to play with consistency and to stay out of trouble.

There are also several NBA players who do not tickle my fancy. Chris Webber is the typical New Age NBA superstar. He gets by strictly on talent and adrenaline, but his lack of understanding of the game is pitiful. Another so-called "franchise player" who I have a problem with is Grant Hill. If he was any softer the spotlights would melt him into a puddle. In my heyday, we would've treated Hill like a rag doll and sent him home crying to his daddy, but today's refs make sure to protect guys like Hill.

So if today's players are a different breed, they require a different breed of coaches to gain their respect. Coaches like me, for example.

It's all about respect, and I *will* be respected.

Another reason why re-entering the NBA from the other side of the bench won't be easy for me is that I don't have a godfather looking out for me. There's no chance that either World B. Free or Earl Cureton will ever be hired as head coaches in the NBA or anywhere else. I did have a close call, though, when Joe Dumars interviewed Rick Mahorn for the Pistons' job in May 2001. "Joe interviewed me twice," Rick said at the time, "so I know that I'm first in line. I'll hire another assistant to coach the guards and it's gonna be me and you, Dawk, on our way to Detroit." But two days later, Dumars hired Rick Carlisle, a white guy who's been an assistant in the league for several years and who has the stuff to be an excellent head coach.

Because they played together in Detroit for several years, Dumars and Mahorn knew each other inside-out-and-sideways. Dumars knows Mahorn is his own man and will not be controlled by management. On the other hand, Joe also knew he'd be able to pull all of Carlisle's strings.

For sure, I've got a lot to learn about my new profession. I need to refine my half-court offense. My inbounds plays have to be more attack-oriented. And I need to improve my specialty plays. But I'm getting there. And I'm hopeful that someday an NBA someone will also take a chance on me.

The ValleyDawgs took a chance, and I'd say it worked out pretty well. The only fly in the ointment at the start of the 2001 season was that Sam Unera and Mike Sweet were having disagreements about player personnel decisions. The rosters of minor league basketball teams are notoriously unstable. Throughout the season, players are constantly getting hurt, going home and getting a "real" job, signing with teams overseas, or just plain vanishing. During a normal season, a USBL or IBA or CBA team can run through anywhere from 20 to 30 players. That makes the finding and signing of replacement players a huge priority. Mike and Sam were constantly at odds over who these new players should be. Mike favored older, more experienced players and Sam the younger, hungrier ones. Even if one of Sam's choices was brought in and had a good game, Mike would focus on the player's every mistake. I was caught in the middle, so I tried to pacify both of them. But the bottom line was that Sam was a part-owner and John

Walson's right-hand man. It was Sam who hadn't let Jennings fire me, and it was Sam who claimed my loyalty. Eventually Sam said that the choice of replacement players was totally up to me, but the tug-of-war created a lot of drama around the team.

We started the season with another ragamuffin squad. As part of my total involvement with player personnel I also started dealing with (*ugh!*) agents. I let one of them talk me into bringing one of his clients into training camp and it turned out to be love at first sight. Corey Hightower was left-handed but he had the skinniest, crookedest legs I'd ever seen on a basketball player. He looked like some wacko who couldn't possibly have any kind of a game. But I've always liked that kind of player, a guy who has to bust his ass to keep up with the thoroughbreds.

Some of the others were: Terrance Roberson, a talented scorer who could run like someone was chasing him with a gun, and Mitch Foster, a USBL veteran and minimally talented big man who always played his heart out. In the backcourt, I rotated a trio of mini-sized point guards: Kareem Reid, Tim Williams and Amaju Gaines (who we called Jamuli Porkchop). Since the USBL would be previewing the NBA's new rules allowing zone defenses, I wasn't afraid of having any of these three posted up. These guys were so quick that I didn't need a five-man press to squeeze the ball. On paper, we didn't look like much. But we could run like a perpetual motion machine.

Once the season was underway, I continued my tradition of wearing loud-colored suits to the games. I had a fire-engine red suit I wore with a matching T-shirt. Also a yellow suit, and a purple suit that made me look like a big black Barney. To surprise the fans, I'd sometimes show up wearing a business suit and a necktie. Then I'd hit them with dress sandals, slacks and a flower-print shirt. We had some fans coming to the games just to see what I would be wearing. That's entertainment. For the third season in a row, the ValleyDawgs led the USBL in attendance.

Some things did change, though. I was learning not to be so hard on the referees. I still wasn't sending them Christmas cards, but sometimes I'd let them know if I thought they made a nice call. I even learned their names so I could talk to them. "Hey, Jesse. I thought he took three steps on that one." And for the first time ever, the refs were actually being polite to me! "Okay, Darryl. I'll take a closer look next time."

I also accepted the fact that most referees (especially the vertically-challenged runts) did not like a normal-sized guy like me hovering over them on the sidelines. A few refs would call techs on me just to make me sit down. After a one-sided dialogue I had with a little white referee, I finally understood that the real issue was control, or at least the appearance of control. "What kind of call is that?" I asked him.

"I'm in charge of you, Coach, and I'm in charge of the ball game. I am not here to make you happy, understand? So sit down and shut up."

The ValleyDawgs came out of the gate at full speed, but then we had a disastrous road trip, losing seven of nine. All of a sudden, people in the media and in the organization were stabbing me in the back. The losses were all my fault. I let the players get away with too much. Darryl Dawkins was a joke after all. Then someone who talked often with Mike Sweet told me Sweet was making critical statements about me. A couple of colleges (including LaSalle and Drexel in Philly) were considering interviewing me for their coaching vacancies, but when they backed away I suspected Mike was leaking negative stuff about me.

Anyway, after that road trip, I decided we needed more size. So I brought in Ronnie Fields and also a tough rebounder named Tunji Awajobi, who ate nails and spit out iron filings. Then Mike Sweet worked hard to sign Keith Closs, a light-skinned, beanpole seven-foot-three center who'd played three full NBA seasons with the Clippers. We were able to get Closs because he was in a complicated arbitration situation with the Clippers over $2,000,000, and if Closs wasn't playing somewhere, he'd forfeit any chance at the money. Closs could block shots without leaving his feet, could run like a guard in heat, had a nice touch around the basket, but was a giant-sized pain in my ass.

The Clippers had cut him because of a series of off-court incidents and he joined the Dawgs with about a dozen games left in the season. A few days later, we had a road game in Maryland and the team gathered outside the hotel to board the van that would take us to the arena. Closs showed up limping and clutching a big cup of coffee like a drowning man holding a life preserver. "Coach," he said. "I can't go today because I had an accident last night." Unfortunately for Closs, Ronnie Fields had already told me what had really gone down: Closs came back to the hotel at four in the morning drunk as Dean Martin. He'd hurt his foot when he kicked a chair during an argument with his girlfriend, and then he fell asleep in the bathtub.

"Kicking a chair when you're dead drunk ain't my idea of an accident. Damn, Keith. We need you to be playing."

"I ain't been kicking no chair, Coach. You're listening to the wrong people."

"Get the fuck out of my face," I said.

"All right, I'll get out of your face." Then he walked around to the other side of the van muttering just loud enough for me to hear, "I kick dark ass. I kick dark ass."

Damn! Maybe the motherfucker *was* crazy.

I put my bag down, turned to him and said, "You do what? I'll beat your motherfucking ass right here!"

Closs made a quick about-face and ran into the hotel. "You better be outta here before we get back!" I shouted after him.

So we won the game, and on the ride back to the hotel the guys were all over me. "What do you think, Coach? You gonna give him another chance? Is he outta here, or what? Come on, Coach, give him a break."

I had to think hard about the situation. I knew that we had no hope of winning the championship without Keith. But did the ends justify the means? How much shit would I be willing to eat just to win? Or was Keith just another knucklehead from the ghetto who didn't know how to act in the real world? What the fuck? In the end, I decided to at least listen to what Keith had to say for himself. When we got back to Allentown, I told the guys this: "I'm gonna be at Banana Joe's tonight. If Keith shows up, I'll hear him out. That's the best I can do."

So there I was, having a few drinks when Keith walked over and asked if he could sit down at my table. All right. Then he started talking: "It's been like this all my life, Coach. I know I'm a fuck-up. I'd be a fool if I tried to deny it. But whenever the shit hits the fan, Coach, everybody always gives up on me. Please don't do the same thing, Coach. Stick with me through this. Don't leave me. Please give me another chance and I'll give you everything I got."

So we shook hands and we hugged and I said, "See you tomorrow at practice."

Keith couldn't play for the next couple of games because his toe was still swollen, but after that, he was Superman. In one crucial game near the end of the season he blocked nine shots and changed about a dozen more. If Keith ever gets invited to another NBA camp, I guarantee that he'll make the team.

Toward the end of the season we picked up another high-stepping big man, Frantz Pierre-Louis, a player who needed a lot of personal attention. If two things in a row went wrong for him, Frantz would go into a funk and I'd have to take him out of the game in a hurry. His biggest difficulty was that the referees wouldn't let him wipe the sweat from his eyes without calling a foul on him.

"Coach," Frantz would moan, "why're they fucking with me? Why won't they let me play my game? I'm ready to go home, man."

"I understand exactly how you feel," I said, "because I went through the same bullshit. But if I would've let the refs drive me from the game, I wouldn't be sitting here right now. And on my 45th birthday, my lovely NBA pension plan wouldn't have kicked in for the rest of my life. You've got to keep playing, Frantz. You've got to keep living. Hard times always pass if you do the best you can."

Then he'd go back in the game and kick ass.

These were a good bunch of people to go to war with, but like everybody else, they had their idiosyncrasies. Kareem Reid was from New York and everything was "nigger" this and "nigger" that. White people couldn't get away with calling a black person nigger, but black folks commonly use that word among themselves. Still, it didn't sit right with me. "Nigger is a word designed by white people to indicate that black people are inferior life forms. So why are you guys perpetuating that bullshit?"

"Aw, Coach," Kareem said. "It doesn't have the same negative meaning when we say it."

All right. But every time I heard Kareem say "nigger" I'd give him a mint and say that his breath smelled. After a while, Kareem chilled out.

Playing the running game, I had 10 guys in my rotation, which meant that two players rarely got off the bench. Dennis Edwards, who could score despite having the ugliest, herkiest, jerkiest jump shot in captivity, sat because his rebounding and defense weren't up to par. Jeremy Hyatt could shoot the lights out and won some games with last-second threes, but couldn't run. While Jeremy accepted his role, Dennis never stopped complaining.

I tried to play everybody enough to keep them sharp. But it was an impossible task. To survive at the end of the bench takes a certain kind of inner strength. Guys like Dennis and Jeremy just had to find their own way to keep their chops up in case somebody got into early foul trouble or somebody got hurt. "You got to be ready when I call on you," I told Dennis, "but you've trapped yourself in a vicious cycle. You're sitting on the bench pouting and bitching so much that when you do get into the game you can't concentrate, so you can't help but fuck up, and you wind up back on the bench."

We had a slight edge as we headed into the post-season tournament because all the games were played in Allentown. Sam told us that if we won the championship we'd each be getting a bonus of $4,000, so we called the playoffs "the paper chase." To collect, we needed to win three games in three nights.

First up was the Florida Sea Dragons, led by their brilliant coach, Kevin Mackey. Before the game an owner of one of the other franchises said to Mike Sweet, "You guys had a hell of a run, but Mackey never loses games like this. Sorry, Mike. That's just the way it is."

I have the utmost respect for Mackey because he always knows what he's doing and he knows how to motivate his players. But there was some trouble brewing on his team and the upshot was that a couple of his players weren't happy with Mackey's style of coaching so they went home just before the end of the regular season. The lesson seemed to be that no matter how good a coach is, he can't please everybody.

Hmmm. I wondered if I had to reconsider my dissatisfaction with the likes of Billy Cunningham, Larry Brown and Dave Wohl .... Hell, no!

Anyway, we were at the top of our game and the pressure put on by my little guards was ferocious. Halfway through the fourth quarter we were ahead by 14 points. I knew that teams with big leads late in ball games will often relax, so I kept after my guys: "This game ain't over, so don't start fucking around out there. Anybody who starts to cruise is going to sit." Sure enough, we began taking bad shots and bullshitting around on defense, and our lead shrunk to six.

Any time I want to yell at my team and cuss them out during a timeout, I'll never do it near the sideline. Instead, I'll turn my back to the crowd and convene our huddle out on the court. "You're gonna get your ass beat," I told my players. "You're gonna lose your bonus and you're gonna go back home feeling like shit. And it's gonna be your own fucking fault. You let a beaten dog hang around long enough, he'll reach up and bite you on the ass."

That did it. We won the game going away. After we said our prayers in the locker room, we piled our hands in the middle of another huddle and shouted our playoff chant: "ONE, TWO, THREE, PAPER CHASE!"

Game number two was against an explosive team from Brooklyn that featured several outstanding one-on-one players and a couple of fearless rebounders. The Brooklyn Kings were coached by George Johnson, a black guy who had a long career in the NBA, and was a great person and an outstanding coach. More than any other team in the tournament, the Kings scared me the most.

One thing working against us was that Frantz Pierre-Louis was going to miss the game because he was getting married in New York. Without Frantz's size and quickness we were in for a struggle.

I had managed to convince my team that it was the defense that keyed the offense. By forcing our opponents to take difficult shots we could really get our running game rolling. And I also took a page from Stan Albeck's defensive philosophy: "No middle. Always push the ball sideline and baseline. No fucking middle!" For the Brooklyn game, I also changed some of my defensive rotations just to give them a different look. For the first time, I was feeling comfortable and confident about tinkering with my game plan. "Instead of going here, this time go there." When a coach's adjustments work, he earns his players' respect and they'll play harder and with more confidence. "Yeah, Coach got his shit together!"

Well, we broke into a 13-point lead early in the fourth quarter and the guys relaxed into the same showboating bullshit, and our lead dwindled to six. So I had to call a timeout, move our huddle onto the court and give them hell: "I've already seen this fucking movie! Don't you motherfuckers realize that the other guys are also professionals? Don't you understand that they don't like being embarrassed? Didn't you guys learn from last night's game?" I made a couple of substitutions, we ran our lead back up to 13, and the game was ours.

My daughter, Dara, had come over from Philly to watch the playoffs and we went to Bennigan's after the game. "Daddy, you really look tired."

"Yeah, those were the two hardest games I've ever coached."

Usually, I'll have a few drinks then stop by a club to help myself unwind. But I was already so unwound that I went straight to bed. Before I went to sleep, I prayed, not necessarily to win the championship game, but simply for the energy and the inspiration to be at my best.

Our last hurdle was the previous season's champs, the Dodge City Legend, coached by a down-to-earth white guy named Kent Davison. Now, Davison was a really smart cookie, and he proved this by hiring Cliff Levingston as an assistant. With Levingston handling the big men and dealing with the blacks, Dodge City was a very resourceful squad.

We played our home games at the Stabler Arena on the campus of Lehigh University and as I pulled into the parking lot before the game, I saw Frantz getting out of a car with his wife and an older man. And I knew that the man was Frantz's daddy. He wanted his father to be there to see him play, which meant that Pierre-Louis was going to have the game of his life.

In the locker room, Frantz gave another indication that he was primed for the ball game. "I was saving myself for the game," he said. "I didn't drink at the wedding, and I didn't consummate the marriage."

Also, before he left, Frantz had been on the starting five, but I wanted to use the same opening lineup that we used against Brooklyn. Now, when I was a young buck I felt slighted when I had to come off the bench. This is exactly how most young players feel. From a coach's standpoint, however, I saw the situation very differently. When the backup center for my team comes in, the other team's starting center has a natural letdown. Yeah, the number one man is out, and the number two man is in, and since I'm the number one for my team, I don't have to play as hard to play well. Also, if my second-string center is as good as, or even better than, my starting center, when he's matched against the other's team's backup, the advantage swings to my team. In any case, Frantz had no objection to coming off the bench and, as expected, played his ass off.

I wore my gold suit, and once the lights switched on my weariness switched right off.

The game was tight for the first half and we were up by two at the break. But there were signs that the Dodge City players were wearing out. I made some more adjustments in our defensive rotation and when the game resumed, we slowly began to pull away. It's hard to single out individual exploits, but Ronnie Fields played out-of-his-ass on defense, Tim Wynn made a crucial steal, Kareem Reid was more unselfish than usual, Terrance Roberson and Jeremy Hyatt made huge contributions, Keith Closs sealed the middle and Frantz finished with 21 points and 18 rebounds. The game and the championship belonged to us.

After the final buzzer, the crowd poured onto the floor and everybody was hugging and celebrating. Nobody was happier than my unofficial assistant coach (and former heavyweight champion) Larry Holmes, who lived in nearby Easton. (Whenever we had a bad first half, Larry always had the same remedy: "Let me go in the locker room and beat the shit outta them.") John Walson Jr. and Sam Unera accepted the trophy from the commissioner and we all touched it like it was the Holy Grail. When some of the commotion petered out, the team gathered in the locker room for our normal post-game prayers. Then we went back out and signed autographs for the fans.

There were so many people I wanted to thank that I couldn't get to them all. It took me two days of phone calls to reach out to everybody—so many that I'm afraid to start naming them here because I'm liable to forget somebody. The owners threw us a wonderful celebration party and, in addition to the bonuses, gave us each a big ebony championship ring with a diamond in the middle.

For that time and that place, winning the USBL championship was as good as it got. Who knows? Maybe somewhere down the line I may be able to coach in the NBA and win a championship there.

19

Chocolate Thunder's Blunders

L ife is pretty good these days, and except for all the time and money I wasted convincing myself that I was in love with the wrong women, I have no other grounds for any serious complaints or regrets. None. I can even look at today's players and see how incredibly wealthy they are, and not feel the slightest twinge of envy. When great players like Oscar Robertson and John Havlicek were making $100,000 a season, my generation was getting paid up to $700,000. Nowadays guys are getting $7 million and beyond. Hey, the Bible tells me not to be envious because the Lord can pour good and bad out of the same cup. Everybody eventually gets what they deserve so I'm perfectly satisfied with what the Lord has given, and continues giving, to me.

That's why I'm always smiling and trying to make everybody I see feel good about themselves. If I pass by somebody who's frowning I'll say, "C'mon, baby, smile. It can't be all that bad, can it?" If I see an old lady coming out of church, I might say, "Oh, girl, you sure look good. You got that thing on rotisserie." There's no disrespect and nothing sexual intended, so they'll always laugh and say, "Thank you."

Looking back, I find it interesting that so many veteran basketball watchers have more regrets about my playing career than I have myself. Their common complaint is that I should have been a much better player than I was. In self-defense I just look at all the great scorers I played with: From George McGinnis to Doctor J, from World B. Free to Otis Birdsong, from Sugar Ray Richardson to Karl Malone. What I'm saying is that I believe my development was stunted because

I was seldom given the ball and put in situations where I had to produce, where I was The Man. I did respond in New Jersey when Stan Albeck called my number in clutch situations. And in Philly, I more than held my own in three championship series against the likes of Bill Walton and Kareem Abdul-Jabbar.

A look at the record book also shows that I was much more than just a backboard breaker and a merry dunkster. With a lifetime percentage of .572, I finished as the fifth-best field-goal shooter in NBA history. And I set the New Jersey Nets' record when I blocked 13 shots in a game against Philadelphia. Also, I lasted in the league for 14 seasons so I must have been doing something right.

People also ask me if I've ever considered finding a "normal" job outside of basketball. Only two possibilities ever attracted me: Being a disc jockey on the radio, or counseling at-risk kids. But these were only passing fancies because I've always had a passionate love affair with the game. Sometimes I still dream that I'm playing and I'll wake myself up trying to block somebody's shot. Or I'll dream that I'm coaching a ball game and wake up hollering at a referee who made a bad call, or at a player who didn't run the play right. I want to coach basketball until I die. That's my normal job.

Even so, now that I'm middle-aged, and probably closer to the end of my life than to the beginning, I can see my past from a different perspective. When I was younger and I was messing around with drugs and women, I knew that what I was doing was wrong. I'd spent too much time with my grandmother not to know this. So through it all, I did feel some brief periods of remorse. But like most young people I was very headstrong so I could also find a way to rationalize my behavior. I was only hurting myself. Or, it's not such a big deal anyway. When that didn't work and I still felt guilty, I remembered how my father always used to quote *Romans 8:38*: "No power or principalities, nor things that come, nor things that pass, shall separate us from the love of Christ." Of course, Daddy was a hard-drinking man, so he'd add this: "Do you think this little bit of liquor will keep me from the love of Christ? And do you think that me being with that woman over there can keep me from the love of Christ? If you do, then man, you must be crazy. Because no matter how many times I may fall, if I can clean out my heart, then I'll always be forgiven. Always."

I'd also heard several preachers give the same kind of witness: "I was out in the world just like you. Everything you did, I also did. Doing drugs and alcohol and chasing women. But God saw fit to smile down on me and save my life. He'll do the same for you, but you've got to want it."

I truly believed that if I confessed in my heart and repented of my wrongdoing, I would be forgiven. So no matter how much "fun" I was having, I always had a sense that I couldn't keep on walking such a crooked path. I can't even count the times when I vowed to confess, repent, and straighten up, starting right now. *Uh oh! I did it again.* Well, starting right now! *Uh oh!* Okay, right now! *Uh oh!* ... That's exactly what happens when you're young and you swear you're going to be young forever.

Among other things, I've also learned that bad times are the best teachers, because that's when we pray from the bottom of their hearts, and that's when we know that God is always there. Also, that a church is only a building, and that the real church lives in the hearts of us all. Most importantly, I've learned that the light is always brighter when you're coming out of darkness.

Now, I'm not interested in mounting a pulpit or a soapbox. All I mean to say is that the experiences I've been through, the wild oats that I sowed, the deaths that grieved me, the financial problems, the physical and mental anguish, all these have made my faith stronger. And I know now that the darkness in my life has really been my biggest blessing. A blessing that I want to, and have to, share.

While I was something of an oddity when I came out of high school and went straight into the NBA, in the last six years there've been more than a dozen players who were given the same opportunity. Some of them turned out to be all-stars like Kobe Bryant, Tracy McGrady and Kevin Garnett. Some couldn't make the grade. And dozens more declared their eligibility for the NBA draft and then were ignored. Whether they're celebrities or obscurities, these are the kids whose lives I can touch. I can tell them from personal experience about how certain women and certain drug dealers will be looking to entrap them. I can tell them about the importance of standing on their own two feet, about controlling their own finances, about not wasting their precious time and energy.

It's much easier for schoolboys to be productive pros these days because nobody begrudges them their good fortune, and because the talent in the NBA has been severely diluted. I only go back to 1975 when the NBA had 18 franchises, yet now there are 29 teams in the league. Counting players on the injured list, that adds up to 165 modern-day players who would not have been good enough to play when I was a rookie. Back in the day, a player's talent had to cover the entire court—shooting, defense, rebounding, passing and handling. But nowadays, guys can be specialists and still thrive. Chris Dudley, for example, has played 17 years even though he still can't score with a pencil. And Dell Curry's been around for 16 seasons even though he still can't guard his own shadow. But kids are still kids, and they still need to be counseled by someone who can understand their problems.

For all these reasons and more, I think I have something valuable to contribute to the game, whether in a program for kids in the hardscrabble streets of some urban ghetto, or on a spick-and-span college campus, or in the low-rent minor leagues, or even in the hallowed arenas of the NBA.

I have been blessed recently by my marriage to Janice, and with the life we've built together in Pennsylvania with our kids, and with a great cast of Lehigh Valley people: Sam Unera, my Guardian Angel; John Walson of Service Cable TV; Joe, Jackie and Joey Straub; Paul Basile and family; Larry (The Champ) Holmes and family; Rick Nash; Hakadeen (A.K.A. Uncle Reggie) and Dave Keyes. For business opportunities, I rely on my good friend and business representative, Martin Gover. One of my greatest joys is being able to call Artis Gilmore my idol and long-time friend. And a special thanks to all my nieces and nephews.

My days are spent coaching the USBL's ValleyDawgs, and volunteering in the community, working on programs for kids like 'Say No To Drugs', 'Stay In School' and 'Hands Are Not For Hitting.' My other pastime is harassing my in-laws, John and Debbie and Doug and Diane.

The good news is that I'm not quite the same Darryl Dawkins I used to be. The main difference being that I've moved to a new section of Lovetron that can only be seen from the dark side of the moon. It's called "Let's Get It On."

Maybe someday I'll meet you there.

Statistics and Facts

KEY DATES
⊕ May 29, 1975: Drafted fifth overall by the Philadelphia 76ers.
⊕ October 27, 1975: Makes NBA debut vs L.A. Lakers.
⊕ November 5, 1975: Scores first points, with six points vs Chicago.
⊕ November 13, 1979: Breaks a backboard for the first time against the Kings in Kansas City.
⊕ December 5, 1981: Breaks leg against New Jersey Nets.
⊕ August 27, 1982: Traded by Philadelphia to New Jersey in exchange for a first-round pick in 1983 (Leo Rautins, taken 17th) and $700,000.
⊕ October 8, 1987: Traded by New Jersey to Cleveland Cavaliers with James Bailey in exchange for John Bagley and Keith Lee.
⊕ October 8, 1987: Acquired by Utah Jazz from Cleveland along with Mel Turpin and a future second-round draft pick. Dell Curry, Kent Benson, and a future second-round draft pick went to Cleveland.
⊕ November 26, 1987: Acquired by Detroit Pistons from Utah in exchange for second-round picks in 1988 and 1990, plus cash.
⊕ February 23, 1989: Waived by Detroit.
⊕ October 7, 1994: Signed with Sioux Falls Skyforce of the CBA
⊕ November 14, 1994: Signed with the Harlem Globetrotters.
⊕ November 21, 1995: Re-joins Sioux Falls Skyforce of the CBA.
⊕ January 17, 1996: Played in the CBA All-Star Game for the National Conference at the Sioux Falls Arena.
⊕ June 23, 2000: Plays one game with the Pennsylvania ValleyDawgs of the USBL as playing-coach.

FACTS
⊕ Still holds single-season NBA record for personal fouls with 386, set in 1983-84. He also holds the next highest mark with 379 in 1982-83.
⊕ Lead league in personal fouls in three seasons, tied for first on all-time list with George Mikan, Vern Mikkelsen and Shawn Kemp.
⊕ Fouled out of 23 games in 1982-82, the third highest mark in history.
⊕ NBA uniform numbers: 53 (PHI, NJ); 50 (DET), 45 (UTAH).
⊕ Lifetime field-goal percentage of .572 (3,477 out of 6,079), tied for fourth-best in NBA history.
⊕ Played in NBA Finals three times with Philadelphia: 1977 vs Portland; 1980 vs L.A. Lakers; 1982 vs L.A. Lakers.

DAWKINS, DARRYL, 'Chocolate Thunder', 'Double D'
Born: January 11, 1957   6'11", 252-270 pounds

Maynard Evans High School, Orlando, Florida
Drafted: 5th overall 1975 by Philadelphia 76ers

NBA

Team	Year	G	MIN	PTS	PPG	FG	FGA	FG%	FT	FTA	P3	P3A	O-RB	D-RB	TOT	BLK	AST	PF
PHI	75-76	37	165	90	2.4	41	82	.500	8	24	—	—	15	34	49	9	3	40
PHI	76-77	59	684	310	5.3	135	215	.628	40	79	—	—	59	171	230	49	24	129
PHI	77-78	70	1722	820	11.7	332	577	.575	156	220	—	—	117	438	555	125	85	268
PHI	78-79	78	2035	1018	13.1	430	831	.517	158	235	0	6	123	508	631	143	128	295
PHI	79-80	80	2541	1178	14.7	494	946	.522	190	291	0	0	197	496	693	142	149	**328**
PHI	80-81	76	2088	1065	14.0	423	697	.607	219	304	0	0	106	439	545	112	109	316
PHI	81-82	48	1124	528	11.0	207	367	.564	114	164	0	2	68	237	305	55	55	193
NJ	82-83	81	2093	968	12.0	401	669	.599	166	257	0	0	127	293	420	152	114	**379**
NJ	83-84	81	2417	1357	16.8	507	855	.593	341	464	2	5	159	382	541	136	123	**386**
NJ	84-85	39	972	527	13.5	192	339	.566	143	201	0	1	55	126	181	35	45	171
NJ	85-86	51	1207	778	15.3	284	441	.644	210	297	0	1	85	166	251	59	77	227
NJ	86-87	6	106	57	9.5	20	32	.625	17	24	0	0	9	10	19	3	2	25
UTA	87-88	4	26	6	1.5	1	7	.143	4	12	0	0	2	3	5	1	1	10
DET	87-88	2	7	4	2.0	1	2	.500	2	3	0	0	0	3	0	1	1	4
DET	88-89	14	48	27	1.9	9	19	.474	9	18	0	0	3	4	7	1	1	13
Career		726	17235	8733	12.0	3477	6079	.572	1777	2593	2	15	1125	3307	4432	1023	917	2784
Playoffs		109	2734	1375	12.6	542	992	.546	291	414	0	7	160	505	665	165	119	438

LEGEND: G: Games; MIN: Minutes; PTS: Points; PPG: Points Per Game; FG: Field Goals; FGA: Field Goal Attempts; FG%: Field Goal Percentage; FT: Free Throws; FTA: Free Throw Attempts; P3: Three Point Shots Made; P3A: Three Point Shot Attempts; O-RB: Offensive Rebounds; D-RB: Defensive Rebounds; TOT: Total Rebounds; BLK: Blocks; AST: Assists; PF: Personal Fouls; **BOLDFACE:** Led league.

ITALY

Team	Year	G	MIN	PTS	PPG	FG	FGA	FG%	FT	FTA	P3	P3A	O-RB	D-RB	TOT	BLK	AST	PF
Ipifim Torino	89-90	36	1272	791	22.0	324	418	.775	140	202	1	2	65	237	302	64	35	125
Auxilium Torino	90-91	33	1223	700	21.2	283	338	.837	125	178	3	5	100	279	379	55	44	134
Philips Milano	91-92	33	957	513	15.5	198	245	.808	114	150	1	2	83	216	299	29	21	142
Telemarket Forli	92-93	40	1363	710	17.8	287	349	.822	136	183	0	0	112	310	422	34	46	148
Telemarket Forli	93-94	38	1261	740	19.5	300	351	.855	137	204	1	3	93	329	422	43	49	144

CBA

Team	Year	G	MIN	PTS	PPG	FG	FGA	FG%	FT	FTA	P3	P3A	O-RB	D-RB	TOT	BLK	AST	PF
Sioux Falls Skyforce	95-96	22	585	297	13.5	108	178	.607	81	133	0	0	44	102	146	19	53	75

USBL

Team	Year	G	MIN	PTS	PPG	FG	FGA	FG%	FT	FTA	P3	P3A	O-RB	D-RB	TOT	BLK	AST	PF
Pennsylvania ValleyDawgs	2000	1	3	0	0	0	0	0	0	0	0	0	0	0	0	0	0	0

COACHING RECORD

Team	Year	League	REG. W	REG. L	PLAY. W	PLAY. L
Pennsylvania ValleyDawgs	Summer 2002	USBL	14	16	—	—
Pennsylvania ValleyDawgs	Summer 2001	USBL	18	12	3	0
Tampa Bay ThunderDawgs	Winter 2000-01	ABA2000	3	8	—	—
Pennsylvania ValleyDawgs	Summer 2000	USBL	20	10	0	1
Winnipeg Cyclone	Nov. 1999-Apr. 2000	IBA	15	21	—	—
Pennsylvania ValleyDawgs	Summer 1999	USBL	17	8	1	1
Winnipeg Cyclone	Nov. 1998-Apr. 1999	IBA	22	12	3	3
Career			109	87	7	5

COACHING HIGHLIGHTS

⊕ 1998-99: IBA Co-Coach of the Year (with Kevin Mackey, Mansfield).

⊕ 1999: USBL Co-Coach of the Year (with Kevin Mackey, Atlantic City).

⊕ July 1, 2000: Coached Blue team in USBL All-Star Game.

⊕ January 20, 2001: Fired from Tampa Bay ThunderDawgs.

⊕ July 1, 2001: Won USBL Championship with Pennsylvania ValleyDawgs.

⊕ February 9, 2002: NBA Rookie Team Assistant Coach, All-Star Weekend.

INDEX